A NEW DEAL FOR THE AMERICAN PEOPLE

A NEW DEAL FOR THE

AMERICAN PEOPLE

Roger Biles

NORTHERN ILLINOIS UNIVERSITY PRESS
DeKalb 1991

Published by the Northern Illinois University Press, DeKalb, Illinois, 60115
♾ Manufactured in the United States using acid-free paper
Design by Julia Fauci

Library of Congress Cataloging-in-Publication Data
Biles, Roger, 1950–
A new deal for the American people / Roger Biles
p. cm.
Includes bibliographical references.
ISBN 0-87580-161-7. —ISBN 0-87580-554-X (pbk.)
1. New Deal, 1933–1939. 2. United States—History—1933–1945.
I. Title.
E806.B496 1991 90-27715
973.917—dc20 CIP

Jacket/cover photograph courtesy of the Franklin D. Roosevelt Library

For Brian, Jeanne, and Grant

Contents

Acknowledgments

This book relies on the large secondary literature covering the New Deal, and I am indebted to the many scholars whose published works enriched my understanding of the 1930s. I would like to thank a number of historians who read all or part of this manuscript and offered sound suggestions for revision: Don Green, Jim Huston, Mark Kornbluh, L. George Moses, Bill Mullins, Bruce Stave, Bernard Sternsher, Martha Swain, and Chris Tomlins all contributed to this book but bear no responsibility for any errors or faulty judgments it retains.

The College of Arts and Sciences at Oklahoma State University granted me a sabbatical leave to complete the book. Susan Oliver and Toni Battles typed countless versions of the manuscript and always remained willing to confront additional revisions. My colleagues in the Oklahoma State University Department of History provided a congenial atmosphere in which to work.

Finally, I wish to acknowledge the importance of my family. The book is dedicated to my three children, Brian, Jeanne, and Grant, who perhaps will someday understand why their father spends so much time writing books. Thanks also to my wife, Mary Claire, who continues to support my every endeavor.

A NEW DEAL FOR THE AMERICAN PEOPLE

Introduction

Franklin D. Roosevelt's promise of a "new deal" gave hope to millions of impoverished Americans during the Great Depression, but the intractability of the economic situation left much of his pledge unfulfilled. Their hopes dashed, their prayers only partially answered in most cases, the people's assessment of the president's efforts varied. Judging from the hundreds of thousands of letters received in the White House—over 450,000 the week after Roosevelt's inauguration and an average of 5,000 per day for the next several years—a great number of Americans lionized Roosevelt for his efforts in their behalf. "President Roosevelt is certainly a Saviour to the Country," wrote a Florida man in 1934. "When he spoke it seems as though some Moses had come to alleviate us from our sufferings," exalted an Arkansas City, Kansas, man. Others less lavish in their praise excused the president's shortcomings, crediting him with good intentions. "I am sure," suggested a Seattle letter writer, "the President, if he only knew, would order that something be done, God bless him. He is doing all he can to relieve the suffering." Expressing the widespread belief that less benevolent forces in government undercut the president's efforts, one man wrote that "FDR didn't do all he could; he was held back." A Florida woman echoed, "I love him for all he has done, and I love him for all he wanted to do and could not."[1]

Although many of the correspondents gave the president high marks for his performance, others were embittered by the New

Deal's limitations. "Roosevelt's statement some time ago that no one would starve is just another broken promise," lamented a disillusioned Missouri man. "New Deal?" sarcastically asked another man. "They forgot to cut the deck. That's what we say around here." The combination of prolonged, bitter hardship and heightened expectations fostered by Democratic rhetoric made the New Deal's task all the more exacting. Although a majority of Americans approved of the president's programs most of the time, the New Deal never lacked for critics—constructive or otherwise—throughout the 1930s.[2]

Historians' assessments of the New Deal have fluctuated significantly in the past several decades. Initially, they lauded the Roosevelt administration's achievements. Carl Degler termed the New Deal "the third American Revolution," a pivotal break from the past in ideals, institutions, and practices. For Degler and others, the federal government's assumption of more responsibility for the welfare of the masses constituted a great stride in the maturation of the republic, and the arrival of the guarantor state was a welcomed event. A liberal consensus developed in the academic community, endorsing the expansion of government power, creation of a welfare apparatus, organization of the labor force, subsidization of the farmer, and realignment of political parties. William Leuchtenburg argued that "it is hard to think of another period in the whole history of the republic that was so fruitful or a crisis that was met with as much imagination."[3]

In the tumultuous 1960s, however, radical historians searched for evidence of thoroughgoing change in the New Deal but consistently came away disillusioned. Barton Bernstein succinctly summarized the New Left's analysis. "The New Deal failed to solve the problem of depression, it failed to raise the impoverished, it failed to redistribute income, it failed to extend equality and generally countenanced racial discrimination and segregation." The disastrous economic conditions of the Great Depression created an opportunity for change unprecedented in America's history, but to the radical critics of the nation's political economy the piecemeal alterations that ensued proved disappointing. Golden opportunities lost and existing institutions preserved, the American capitalist system survived. New programs merely shored up unacceptable flaws; imperfections remained.

Paul Conkin concluded, "The story of the New Deal is a sad story, the ever recurring story of what might have been."[4]

By the 1980s, criticisms of Roosevelt and the New Deal had become so commonplace that William Leuchtenburg lamented, "As it now stands, we have a dialectic that is all antithesis with no thesis." Accordingly, a movement away from the excesses of the frequently strident New Left critique began. As Jerold S. Auerbach noted, any analysis of the 1930s reforms that demands nothing less than the absolute rejection of the American capitalist system must inevitably consign the New Deal to failure. A more realistic judgment would consider the feasibility of change in a system grounded in long-standing values, mores, and institutions. Yet the rigor of the New Left critique made it impossible to gainsay the New Deal's shortcomings, particularly its failure to challenge entrenched elites and to address economic inequality. Having largely accepted the accuracy of Barton Bernstein's indictment, many historians have sought to explain the paucity of change by referring to the constraints limiting New Deal reform efforts. A spate of recent studies, including many monographs on state and local reactions to federal initiatives, have underscored the pivotal strength of conservative forces arrayed against the New Deal and the persistent commitment of the American people to traditional values.[5]

The historical scholarship emerging in recent years has dealt with the impact of the New Deal on specific groups, such as women, blacks, and organized labor. A younger generation of historians has been concerned with the impact (intended or not) of federal programs on urban life and politics, as well as on specific regions of the nation, such as the West and the South. The result has been an emerging consensus regarding the limitations of New Deal reform and an understanding of the realities of politics and the resistance to change in local and state institutions. This book mirrors that consensus. As a result, it is written not entirely from the perspective of Pennsylvania Avenue but from the rest of the country responding to directives from the nation's capital. The New Deal's inadequacies, as chronicled both by Reagan conservatives and New Left historians, and its successes, as celebrated by liberals, are all part of the same story—a story that can only be understood with an appreciation for the context of the depression years. Whether the New Deal went too far or not far enough, reforms implemented in the Roosevelt years indelibly shaped American life through the 1980s. And, its critics notwithstanding, New Deal reforms suited most of the American people well enough to secure an enduring place in the society.

CHAPTER ONE

Herbert Hoover and the Great Depression

In the 1920s the economy of the United States won worldwide acclaim for attaining new heights of prosperity. The United States emerged from the nightmare of World War I as a creditor nation and, except for the brief recession of 1921–22, charted an unprecedented course of productivity and economic growth. The gross national product rose an average of 5 percent per year, and industrial output increased by more than 60 percent for the decade. Unemployment seldom exceeded 2 percent. With virtually no inflation and annual per capita income rising significantly (from $520 to $681), purchasing power increased and millions of people enjoyed improved living standards. Consumers chose from an impressive array of such new and affordable products as automobiles, radios, phonographs, washing machines, vacuum cleaners, telephones, and sewing machines. "Coolidge prosperity" seemed irrefutable, and the experiences of the 1920s appeared to validate Herbert Hoover's prediction at the decade's end of poverty's elimination.

But affluence and unshakable optimism notwithstanding, the overall national picture obscured significant problems in some sectors of the economy and especially among certain groups. Alarmingly, over five thousand banks failed in the 1920s, a shocking statistic for a supposedly thriving economy. For all the alleged beneficence of American capitalism, many workers labored in relative poverty. Although wages increased, the average annual worker's income lagged three hundred dollars below the yearly earnings necessary for a minimal standard of living. Organized labor, undercut by company unions and welfare capitalism, limped through the decade with a shrinking membership, few resources, and limited influence. The American Federation of Labor, led after 1924 by the supremely cautious William Green, rarely supported strikers in worker-management confrontations and continued to serve the interests of increasingly outmoded craft unions while ignoring the growing legions of unskilled industrial workers. As a result, while Green's AFL consistently affirmed its desire to cooperate with employers, thousands of powerless workers went unrepresented in their dealings with management.

Workers in some industries suffered especially. Coal miners and steelworkers, for example, saw slight decreases in hours and scant wage increases. According to the National Industrial Conference Board, hourly wages in the bituminous coalfields fell from 84.5 cents in 1923 to 62.5 cents in 1929 and in the steel mills from 41.7 cents to 41.4 cents for the same period of time. In piedmont textile villages, mill girls worked fifty-six-hour weeks for as little as 16 cents an hour. Blacks continued to monopolize the lowest paying, dirtiest, and least desirable occupations; in the postwar years Mexicans, eastern and southern Europeans, and other recent arrivals vied with blacks for the jobs the majority of Americans disdained. Female wage earners made less than males, regardless of skill level, and the gap between the genders widened during the decade.

While a checkered prosperity favored some workers and bypassed others, the situation for the nation's farmers was more uniformly bad. World War I–induced crop shortages in Europe resulted in a bonanza for American farmers, but the postbellum resumption of production abroad, along with the removal of government support, sent agricultural prices plummeting. Improved technology at a time of decreasing demand exacerbated the problem for wheat farmers as well as cotton planters. More than three million farmers left the land during the decade, and many of those who remained lost their land and became tenants and sharecroppers. Through such organizations as the Farm Bureau Federation, farmers lobbied for government intervention to raise farm prices. Twice during the decade Congress passed the McNary-Haugen Act, only to have it vetoed by President

Coolidge. Despite the vigor of their protests, farmers found little sympathy from a populace enjoying a general prosperity.

American affluence was owed, in part, to runaway speculation that resulted in inflated real estate and securities. Evidence of these distended profits surfaced as early as 1926 when the Florida land boom unraveled. Ostensibly caused by a fiercely destructive hurricane, the fall in Florida land values actually stemmed from blindly unrealistic investments; indeed, promoters sold more house lots there than the number of families in the country. Investors ignored the bad news from Florida and patronized the stock market as never before. Stock prices continued to rise, as did the volume of brokers' loans, and the Great Bull Market of 1928, in which industrial stocks soared more than one hundred points during the summer, lent credence to the belief that everyone and anyone could play the market and never lose. Even that paragon of cautious frugality, President Calvin Coolidge, proclaimed stocks cheap at current prices.

Unflaggingly optimistic, investors and economists ignored the warning signs that began to appear in the summer of 1929. Stock prices reached record highs even as evidence of an impending recession—falling wholesale prices, curtailed consumption, reduced industrial production, and rising unemployment—mounted. For the first time in memory, stock prices wavered unevenly in September and early October, but the market always finished strongly. On October 21 stock prices fell suddenly but started back up the next day. Millions of shares of common stock changed hands on October 23, and prices dropped 18 points in a few hours. The following day (Black Thursday) panic ensued as brokers dealt thirteen million shares and stock prices fell alarmingly. Intent on salvaging whatever they could, traders dumped their stock, took their losses, and sent prices spiraling even lower. Several of New York's leading bankers, led by J. P. Morgan, Jr., met that afternoon and resolved to take forceful action. Pooling their vast resources, they dispatched Morgan's personal broker to the exchange to buy large blocks of stock. This dramatic show of confidence by the economy's preeminent financiers appeared to work: trading slowed, prices stabilized, and for several days the panic seemed to be over. President Hoover assured the nation that the economy remained sound and that the financial panic would subside.

The following week, however, the selling frenzy resumed. On October 29 (Black Tuesday) more than sixteen million shares were sold, and industrial stocks lost an average of 40 points. In the following weeks staggering losses mounted. Optimistic pronouncements by Hoover and others had no effect, nor did J. P. Morgan and his fellow moguls attempt another display of confidence. Stocks valued at eighty-seven billion dollars before the crash were worth only eighteen billion dollars by 1933. Millions of investors faced sudden financial disaster, and newspapers reported that countless ruined speculators had thrown themselves from skyscrapers to certain death on the pavement below. These accounts exaggerated the number of suicides, which, in fact, peaked during the worst years of the depression, 1932–34.

No one seemed to have an explanation or a cogent solution. Secretary of the Treasury Andrew Mellon callously suggested: "Liquidate labor, liquidate stocks, liquidate the farmers, liquidate real estate. . . . Values will be adjusted, and enterprising people will pick up the wrecks from less competent people." Former president Calvin Coolidge weakly explained that "when more and more people are thrown out of work, unemployment results." He further concluded, "The final solution to unemployment is work."[1]

Why had the stock market crashed? In part, because the irresponsible inflation of securities had little to do with the health of corporations and much to do with the whimsy of investors. Brokerages relaxed collateral requirements and mandated margins as low as 5 percent. (Margin was the amount of down payment necessary to make a purchase.) No supervisory or regulatory agent monitored stock purchases. Also, the nation's corporate structure rested on shaky ground. Investment trusts used investors' capital to speculate in corporations' securities. Many corporations were, in fact, warrens of holding companies and interlocking directorates with virtually no accountability to stockholders. Some trusts, most notably Samuel Insull's utilities empire, perpetrated fraud and stock manipulation; others were guilty of being capitalized far above their value. As long as profits accrued, these structural deficiencies remained in the background. But when the market faltered, many investors found themselves overextended and consequently defaulted on their obligations.

The stock market collapse signaled the coming of the Great

Depression, but many factors combined to send the nation's economy into its worst tailspin. The remarkable performance of the Great Bull Market in the 1920s diverted attention from several significant problems in the economy. First, the United States operated in an unsettled international economy that never fully recovered from the First World War. The Allies, particularly England and France, owed huge sums of money to the United States and could make their payments only because American investors underwrote German indemnities and reparations to the Allies. By the end of the decade, American investors found the domestic market more alluring and curtailed investment abroad. High American tariffs installed to protect domestic farmers and manufacturers from foreign competition put European debtors at an even greater disadvantage. In 1931 the devaluation of the English pound and the failure of Austria's Kredit-Anstalt (the nation's largest bank) led to frantic bank withdrawals throughout Europe. The collapse of the international economy, which had been kept afloat largely by American credit, meant shrinking export opportunities for American industries and reduced international trade—a disaster at a time when saturated domestic markets led to dwindling consumption. A moratorium on debt payments to the United States would have eased the pressure on European nations, but most Americans, already peeved at the debtors' grudging recognition of their obligations, agreed with Calvin Coolidge, who snapped: "They hired the money, didn't they?"[2]

Another major cause of the depression was the absence of diversification in American industry. Economic expansion in the 1920s relied overwhelmingly on a few key industries, most notably automobiles and construction. When they lost vitality, others lacked the size or productivity to fill the void. At the other extreme, numerous "sick industries," such as mining, railroads, textiles, and farming, made a difficult situation worse, for high unemployment in these businesses retarded purchasing power and depressed whole regions of the country.

Most important, a fundamental maldistribution of income created an anomalous poverty in the midst of plenty. A Federal Trade Commission study found that the richest 1 percent of Americans possessed 60 percent of the country's wealth. The reduction of personal and corporate income taxes during the 1920s further skewed the distribution of purchasing power. In 1929 more than 70 percent of American families survived on an annual income of less than twenty-five hundred dollars, the recognized minimal standard of living. Productivity far outpaced wage increases, with the result that industrial surpluses crammed warehouses to overflowing. American industry remained unsurpassed in its ability to mass-produce consumer goods, but not under conditions in which the majority of the people could purchase them. If corporations had lowered prices or raised wages, purchasing power could have been revitalized. Instead, executives countered dwindling profits with reduced wages, production cutbacks, and layoffs. Resultant unemployment increases only led to less disposable income, another round of contraction, and falling profits. Thus, a vicious downward spiral led the nation into a collective tragedy of plant closings, bankruptcies, and joblessness.

As the economic situation worsened, the modest state of economic intelligence exacerbated the problem. Two weeks after the crash, the Harvard Economic Society reported authoritatively that "a serious depression like that of 1920–21 is outside the range of probability." British economist John Maynard Keynes's ideas of compensatory fiscal policy, which urged the stimulation of private investment through government deficit spending, had not been widely accepted. Most experts, acknowledging their befuddlement at the severity of the downturn, could only advise allowing the crisis to run its course. The idea of government playing a leading role in combating the crisis generated little enthusiasm, and some businessmen argued that the depression would have a salutary effect. Auto magnate Henry Ford said it was a "good thing the recovery is prolonged. Otherwise people wouldn't profit by the illness."[3]

If anything, government monetary policies in the years prior to the crash contributed to the problem. Easily available credit and low interest rates provided an enticing climate for stock market speculation, just as indifference to the banking and securities industries encouraged risk taking. The regressive taxation policies of Secretary Mellon contributed to the maldistribution of income, and high tariff barriers inhibited foreign trade. Governments' benevolence toward big business and hostility to labor unionism—policies firmly entrenched in the nineteenth century—contributed to economic growth but did little to ensure that workers could afford American-made goods.

In the early 1930s the results of business contraction and

flawed economic policy began to be felt. Surviving businesses cut wages and laid off workers. Industrial workers averaged earnings of $25 per week in 1929 but only $16.73 by 1933. That same year the unemployment rolls included roughly thirteen million Americans, fully one-fourth of the work force. For the remainder of the decade, unemployment never fell below 15 percent and averaged almost 20 percent. At the time of the 1932 presidential election, *Business Week* reported 31 percent unemployment nationally, 46 percent in manufacturing, 45 percent in extractive industries, and 35 percent in domestic and personal services. In 1932 steel plants operated at only 12 percent capacity, and 70 percent of the nation's coal miners stood idle. The gross national product fell by 25 percent from $104 billion in 1929 to $76 billion in 1932. Agricultural prices fell 61 percent from 1929 to 1933, and net farm income decreased from $13 billion to $5.5 billion. Farm foreclosures claimed one-third of homesteads; in 1932, for example, creditors sold 60 percent of North Dakota farms for failure to pay mortgages or taxes. On one day in 1932, officials auctioned off one-fourth of rural Mississippi.

The jobless and indigent suffered everywhere but perhaps no more so than in the nation's largest industrial cities of the Midwest and Northeast. By 1932 unemployment rates had risen to a staggering 50 percent in Cleveland, 60 percent in Akron, 80 percent in Toledo, and 90 percent in Gary, Indiana. Philadelphia had 280,000 unemployed, only one-fifth of whom received any relief. In Chicago, public school teachers—who went unpaid for years at a time—fed over eleven thousand hungry children. In city after city the unemployed sold apples and pencils on street corners. Breadlines extended for blocks outside soup kitchens and Salvation Army offices, and thousands sought handouts from restaurants or sifted through garbage cans for food scraps. In 1932 New York City hospitals reported 95 deaths from starvation.

Evicted from their homes and apartments, the dispossessed crammed into crumbling rookeries bereft of gas, electricity, and plumbing. The less fortunate slept in doorways, on park benches huddled under newspapers (Hoover blankets), and on automobile seats salvaged from junkyards. They frequently erected ramshackle quarters out of undressed lumber, corrugated tin, scrap iron, and wooden crates on vacant land or on the outskirts of cities. These desolate settlements, caustically known as

Hoovervilles, lighted cityscapes at night as their denizens warmed themselves in front of rubbish fires in oil drums. In Chicago a shantytown shot up at the edge of the Loop; its residents named the streets Prosperity Road, Hard Times Avenue, and Easy Street. In New York City, hovels dotted the Hudson River shoreline from 72d Street to 110th Street, and a drained reservoir in Central Park became a residential community called Hoover Valley. People too poor to purchase gasoline or license plates sometimes drove Hoover carts, makeshift contraptions made of automobile axles and tires and pulled by mules or horses.

The search for jobs led an estimated two million men to hitchhike and steal away on freight trains bound for warmer climes. An official of the Missouri Pacific Railroad estimated that the number of people illegally riding trains had grown to 186,000 by 1931, up from 13,700 three years earlier. The care and feeding of these transients posed huge problems for embattled cities, whose law enforcement officials patrolled the railroad yards to discourage hoboes from disembarking. Many of this new "floating proletariat" were migrant farm workers. According to Farm Security Administration estimates, over 500,000 farm laborers roamed the countryside during the 1930s. Hundreds of thousands of Oakies, Arkies, and Texies, uprooted by the decade's swirling sandstorms in the dust bowl, headed for California where they settled in unsavory camps along with an undetermined number of Mexicans. Often greeted with violence, many returned to the Great Plains. Finally, California began to deport newcomers, Americans and illegal aliens alike.

Across the nation millions of desperate families sought aid from local public relief systems designed to assist only a fraction of the number suddenly clamoring for aid. In most communities these agencies quickly exhausted their resources. New York City, whose benefits to the needy set the standard, could provide families only $2.39 per week on the average. By 1931 New Orleans had exhausted its revenue and simply ceased to accept relief applications. St. Louis arbitrarily halved its relief rolls in one draconian cut. When the stock market crashed in 1929, virtually no southern cities even operated municipally funded relief bureaus. Birmingham, Alabama, one of the few that did, tried to sell its city parks to raise the necessary funds for operation of the relief agency.

The dearth of public funds led to the tapping of private resources. In Chicago philanthropic interests raised eleven million dollars for unemployment relief; expected to last for one year, these funds were completely dissipated in four months. In Philadelphia the private Committee for Unemployment Relief exhausted its entire three-million-dollar appropriation within a year and disbanded. Its chairman, Horatio Gates Lloyd, a partner in the city's most prestigious financial institution, acknowledged the inability of charitable enterprises to meet the needs of the jobless and called for government action. In city after city, private donations paled before the awesome needs of a massive indigent population.

As local relief funds quickly proved inadequate, state governments were pressured to expand their efforts. Like local governments, however, they faced declining tax revenues and seemingly endless drains on resources. Gerrymandered state legislatures, disproportionately representing depopulated rural areas, frequently chose to ignore hard-hit metropolises. Not until January 1932 did Wisconsin become the first state to establish an unemployment insurance program, and barely a year earlier New York governor Franklin D. Roosevelt created the first state relief organization. While some governors urged restraint based upon philosophical adherence to free enterprise principles, most states failed to respond simply because they were no more able to do so than the cities. The failure of local and state agencies to respond meaningfully to the crisis slowly led to an erosion of confidence. Indeed, the situation offered little hope of improvement. British economist John Maynard Keynes called the situation "one of the greatest economic catastrophes of modern history."[4]

The psychological impact of unemployment and business failure could be devastating to individuals. To many Americans the depression was bewildering, particularly since the nation's productivity remained extraordinarily high. Industrialist Bernard Baruch noted the irony: "In the presence of too much food, people are starving. Surrounded by vacant houses, they are homeless. And standing before unused bales of wool and cotton, they are dressed in rags." Keynes put it more succinctly: "This is not a crisis of poverty but a crisis of abundance."[5]

Coping with inactivity, anxiety over the threatened loss of home and possessions, self-doubt, and demoralization—all these problems surfaced as social workers observed the plight of the unemployed. Heads of households worried about their inability to care for their families. Imbued with the American ethos of rugged individualism and self-help, many of the newly dependent found applying for relief humiliating, and many held out interminably before reluctantly doing so. After months—in some cases, years—of receiving aid, morale deteriorated and apathy set in. A disspirited malaise seemed to blanket the country.

Although many people passively accepted their fate, some of the unfortunate reacted more strenuously. Hostility against the rich flared, usually in fiery rhetoric but occasionally in action as well. In Harlan County, Kentucky, striking miners protesting wage cuts and evictions from company-owned houses ambushed scabs. A full-pitched battle between strikers and deputies left four dead and several wounded. In the Midwest, farmers armed themselves and interceded to halt over 140 foreclosure sales. In 1932 disgruntled farmers formed the Farm Holiday Association and, under the leadership of Iowan Milo Reno, sought to hold produce off the market until prices rebounded. Such a narrowly focused boycott had little impact on gross farm prices, and when violence broke out in Iowa and neighboring states, Reno halted the strike. A hunger march on the Dearborn, Michigan, Ford auto factory resulted in violence and the tragic death of four protestors; the funeral cortege included twenty thousand mourners. Such examples of civil disorder were disquieting, but on the whole very little bloodshed ensued. Probably fewer than 5 percent of the unemployed engaged in protest activities. Given the sordid conditions of the lengthy depression, Americans remained remarkably law-abiding and docile.

Overcome with despair, many Americans reluctantly discarded their deeply held belief in rugged individualism and self-reliance and turned finally to the federal government as a last resort. And in 1929 few Americans seemed better suited to deal with such widespread calamity than the newly elected president, Herbert Hoover. Born in the Quaker community of West Branch, Iowa, in 1874, Hoover grew up in modest circumstances made worse by the death of his father in 1880 and his mother four years later. He lived with several different relatives prior to matriculating in the first class at Stanford University. After graduating with a B.A. degree in geology, Hoover joined a London mining firm for which he worked for more than a decade.

During that time he lived in Australia, Burma, Ceylon, Egypt, France, Germany, India, Korea, Japan, New Zealand, Rhodesia, and Russia, rising in the company's hierarchy and establishing a reputation as a successful businessman. In 1914 the wealthy engineer returned to the United States for the first time in 16 years and confidently proclaimed that if a man "had not made a million by the time he is forty he is not worth much." Thus, the first part of the Hoover legend was complete: the orphan became an overwhelming success through hard work and a shrewd business acumen.[6]

The second part of the Hoover legend, that of the energetic relief administrator whose widely heralded philanthropic activities made him an international figure, began to form during the First World War. As chairman of the Commission for Relief in Belgium, Hoover somehow managed to feed nearly ten million people despite the countless obstacles thrown up by the combatant nations. After the United States entered the war, President Wilson named him the head of the U.S. Food Administration. When hostilities ceased he assumed control of the American Relief Administration, supervising the distribution of food and clothing to over thirty million people on the war-torn continent. As European nations struggled to achieve economic equilibrium and the threat of Communist revolution abated, Hoover's highly publicized activities made him a hero. When the great flood of 1927, the decade's worst natural disaster, rendered thousands homeless in the Mississippi Valley, President Coolidge immediately chose Secretary of Commerce Hoover to coordinate relief efforts. This last episode reinforced the image of the vastly successful Quaker as both the Great Engineer and the Great Humanitarian, an efficient, hard-driving entrepreneur and a selfless steward of the dispossessed. In 1920 several liberal Wilsonians (including New Yorker Franklin D. Roosevelt) encouraged the wildly popular Hoover to seek the Democratic nomination for president; he declined.

Following the election of Republican President Warren G. Harding in 1920, Hoover joined the cabinet and continued to serve as secretary of commerce under Calvin Coolidge. His great success at making a historically insignificant cabinet post into one of high visibility and expanded influence added to his growing reputation as a master bureaucrat. Indeed, Hoover's far-ranging activities lent credence to charges of empire building and usurpation of authority. It was Hoover, for example, and not Secretary of Labor Jim Davis, who sponsored unemployment conferences, pressured the steel industry into surrendering its 12-hour workday, and urged businesses to develop unemployment insurance programs. It seemed that only Treasury Secretary Mellon and Secretary of State Charles Evans Hughes acted forcefully enough to safeguard their own bailiwicks. Most important, Hoover's ubiquity led the public to associate the apparent prosperity of the day as much with the energetic commerce secretary as with the indolent Republican presidents.

Although he had several opportunities to assume more prestigious posts in government, Hoover remained at the Commerce Department because it was the logical place to foster the associational activities he favored. For Hoover the maturation of American capitalism depended upon the ability to rationalize production, maintain individual entrepreneurship, harmonize class relations, and establish a community of interests. The key to his emerging "American system" rested with a voluntary, decentralized network of associations, operating apart from government control, that acted simultaneously for profit and the common good. Hoover saw only failure in the heavy hand of coercive government, believing that America's history ratified the reliance on individual effort. At the same time—and perhaps largely owing to his Quaker upbringing—he steadfastly denied that greater efficiency, business cooperation, and a vigorous drive for greater profit precluded altruism. No proponent of ruthless self-interest, he envisioned a "progressive individualism," whereby trade associations eliminated waste and duplication of effort while their enlightened executives voluntarily acted in the public interest. In other words, his own skill at combining business success with a social conscience could be replicated on a national scale to the mutual benefit of all Americans.

Government did have a role to play in Hoover's American system, albeit a limited one. It could, through committees, conferences, commissions, and other investigative bodies, use its influence to study economic and social problems. It would gather information that, in turn, would be made available to the public for consideration. Government would not determine policy, but rather assist private groups and individuals to make informed decisions. Power would be vested in the civic associations, labor unions, chambers of commerce, trade associations, farm cooperatives, and welfare organizations representing the "new individualism." And thanks largely to Hoover's efforts as secretary of commerce, the number of such national associations grew from an estimated seven hundred at the end of World War I to over two thousand by 1929.

When Calvin Coolidge announced his decision not to seek reelection in 1928, Hoover seemed the inevitable successor. In his nomination acceptance speech, he confidently proclaimed, "We in America today are nearer to the final triumph over poverty than ever before in the history of any land." His perfunctory victory over the Democrat Al Smith, a parochial New Yorker whose liabilities included his unvarnished opposition to prohibition, his Roman Catholicism, and his refusal to campaign widely or tailor his appeal to various audiences, left Hoover in an ideal position to implement fully his American system. A spate of optimistic projections fell into question almost immediately, however, as the stock market crash and deteriorating economic conditions confronted the new president shortly after he settled into the White House. He initially responded by issuing public statements denying the worsening of economic conditions and by blaming Europe for whatever problems existed. Believing that pessimism would only discourage investment and limit production, Hoover radiated optimism despite all the contradictory visible evidence. Because "panic" and "crisis" (the traditional terms for economic downturns) sounded too ominous, he insisted on using the more benign "depression."[7]

From November 19 to 27, 1929, Hoover convened several conferences with the leading spokesmen of industry, finance, agriculture, the Federal Reserve system, and public utilities. The president obtained from these luminaries pledges that they would maintain employment levels and wage rates. With these assurances, he issued another round of optimistic pronouncements and forecast a short duration for hard times. On December 5, 1929, more than four hundred of the nation's leading businessmen met in Washington, D.C., to form the National Business Survey Conference. Guided by National Chamber of Commerce chairman of the board Julius H. Barnes, the conference sought to bolster flagging investor confidence by having conferees pledge to maintain wages, prices, and employment levels. Hoover attended but, true to his view of government as cheerleader, acted simply as an advisor. These efforts to solicit the voluntary support of business failed for, as conditions worsened, businessmen abandoned their pledges and retrenched. The National Business Survey Conference, earlier launched with much fanfare, expired quietly in May 1931.

The crisis in agriculture continued to worsen. Hoover perplexed farmers when he selected Arthur M. Hyde, a Missouri automobile dealer, as his secretary of agriculture, and again when he spurned the McNary-Haugen Bill. He only partially pleased them when he signed the Agricultural Marketing Act in 1929, which created the Federal Farm Board and endowed it with five hundred million dollars to make loans to cooperative associations for the purpose of buying crops to keep them from glutting the market. Critics felt the bill did little to solve the basic problem of agricultural surpluses. At first, the Federal Farm Board sought to collapse the 12,500 existing cooperatives into a handful of national associations representing each of the major farm products. When that failed, the board urged farmers to destroy a portion of their crops—a suggestion for voluntary action that farmers studiously ignored. Afraid that mandatory production controls would undermine American individualism, Hoover drew back from further changes and watched the Agricultural Marketing Act end in failure.

Farmers looked with grave concern on Hoover's role in tariff revision. Senator George W. Norris of Nebraska led a coalition of western Republicans and Progressive Democrats to include an export debenture plan as part of a new tariff bill. The Hawley-Smoot Tariff approved by Congress in 1930 lacked such a provision and raised duties on both manufactured items and farm products to record levels (Rates increased on more than 900 manufactured goods and over 70 farm products). Fearing foreign reprisals and higher consumer prices, over one thousand economists petitioned Hoover to veto the bill. He refused. As the economists feared, other nations erected equally steep tariff barriers and American exports declined by half between 1930 and 1932.

Increasing unemployment and widespread misery led to repeated calls for more action from Washington. When New York congressman Fiorello LaGuardia warned that "this depression with its attendant unemployment has reached a state where the safety of the republic is threatened," Hoover retorted, "Prosperity cannot be restored by raids upon the public treasury." Replying to congressional calls for public works, the president charged, "They are playing politics at the expense of human misery." Hoover responded to the calls for government action but in his own fashion. In the early months of 1930 he signed two bills allocating hundreds of millions of dollars for the construction of public buildings and highways, then announced that he had "done enough in the matter of increased Federal expenditures for public works."[8]

In October 1930, Hoover formed the President's Emergency Committee for Employment (PECE), an organization designed to coordinate state and local relief efforts—but not to spend federal money for relief. Colonel Arthur Woods, PECE's first administrator, worked with state governors to establish over three thousand relief committees of leading citizens. Woods, who advocated more extensive federal action, resigned in April 1931 when Hoover resisted, and the committee, renamed the President's Advisory Committee for Employment (PACE), languished for several months under a caretaker. In August 1931, PACE was replaced by the President's Organization on Unemployment Relief (POUR), headed by American Telephone and Telegraph's Walter S. Gifford. Hoover told Congress that increased federal spending "would destroy confidence" and "jeopardize the financial system, and actually extend unemployment." Gifford concurred, adding that "no new public works initiatives were contemplated." In fact, Gifford admitted, he did not know how many families were unemployed or how many received relief—nor did he think "the data would be of any particular value." Repeatedly, Hoover sanctioned the creation of government agencies to confront the unemployment conundrum but insisted that their role be solely hortatory.[9]

In the waning months of 1931, with economic conditions undeniably worsening all around him, Hoover rejected recovery plans propounded by Gerard Swope, the president of General Electric, and by the U.S. Chamber of Commerce. With the failure of Europe's central banks and the apparent collapse of the German government imminent, Hoover at last admitted that the United States was not on the verge of recovery. Recognizing the need for sweeping measures, Hoover still insisted that private business take the lead. On October 4, 1931, he met secretly with several dozen banking and financial leaders at Andrew Mellon's New York City apartment, arguing for cooperative action to restore confidence and encourage investment. The bankers, many of whom thought Hoover's plans unworkable and hoped for more government involvement, agreed to organize the National Credit Corporation, but only after the president agreed to revive the War Finance Corporation if the private agency's efforts fell short. The National Credit Corporation opened for business on November 7, 1931, empowering its member banks to lend other member banks money from a five-hundred-million-dollar fund. The conservative bankers made loans extremely hard to get by establishing hefty collateral requirements, appraising securities at depressed market values, and providing loans at only 40 percent of collateral's market value. Nor would they accept real estate as collateral at all. Loans only went to member banks and since the institutions facing the gravest danger often could not afford the 2 percent membership subscription fee, they could not receive the loans. Of the one-half-billion dollars allotted, the NCC lent only about ten million dollars by December. Critics charged that even the five-hundred-million appropriation fell far short of need.

By year's end financiers had already adjudged the National Credit Corporation a failure. The nation's healthy banks had no intention of endangering their own positions by assuming the questionable assets of weaker banks. Even Treasury Secretary Andrew Mellon denied Hoover's plea that he save the Bank of Pittsburgh. The grand experiment in enlightened cooperation, potentially the centerpiece of administrative efforts to combat the depression, collapsed of narrow self-interest. Many believed that the banker's halfhearted efforts resulted from Hoover's guarantee of federal action if the experiment failed, thus handicapping the private agency from the start. The president agreed, positing that individualism had not really failed; it had been undermined by the selfishness of a few capitalists hoping for government aid.

In June 1931, Hoover moved boldly on several fronts, enlisting the federal government as never before in the fight for economic recovery. First, he announced a moratorium on all international debts, public and private. Variously praised as an act of magnanimous statesmanship and damned as long overdue, the action undeniably charted new paths of executive leadership. Unfortunately, the moratorium exerted no appreciable impact on the moribund world economy. He also supported increased funding for federal land banks and the creation of government-supported home loan banks; both measures were designed to forestall mortgage foreclosures through government intervention. Further, Hoover backed the Glass-Steagall Banking Act, which strove to aid American banks in meeting the demands of overseas depositors and to limit the withdrawal of gold from the country. The Federal Reserve Board increased the discount rate from 1.5 to 3.5 percent, ostensibly so that foreign capital would not be withdrawn. This undoubtedly preserved the gold standard but elevated the cost of borrowing.

In his most ambitious venture, Hoover asked Congress to create the Reconstruction Finance Corporation (RFC) with five hundred million dollars in capital and the authority to borrow two billion more. The RFC would be empowered to make loans primarily to banks, building and loan associations, insurance companies, and railroads. Hoover theorized that the best approach would be to invigorate the commanding heights of the economy, and the resultant investment increases would benefit the masses through rising employment. Congressman LaGuardia called the RFC legislation "a millionaire's dole. . . . It is a subsidy for broken bankers—a subsidy for bankrupt railroads—a reward for speculation and unscrupulous bond pluggers." Speaker of the House John Nance Garner insisted on loans to small businesses and individuals as well, but Hoover accused him of trying to make the RFC "the most gigantic banking and pawnbroking business in all history." After only token resistance, both houses of Congress overwhelmingly passed the landmark measure. Hoover could justifiably contend that no president had ever taken such sweeping measures in peacetime. Even Progressive stalwart George Norris marveled that he had never contemplated "putting the government into business as far as this bill would put it."[10]

Within two weeks after the bill's passage, the RFC was granting over one hundred loans daily. During February and March 1932, the RFC approved 974 loans, of which $160 million went to banks, $60 million to railroads, and $18 million to various lending institutions. Banks failed less frequently and bank deposits increased, but no industrial recovery followed. By insisting on lofty 6 percent interest rates, the RFC made loans inaccessible to many potential borrowers. Those bankers who did receive the loans apparently chose to safeguard their own assets rather than increase their lending. By July the government agency had lent over $1 billion to over four thousand banks, trust companies, and railroads. Still, the economy sputtered. Critics charged that conservative lending policies favored the largest, healthiest banks while ignoring the ones most in need of assistance. Protest increased when the RFC lent $90 million to the gigantic Central Republic Bank of Chicago while simultaneously refusing to lend the City of Chicago $70 million to pay its municipal employees and teachers. The highly publicized affair was a public relations disaster for Hoover and his increasingly unpopular trickle-down economic policy.

Although an ardent believer in fiscal conservatism and a balanced federal budget, Hoover allowed a huge deficit to accrue. The 1931 fiscal year yielded a $903 million shortfall, and 1932 promised a $2 billion overdraft. Unbalanced budgets resulted in large part from shrinking tax revenues. Mindful of his violation of economic orthodoxy, on June 6, 1932, Hoover signed a new revenue bill that raised individual and corporate levies nearly to World War I levels. The granting of RFC loans to corporate giants while raising income taxes further sullied the president's reputation. Moreover, he had consistently rejected calls for federal relief and employment programs, monotonously delivering stale paeans to individualism and voluntarism. By the summer of 1932, however, the disappointment of the RFC finally drove Hoover to consider yet another deviation from his firmly held ideology; he began to consider a large-scale public works effort.

For months Progressive forces in Congress had fought for federal aid to the unemployed, always with Hoover antagonistic. A $500 million emergency construction bill by New York senator Robert F. Wagner, a revision of an earlier draft by John Nance Garner, sailed through Congress only to be vetoed by Hoover. A new bill, drawn to the specifications of Hoover and Secretary of the Treasury Ogden Mills, subsequently went to the president, who signed it on July 21, 1932. The Emergency Relief and Construction Act, an amendment to the RFC bill, provided $1.5 billion for public construction of income-producing projects, $300 million in loans to states for direct relief, and $200 million for the liquidation of ruined banks. While the Emergency Relief and Construction Act constituted another milestone in the federal government's assumption of responsibility for the commonweal, the effort ultimately proved frustrating. The sums allocated fell far short of the amount necessary to care for the millions in need; for example, Pennsylvania could only borrow enough money from the RFC to provide its unemployed workers 3 cents per day. Moreover, bureaucratic delays kept the programs from being implemented promptly.

Clearly, Herbert Hoover was not a do-nothing president, nor did he slavishly follow the dictates of rapacious businessmen. Initially rejecting legislative and executive action, he preferred to rely upon private resources to combat the depression. This would be far preferable to the dole, which threatened to sap the initiative and sturdy independence of the American people. He hoped that government involvement could be limited to the gathering of data, the provision of expert advice, and the dissemination of educational materials. His refusal to endow government with coercive powers to use against recalcitrant businessmen, however, doomed his associational dream for America. As voluntarism came up short, he launched unprecedented federal government forays into the marketplace, doing more than any other peacetime chief executive had ever attempted. (To combat recessions in 1907, 1914, and 1921, Presidents Theodore Roosevelt, Woodrow Wilson, and Warren Harding had launched modest federal relief programs but nothing on the scale chanced by Hoover.) In fact, many of his departures laid the foundations for subsequent New Deal programs: the Agricultural Marketing Act paved the way for federal farm price supports, the Emergency Relief and Construction Act's public works projects formally passed to Harold Ickes and the Public Works Administration, and the Federal Emergency Relief Administration received five hundred million dollars to continue RFC-sponsored relief. In several other instances New Dealers modeled supposedly innovative programs after existing Hoover agencies, leading revisionist historians to emphasize correctly the continuity spanning the 1932 election.[11]

But these new departures by Hoover had severe, even debilitating, limitations. The RFC, like other creations, came to life as a temporary agency empowered to issue debentures (not bonds) and hamstrung by the provision that all public works must be self-liquidating. Hoover's obeisance to the notion of an enlightened business community kept him from investing in government the support he willingly offered to private entities.

His insistence that European conditions derailed American recovery showed an appreciation for the interdependence of capitalist nations but also caused him to ignore the severe weaknesses in the national economy that cried out for attention. Nothing undermined Hoover's attempts to restore prosperity more than his tardy and often minimal attempts at innovation; indeed, the phrase "too little, too late" often accurately characterized his efforts. Historian Albert U. Romasco summarized the Hoover record:

> The President's distaste for enlarging federal authority, together with his analysis of the depression, accounts for his determined opposition to expanding federal activities which he himself had started. . . . Herbert Hoover's great achievement was that he led the nation in its struggle against depression; the fact that he forestalled others from continuing and widening the experiment was his great failure.[12]

While later generations of historians have treated Hoover's presidency more kindly, his contemporaries pitilessly condemned his performance. Ironically, the man known only a short time earlier as the champion of the unfortunate found himself widely pilloried for his apparent insensitivity. His reserved demeanor, once seen as coolly professional, suddenly seemed cold, distant, aloof. Repeated assurances that conditions were improving, an analysis obviously far off the mark, failed to bolster investor psychology and did nothing for his credibility. When Hoover stated in 1932 that "no one has starved" and opined that "hoboes, for example, are better fed than they have ever been," a suffering nation recoiled in disbelief.[13]

Hoover's already dismal reputation received a crushing blow from the Bonus Army episode in the summer of 1932. World War I veterans, voted by Congress to receive a bonus in 1945, complained bitterly when the president cited the need for balancing the national budget and refused their entreaties that the gratuity be paid early. In June more than twenty thousand conscripts in the Bonus Expeditionary Force arrived in Washington, erected makeshift camps, and lobbied strenuously for congressional approval of early payment. When Congress voted negatively, some dispirited veterans vacated the camp but most remained. Washington, D.C., police moved to evict marchers from abandoned buildings, a brief riot erupted, and two veterans were killed. Persuaded that the B.E.F. had become a breeding ground for radicalism, the president ordered police and the U.S. Army to confine the veterans to their encampment. Disregarding these orders, Army Chief of Staff General Douglas MacArthur led infantry and cavalry regiments, convoyed by tanks, into the camp, lobbing tear-gas containers and wielding bayonets, and drove the B.E.F. out of the city. The casualties included more than one hundred injured veterans and one dead infant. Hoover refused to condemn MacArthur's excessive zeal and assumed full responsibility, justifying the tragedy with references to communist activities in the Bonus Army. To millions of Americans this episode merely reaffirmed Hoover's callous disregard for the downtrodden, and his belief that the radicals controlled this loyal group of veterans indicated how isolated and uninformed he had become in the White House.

The sullen national mood and Hoover's unpopularity foreboded ill for the Republican party in the 1932 election. Since failure to support the incumbent would be tantamount to admitting blame, the Grand Old Party somberly nominated Hoover and prepared for the worst. The Democrats, flush with optimism, gathered in Chicago assuming that whomever the nominating convention chose would be a sure winner in November. Not surprisingly, the party suffered no shortage of eager candidates. The list of presidential aspirants included Speaker of the House John Nance Garner; Maryland governor Albert Ritchie; the 1928 candidate, Al Smith; former secretary of war Newton D. Baker; and New York governor Franklin Delano Roosevelt, among others.

By the time of the convention Roosevelt's tireless cultivation of Democrats across the nation and his renown as the innovative governor of the nation's largest state made him the man to beat for the nomination. Being damp (advocating local option on prohibition) made Roosevelt more acceptable than Al Smith to Democrats in the rural South and Midwest. His many speeches on behalf of the "forgotten man" clearly cast him as the party's liberal candidate, as did the staunch opposition of the Democrats' conservative leadership. Conservatives like financier Bernard Baruch and John J. Raskob, the DuPont executive whom Al Smith had installed as chairman of the Democratic National Committee, had kept the party afloat in the 1920s—frequently by spending their own money. To them Roosevelt seemed dangerously radical. They found a forceful ally in Al Smith, who took umbrage at how little Governor Roosevelt had sought his advice in recent years. Solidly in league with the Baruch-Raskob forces, an increasingly conservative Smith attacked Roosevelt's references to the "forgotten man" as shameless demagoguery. No longer friend or mentor to the Democratic frontrunner, Smith became the point man for the party's right wing and in the process alienated many who had supported him in 1928.

Because nomination required a two-thirds majority, a Stop Roosevelt coalition was able to deny the governor victory through three ballots, but Garner's switch on the fourth vote commenced the stampede that gave Roosevelt the nomination. In a sharp break from custom, the nominee flew to Chicago from Albany and addressed the delegates in person. In his acceptance speech he pledged himself to a "new deal" for the American people, thereby inserting a new phrase into the political lexicon. Precisely what it meant remained a mystery throughout the campaign, as did, many observers felt, the Democratic candidate.

Franklin D. Roosevelt, a distant cousin of former president Theodore Roosevelt, had been a prominent Democrat for almost a generation. A member of the Dutchess County, New York, landed gentry, Roosevelt grew up with all the privileges common to a Hudson Valley aristocrat. He attended the best schools (Groton, Harvard, and Columbia Law School) without academic distinction and indifferently labored for a New York City law firm before entering politics. As a New York state legislator he earned the reputation of an anti–Tammany Hall reformer. Beginning in 1913 and continuing through the First World War, he served as assistant secretary of the navy. In 1920 he received the Democratic nomination for vice-president and, along with presidential candidate James M. Cox, lost in a landslide to the Republican ticket headed by Warren G. Harding. The following year he contracted poliomyelitis and lost the use of his legs, apparently bringing an abrupt end to his promising political career. Although he never regained full ambulatory power, he valiantly underwent countless hours of torturous therapy and became partially mobile with the help of braces, crutches, and wheelchairs. In 1924 Roosevelt made a triumphant return to national politics, nominating Al Smith for president in the widely acclaimed "Happy Warrior" speech. When Al Smith sought the presidency in 1928, Roosevelt ran for governor of

New York. Although Smith failed to carry his own state, Roosevelt narrowly won and overwhelmingly retained the governorship two years later. By establishing the first statewide unemployment relief system, Roosevelt gained national acclaim as a caring reformer unlike the nation's beleaguered chief executive.

Widely reputed to be an amiable dilettante of little substance, Roosevelt did not strike many of those who knew him in 1932 as having the wisdom, skill, or toughness necessary to lead the nation in its most trying hour. Esteemed journalist Walter Lippmann spoke for many when he judged Roosevelt "a pleasant man, who, without any important qualifications for the office, would very much like to be President." Supreme Court Justice Oliver Wendell Holmes condescendingly remarked that Roosevelt possessed a "second-class intellect" but, fortunately, a "first-class temperament." To a great extent the nominee lent substance to such an analysis by conducting a vague, often contradictory, campaign in which he frequently declined to consider specific problems. Roosevelt campaigned vigorously (no doubt in an effort to assure the electorate that his physical disability would not impair his performance as president), but his speeches usually espoused only shopworn platitudes. The ephemeral quality of his public addresses doubtless stemmed from the cautious approach to the election suggested by Hoover's unpopularity. Virtually assured of election, why should the Democrat take controversial positions? Moreover, much of Roosevelt's vagueness simply reflected his lack of a coherent program to present.[14]

As frustrated Republicans complained, Roosevelt "was all over the map" in his political analyses—in Herbert Hoover's words, a "chameleon on plaid." More surprising yet, in light of subsequent developments, the Democratic candidate frequently lambasted the incumbent for doing too much rather than too little. In Pittsburgh Roosevelt denounced Hoover for his failure to balance the budget; in Columbus, Ohio, for "overregulation." At Topeka, Kansas, Roosevelt outlined his farm policy and somehow managed to include all the various agriculture proposals then in vogue. To the Commonwealth Club in San Francisco he gave an unabashedly liberal speech, calling for a planned economy and a more equitable distribution of wealth. And in Portland, Oregon, he promised to "protect the welfare of the people against selfish greed," adding, "if that be treason, my friends, then make the most of it!"[15]

Although Roosevelt occasionally dissembled and at times sounded clearly conservative chords, a liberal tone emerged from his campaign. He called for social insurance, national planning, the development of public power, and a host of reforms spawned in the pre–World War I Progressive Era. Most important, he affirmed the need for more sweeping government action than Hoover had been willing to countenance. During the campaign Hoover stated that "the sole function of government is to bring about a condition of affairs favorable to the beneficial development of private enterprise." Roosevelt countered in clear and unmistakable terms: "I assert that modern society, acting through its Government, owes the definite obligation to prevent the starvation or the dire want of any of its fellow men and women who try to maintain themselves but cannot."[16]

For all the similarities and obscurities, the two candidates offered the electorate a clear choice in 1932. Much has been made of the differences in tone and style between the aspirants—Hoover the humorless, dour engineer grimly defending his administration, and Roosevelt the buoyant optimist, evoking warmth and compassion. But the contrast ran deeper and Hoover repeatedly inveighed against his opponent's "economic radicalism." Late in the campaign in New York's Madison Square Garden he intoned, "This campaign is more than a contest between two men. It is more than a contest between two parties. It is a contest between two philosophies of government." Roosevelt's election in 1932 reflected the American people's desire that government take an active role as an agent for human welfare.[17]

Whatever coherence the Roosevelt program had resulted from his collaboration with a small group of advisors known as the Brains Trust. In March 1932, the New York governor sought the services of several Columbia University professors he originally referred to as his "privy council." Old-line politicians like Louis McHenry Howe, Jim Farley, and, to a lesser extent, Edward M. House continued to counsel the candidate on vote-getting matters, but the Brains Trust increasingly hammered out the substance of what would be the New Deal. The first Brains Truster was Raymond Moley, a political scientist at Columbia's Barnard College, whose humble origins and sympathy for the downtrodden showed through in the "forgotten man" speech he wrote for Roosevelt early in the campaign. Rexford Guy Tugwell, a specialist in agricultural economics, returned from a 1927 trip to the USSR so impressed with collectivized farming that he thereafter advocated economic planning as the solution to the depression. Adolf A. Berle, Jr., coauthor of the highly influential *The Modern Corporation and Private Property,* recommended business-government cooperation as the optimal economic arrangement in complex industrial societies. Other academicians contributed at various times to Roosevelt's speeches, but the Brains Trust remained largely under the influence of these three charter members.

Moley, Tugwell, and Berle rejected the economic thinking of Louis Brandeis, Felix Frankfurter, and their followers, who argued for free markets and retreat to small-scale units of production. Alternatively, the Columbia trio endorsed the approach outlined in Charles Van Hise's *Concentration and Control* and Herbert Croly's *The Promise of American Life,* which called for government regulation—not destruction—of big business. The Brains Trust sought government intervention only on a limited scale, a balanced federal budget, and expanded relief and public works programs as temporary emergency measures. Tugwell valued planning as both an end and a tool, but collectively the men advanced it only when necessary for recovery. Roosevelt's inchoate program in 1932, developing through his interaction with these like-minded advisors, put domestic recovery before international agreement; more specifically, it called for relief and public works funded by an emergency (unbalanced) budget, some form of social security and unemployment insurance, and federal aid to farmers. Although not fully conceived and lacking in detail, this was the program Franklin D. Roosevelt submitted to the American electorate in 1932.[18]

In an anticlimax, Roosevelt won handily in November. The president-elect collected 57.4 percent of the popular vote to Hoover's 39.7 percent; the incumbent managed to carry only Pennsylvania, Vermont, Connecticut, New Hampshire, and Maine in the electoral college. Democrats assumed control of both houses of Congress, by margins of 59 to 36 in the Senate and 313 to 117 in the House. Arguably, no incoming president had ever enjoyed such a resounding mandate—and no incumbent ever left office so thoroughly repudiated and so vastly unpopular. The outcome of the 1932 election also presaged a realignment of the two political parties. The Republicans, who had dominated national politics since the 1890s, surrendered primacy to the Democrats, who have remained the majority party into the 1990s. Unfortunately, more than four months passed between the election and the inauguration—the Twentieth Amendment to the U.S. Constitution, ratified the following year, narrowed the length of time by about half—and as a lame duck, Hoover struggled fitfully to manage an economy that seemed to worsen daily.

After what appeared to be genuine improvement in the fall of 1932, the winter brought record unemployment levels. Hoover contended that his policies had finally begun to work, but the election of the dangerously radical Roosevelt punctured business confidence and undermined the recovery. Determined not to recede quietly from the scene, the president sought to enlist his successor in action against the worsening conditions. Working with Treasury Secretary Ogden Mills and Secretary of State Henry L. Stimson, Hoover tried to persuade the president-elect to endorse the current administration's policies. This amounted, suspected Roosevelt, to nothing more than an attempt to abort the New Deal. On November 22, 1932, Roosevelt and Hoover met at the White House to discuss possible courses of action after the expiration of the foreign debts moratorium in December. Roosevelt listened to Hoover's suggestion that the president-elect endorse the administration's proposal to reconstitute the debt commission but remained noncommittal. In late December at another White House conference, Roosevelt again declined to take a position on the debt problem before his inauguration. Roosevelt did not share Hoover's view of the primacy of international causes of the depression and intended to place more emphasis on domestic recovery programs. Equally important, the president-elect refused to share responsibility with an administration over which he exercised no control; nor would he support policies that might limit the choices available to him later as president.

Hoover persisted in the effort to recruit Roosevelt as a kind of junior partner in his administration's last days, then pilloried the New Yorker for his failure to join the team. Hoover's call for a sales tax, government retrenchment, and bankruptcy legislation generated little enthusiasm in Congress and even less among the thoroughly disillusioned American public—especially so because it was played out before the backdrop of the sensational Pecora hearings. In January 1933, the congressional investigation into the stock market collapse, suspended since June 1932, resumed on an enlarged scale. As the newspapers reported in excruciating detail, leading bankers admitted shocking breaches of ethics and exceedingly stupid decisions. Prodded relentlessly by the skillful committee counsel, New York attorney Ferdinand Pecora, the once-venerated financiers exploded their own image of wisdom. Businessmen sank to even lower repute, as did the accommodating president, who had sung their praises and charted America's future course in the path of their enlightened leadership.

In February the American banking system, steadily declining for months, seemed on the verge of total collapse. As public confidence ebbed, panic-stricken depositors stood in long lines to withdraw whatever money they could before the inevitable bankruptcy declaration. Mob psychology led frightened customers to demand their cash from otherwise stable institutions, and the untenable demands for funds created self-fulfilling prophesies of deposit shortages. On February 14, the governor of Michigan declared a "bank holiday," closing the state's 550 banks. Other states followed suit. By inauguration day, over 5,000 banks nationwide with deposits of $3.4 billion dollars had closed their doors. When Governors Herbert Lehman of New York and Henry Horner of Illinois suspended banking on March 4, every state in the union but one had severely restricted financial activity. The very foundations of the American economic system seemed to be crumbling.

Hoover wrote to Roosevelt urging him to issue a public statement that would restore public confidence and end the banking crisis. Such a statement should pledge no currency inflation, a balanced budget with additional taxes if needed, and no issuance of government securities—in other words, an endorsement of Hoover's policies. Hoover wrote to Pennsylvania senator David Reed, "I realize that if these declarations be made by the President-elect, he will have ratified the whole major program of the Republican Administration; that is, it means the abandonment of 90% of the so-called new deal." Roosevelt believed that the banks were likely to fail and a statement of confidence by him would have little effect other than to link his name to the debacle. As he told one of his advisors, "Let them bust; then we'll get things done on a sound basis."[19]

Treasury Secretary Ogden Mills urged Hoover to use war powers invested in the executive (under the World War I Trading with the Enemy Act) to solve the financial crisis by declaring a national bank holiday. Because Attorney General William D. Mitchell questioned the legality of such a move, Hoover resolved to do it only with Roosevelt's explicit concurrence. The president-elect again demurred, suggesting that Hoover did have the authority to proceed but that, in any event, the responsibility for official action continued to rest with the current administration. On March 3, the day before the inauguration, Hoover ignored the advice of Treasury Department officials who argued that only a national shutdown could save the banking system. He did nothing, other than label the incoming president's failure to cooperate as the act of a "madman." (Two days after taking the oath of office, Roosevelt declared the national banking holiday.) An overwrought Hoover left office burdened with a sense of impending calamity. "We are," he concluded, "at the end of our string."[20]

By contrast, Roosevelt exuded cheerful optimism as he prepared to assume command. Family and friends marveled at his imperturbable calm—as did the public when a crazed assassin failed in his attempt to murder the president-elect on February 15, 1933, fatally wounding Chicago mayor Anton Cermak instead. For more than four months, Roosevelt had quietly reposed on the sidelines as conditions worsened. The banking crisis raised the level of apprehension to new heights at the very end of Hoover's stewardship. A frightened America awaited the changing of the guard, not knowing what Roosevelt would do but hoping for the best. What changes would the New Deal bring?

CHAPTER TWO

The Hundred Days

March 4, 1933, the day of Franklin D. Roosevelt's inauguration, was blustery and damp in the nation's capital. Because of the death of Montana senator Thomas J. Walsh, the president-elect's choice for U.S. attorney general, flags flew at half-mast. Further adding to the sense of gloom, virtually all of the country's banks had closed and the nation's financial machinery sat idle. Soldiers with machine guns lined the Pennsylvania Avenue route from the White House to the Capitol taken jointly by the outgoing and incoming presidents. As their limousine moved slowly toward Capitol Hill, Roosevelt tried several times to engage Hoover in conversation. Distracted and phlegmatic, Hoover bit off one-word responses and stared blankly ahead. Finally, Roosevelt gave up and began waving genially to the cheering bystanders. The two men never saw each other after that day.

After taking the oath of office on the Capitol steps from Supreme Court Chief Justice Charles Evans Hughes, Roosevelt, bareheaded and coatless, braced himself against the biting wind and solemnly delivered his inaugural address. "I am certain that my fellow Americans expect that on my induction into the Presidency I will address them with a candor and a decision which the present situation of our Nation impels. . . . So, first of all, let me assert my firm belief that the only thing we have to fear is fear itself—nameless, unreasoning, unjustified terror which paralyzes needed efforts to convert retreat into advance." What had led the nation into such economic calamity? The banking community, he alleged, which had erred repeatedly and now abdicated leadership. In Roosevelt's metaphorical terms, "the money changers have fled from their high seats in the temple of our civilization." As Hoover sat impassively nearby, Roosevelt continued his criticism of materialism and unchecked profit seeking. With special emphasis he intoned, "This nation asks for action and action now!"[1]

Moving into his peroration, Roosevelt seemed to grow more solemn. He preferred to work closely with the legislative branch but proclaimed that he might need to assume temporary authority to work effectively. If that happened, he said, "I shall ask the Congress for the one remaining instrument to meet the crisis—broad Executive power to wage a war against the emergency, as great as the power that would be given to me if we were in fact invaded by a foreign foe." In the recent election the people had cast their vote for forceful action, for leadership. "In the spirit of the gift," he asserted, "I take it." A few perfunctory words concluded the address, the president left for the inaugural parade, and the crowds shuffled away. The promise of action, the indomitable optimism, and the forcefulness of Roosevelt's demeanor elevated the spirit of the thousands of people huddled in the Washington mist and the millions listening to him on radio. One of the few negative reactions came from the president's wife, Eleanor, who termed the inauguration "very, very solemn and a little terrifying." Perceiving a sense of desperation in the crowd, she lamented the fact that "when Franklin got to that part of his speech when he said it might become necessary for him to assume powers ordinarily granted to a President in war time, he received his biggest demonstration."[2]

The new president wasted little time in fulfilling his promise for immediate action. The next day he summoned Congress into an emergency session to begin on March 9. At 1:00 A.M. on March 6, under the authority of the World War I Trading with the Enemy Act, Roosevelt declared a national banking holiday. This gave the new administration three more days to devise banking legislation. Ignoring the cries of Progressives to nationalize the banks, the president relied on the men remaining from the previous administration in the Treasury Department and the Federal Reserve Board to institute the very measures Hoover had urged on Roosevelt during the interregnum. At noon on

March 9, Congress convened and promptly considered the Emergency Banking Act. With no copies of the bill available, rapt legislators listened as the specifics were read to them. Speaker of the House Joseph Byrns proclaimed a 40-minute limit to debate and no opportunity for amendment. At 4:05 P.M. the House approved by voice vote; scarcely three hours later the Senate approved by a vote of 73 to 7. Roosevelt signed the bill that evening.

The Emergency Banking Act legalized the recently proclaimed banking holiday and empowered the secretary of the treasury to reopen financially sound institutions. Unsound banks would remain closed under the supervision of "conservators." On March 12 Roosevelt devoted his first fireside chat to a thorough, if somewhat simplified, explanation of the banking situation. Like so many of his radio addresses, Roosevelt's banking message was a rousing success. Clear, concise, and persuasive, it gave the American people an understanding of the problem and the feeling that something would be done to solve it. The next day banks began reopening, and in the following weeks deposits exceeded withdrawals. By the end of March a majority of the nation's banks had reopened, and after another two months over 90 percent of deposits were available again. The banking crisis was over.[3]

Roosevelt's decision to resuscitate the existing financial system rather than substitute an entirely new arrangement drew fire from the political left. Socialist Norman Thomas complained, "It has re-established a banking system when it was on the verge of ruin." Bronson Cutting, Progressive senator from New Mexico, later wrote: "I think back to the events of March 4, 1933 with a sick heart. For then . . . the nationalization of banks by President Roosevelt could have been accomplished without a word of protest. It was President Roosevelt's great mistake." A disgruntled North Dakota congressman charged that "the President drove the money changers out of the capitol on March 4th, and they were all back on the 9th." Roosevelt remained equally cautious by refusing to support additional legislation providing for government insurance of deposits. With the full support of the bankers, he argued that the necessary refinements had been made.[4]

Roosevelt originally planned only to secure emergency banking legislation from the special session of Congress, but the ease with which that was accomplished led him to keep the legislature in Washington and pursue economic recovery initiatives immediately. Recognizing that pensions paid to veterans (about 1% of the total population) constituted almost one-fourth of the 1933 budget, Roosevelt charged Budget Director Lewis Douglas to devise suitable economy measures. The resultant Economy Bill, quickly passed by a compliant Congress on March 11, reduced veterans' benefits and authorized the president to cut salaries of federal workers up to 15 percent. In May a second Bonus Expeditionary Force of approximately one thousand veterans descended on Washington to protest. Unlike Hoover, Roosevelt met the potentially volatile situation adroitly. He provided the migrants with tents, showers, latrines, and mess halls. Eleanor Roosevelt visited the encampment, prompting one impressed veteran to say, "Hoover sent the army; Roosevelt sent his wife." This Bonus Army disbanded in short order.[5]

The president's success in defusing veterans' protest did not obscure the fact that his first two measures reflected little of the liberalism his supporters expected. Both bills seemed cautious and conservative—in fact, exactly the tack Herbert Hoover would have taken. Moreover, the budget cutting would surely prove deflationary at a time when just the opposite approach seemed necessary. The third measure, though much more popular, still gave no evidence of a "new deal." Anticipating the repeal of the Eighteenth Amendment, Roosevelt urged Congress to pass a law permitting the consumption of beer and light wines. The nation cheered when Roosevelt signed the bill on March 22, but the critics continued to express disappointment at the apparent lack of significant action. The liberal *New Republic* warned, "Perhaps many of those interests who cheered him for his first three successes would soon be sneering at the greatest President since Hoover."[6]

On March 16 Roosevelt sent Congress an omnibus agriculture bill—at last a substantive measure reflecting some of the action promised the previous year. Throughout the campaign Roosevelt had reaffirmed his belief that any recovery program must start with restoring some vitality to the demoralized farmers, without whose purchasing power industrial surpluses could never be reduced. In several speeches Roosevelt advocated the domestic allotment program, a plan espoused by Montana State College professor M. L. Wilson, whereby farmers would reduce production in return for price subsidies. A December 1932 conference of leading farm groups revealed a growing sentiment for domestic allotment, but other plans continued to attract support. Most notably, many experts remained committed to McNary-Haugenism, which called for a protective tariff on agricultural products and the sale of surpluses by government to foreign markets. A March 1933 gathering of farm leaders approved a compromise approach authorizing numerous methods to be employed at the discretion of the secretary of agriculture, Henry A. Wallace. For four days and nights Wallace and three other draftsmen wrote the bill that Roosevelt submitted to the legislature.

The Agricultural Adjustment Act contained something to please—and frustrate—everyone. Domestic allotment remained the heart of the bill, but it also contained elements of McNary-Haugenism such as marketing agreements and export-inducing government subsidies. To appease conservative critics and ensure that the administrative agency would be self-financing, the allotment payments to farmers would be provided by taxing the processors of farm products. Reliance on such a regressive tax, which would no doubt be passed along to consumers in the form of higher prices, reflected Roosevelt's fiscal conservatism. Finally, the bill included an emergency farm mortgage act and the so-called Thomas Amendment, a fiduciary measure that authorized the president to remonetize silver or otherwise inflate currency.

For the first time one of Roosevelt's administrative measures met fierce resistance in Congress. Agricultural processors' lobbyists descended upon the capital to protect their clients' profits, while liberals balked at a regressive tax to fund allotments. Progressive senator Burton K. Wheeler of Montana charged that the AAA would help the "commuting farmer" but not the "dirt farmer." Congressional conservatives recoiled at the sudden departure from the "safe" earlier legislation, especially objecting to the economic planning and government control inherent in domestic allotment. Representative Joseph W. Martin of Massachusetts lamented, "We are on our way to Moscow." To counter conservative opposition, Roosevelt approached Bernard Baruch to head the Agricultural Adjustment Administration. When the wealthy financier declined, the president persuaded George N. Peek, the creator of McNary-Haugenism, to take the position. Peek's establishment credentials, especially his association with financier Bernard Baruch, mollified initial opponents in the

Senate who insisted on a conservative administrator to head the new agency. After nearly two months of discussion the House passed the farm bill by a 315–98 margin and the Senate by 64 to 20.[7]

In his nomination acceptance speech Roosevelt had spoken of paying unemployed men to perform conservation tasks in the nation's forests—an expansion of a program he pioneered as governor of New York. On March 21 he asked Congress to create the Civilian Conservation Corps (CCC), which would employ a quarter of a million young men to plant trees, drain swamps, build dams, construct reservoirs, and generally refurbish forests, parks, and beaches. Roosevelt prided himself on being a conservationist, a great lover of the outdoors, and he took a special interest in the creation of the CCC. Moreover, he claimed sole responsibility for the idea and hoped to see his vision vindicated. In lofty terms he explained how hard work in nature would build sturdy bodies and elevate the spirit of the suffering youth from the benighted cities. Accordingly, he exulted when Congress approved the measure by voice vote on March 31.

Aiming to get the young men laboring for the CCC as quickly as possible, Roosevelt chose to work through existing federal agencies. The Department of Labor recruited the men, the War Department operated the camps, and the Departments of Agriculture and Interior jointly supervised the projects. To coordinate the enterprise Roosevelt chose Robert Fechner as CCC director. Opposition from organized labor, concerned with the agency's low wage rates, dissipated with the selection of Fechner, an American Federation of Labor vice-president. Unmarried men between the ages of 18 and 25 volunteered for six months, renewable up to two years, and received $30 per month, $25 of which went to their families back home. At its peak the CCC employed five hundred thousand men in twenty-five hundred camps and, though created as a temporary measure, survived until 1942. A few critics assailed the CCC as a forerunner of fascism or Hitlerism, but public response remained overwhelmingly positive. Roosevelt proudly claimed that the CCC was the most popular of the New Deal agencies.

For all its virtues the CCC benefited relatively few of the cities' unemployed millions. On March 21 Roosevelt asked Congress for the funds to create a federal relief agency patterned, on a much larger scale, on the Temporary Emergency Relief Administration (TERA) he had created in New York. The bill creating the Federal Emergency Relief Administration (FERA), drafted by Senators Robert M. LaFollette, Jr., of Wisconsin, Robert F. Wagner of New York, and Edward P. Costigan of Colorado, called for five hundred million dollars for federal grants to states. These grants would be distributed in two ways: on a matching basis, three state dollars for every federal dollar, for roughly half the awards, and unconditional federal grants where financial exigency precluded state contributions for the rest. In both cases, state administration of the awards ensured decentralization and the federal government would have no direct contact with relief recipients. The FERA would provide some relief for the unemployed but would emphasize work relief for the employable. Congress passed the bill on May 12, and the agency commenced operation one week later when Roosevelt appointed as its administrator Harry L. Hopkins, who had occupied the same position at the TERA in New York.

Roosevelt also resolved to address during the special legislative session the problems of the securities industry. The continuing Pecora investigation kept the stock market crash and its fallout a topic of great interest among the outraged public. The Emergency Banking Act had restored confidence in the nation's banking system but, as Roosevelt keenly appreciated, faith in the stock exchanges would have to be restored as well. On March 29 the president called for a law allowing federal supervision of investment securities. Any business interested in selling new securities in interstate commerce would be obligated to provide the government with complete information or face stiff penalties. To the traditional caveat emptor, Roosevelt insisted, must be added, "Let the seller beware."[8]

The drafting of such a bill proved an extraordinarily difficult task. Revering the stock market as the last bastion of totally unfettered free enterprise capitalism, the business community looked askance at any government intrusions. Several New Dealers tried their hand at appeasing both business and congressional critics, but without success. Finally, two Felix Frankfurter protégés from Harvard University, James M. Landis and Benjamin V. Cohen, produced a satisfactory product. The Securities Act required full disclosure but gave government limited power; it did not have the authority to deny approval but could delay issuance of securities pending further documentation. Wall Street lawyers still objected to the vast expansion of government power and to the provision that company executives would be held personally liable for misstatements. Congress approved, however, and Roosevelt signed the bill on May 27, 1933.

The following year Roosevelt completed the process of securities reform by presenting a bill to regulate the stock exchanges. This companion piece to the 1933 law, written by Benjamin Cohen and another Frankfurter acolyte, Thomas G. Corcoran, met with even fiercer resistance from Wall Street. Representative Sam Rayburn, one of the cosponsors of the legislation, called the opposition "the most powerful lobby ever organized against any bill which ever came up in Congress." The new law superseded the old by requiring full information not only from new securities but from all securities engaged in trading. It went even further, authorizing the federal government to supervise all trading as well as to regulate margin requirements. Originally assigning administration to the Federal Trade Commission, the bill underwent revision to invest operating authority in a new agency, the Securities and Exchange Commission (SEC). Earning himself the undying enmity of the financial community, Roosevelt signed the Securities Exchange Act on June 6, 1934.[9]

The great collision with business still a year in the future, the New Deal continued to take shape in the spring of 1933 as Roosevelt produced more requests for legislative action. In April he turned to the question of public power in the Tennessee Valley. In the late nineteenth century the advent of hydroelectric power, coupled with a rising environmental consciousness, launched a national debate about the private exploitation of natural resources and the public good. In the Progressive Era this became an increasingly popular issue—in good part due to the efforts of Franklin Roosevelt's cousin, Theodore—and a vital battleground between big business and its critics. During the First World War President Wilson authorized the use of a dam on the Tennessee River near Muscle Shoals, Alabama, for the production of synthetic nitrates—largely to produce explosives. Nitrates could also be used to produce fertilizer, a commodity sorely needed in the impoverished soil of the South. After the war the question of what to do with the Muscle Shoals facilities (a dam and two power plants) became the focus of the public power controversy.

Perhaps no issue engaged the congresses of the 1920s more than the fate of Muscle Shoals. When President Harding announced his desire to sell the project to private interests, auto magnate Henry Ford attempted to lease the facilities for a nominal fee. George W. Norris of Nebraska, chairman of the Senate Agriculture Committee, managed to derail Ford's efforts. Between 1921 and 1931 Norris introduced into Congress six bills empowering the federal government to operate hydroelectric plants on the Tennessee River. Two bills passed only to be vetoed by Coolidge and Hoover, the latter condemning the idea of public power as "a negation of the ideals upon which our civilization is based." Although consistently frustrated, Norris did manage to keep alive the possibility of government ownership pending the election of a president congenial to such aims. As governor of New York Roosevelt had forged a sterling record on conservation generally and public power specifically and, as a result, Norris campaigned for him in 1932. Roosevelt's election meant for the Nebraska senator and other Progressives the final realization of their dreams.[10]

In fact, Roosevelt's many ideas for development in the Tennessee Valley exceeded the plans favored by Norris. For the seven southern states touched by the river the president envisioned, in addition to hydroelectric power, flood control, soil conservation, diversification of industry, afforestation, and elimination of marginal farm land—all made possible by an unprecedented amount of centralized planning cutting across state lines. Inevitably, the proposal met considerable resistance from those fearful of expanding federal government influence. No New Deal program raised more charges of socialism, especially since government-produced and distributed electric power would compete with private power companies in the marketplace. Representatives of the power companies decried government intrusion, arguing incongruously both that no market existed for increased electricity production and that the loss of this additional business would decimate the securities of existing companies. Spearheaded by Norris and Tennessee senator Kenneth D. McKellar, TVA legislation survived the utilities companies' opposition. As a beaming Norris looked on, Roosevelt signed the bill.

In subsequent years observers have rightfully lauded the TVA for the many benefits it brought to the people of the Tennessee Valley, but modernization exacted a stiff price. New dams flooded farms, homes, schools, and churches to form the system's lakes, and the relocated inhabitants often left reluctantly. Those who remained questioned whether the TVA needed to construct so many dams. Critics noted the irony when the authority erected electrical plants fueled by strip-mined coal, thereby denuding part of the region it supposedly existed to conserve. When TVA later converted to nuclear power, the replacement of outmoded facilities and anachronistic technology cost billions of dollars and brought charges of shortsighted, fiscally irresponsible management. The project meant a higher standard of living for many and it brought a backward, isolated region more fully into the national mainstream, but the high cost of progress left many denizens of the region viewing the TVA as a mixed blessing.

Three days after sending the TVA bill to Congress, Roosevelt sent legislation to address the problem of home mortgage foreclosures. With Americans losing their homes at the rate of one thousand a day by 1933, even Hoover supporters admitted that his much ballyhooed Federal Home Loan Bank had failed. By April home owners found it nearly impossible to obtain mortgages or renew existing ones. The Home Owners Loan Corporation (HOLC) would refinance home mortgages by establishing the federal government as a second source of credit. During its first three years the HOLC spent more than three billion dollars and refinanced more than one million homes. Eventually it insured over 20 percent of the nation's nonfarming dwellings. In so doing the HOLC saved the real estate market and the construction industry, while earning the profound gratitude of the American middle class.

Americans of all classes and political persuasions marveled at the frenetic pace of activity in Washington under the new administration. Thousands of idealistic, aspiring men and women came to the capital flush with ideas and energy. Convinced they were fighting the good fight, they never doubted their effectiveness. One recent arrival to Washington exclaimed, "You feel like charging Hell with a bucket of water." Many of these New Dealers hailed from the East Coast, but they represented all regions and backgrounds. No longer did the "best and brightest" head for Wall Street; instead, they opted for Washington and public service. Brash, frequently overbearing, but never lacking in ideas, they transformed the staid, sleepy southern city into a beehive of activity. Of course, not all of the government veterans approved. George Peek described the immigration acidly. "A plague of young lawyers settled on Washington. . . . They floated airily into offices, took desks, asked for papers and found no end of things to be busy about. I never found out why they came, what they did or why they left." No one, however, could deny their industry. Crafting legislation, creating and then staffing massive new bureaucracies, the New Dealers performed an awesome amount of work in a short time and left as their legacy a vastly expanded federal government. In the torpid days of depression America, this seemed all to the good.[11]

As the relentless New Deal activity continued, however, economic recovery lagged in the spring of 1933. The money question increasingly took center stage. Since so many of the administration's early measures had been deflationary, Roosevelt himself recognized the need for currency inflation. Western Progressives, many of them holdovers from the William Jennings Bryan wing of the Democratic party that favored free silver, urged a cheaper dollar for relief to debtors. On the other hand, several key administrative figures like Lewis Douglas and James Warburg argued strenuously for fiscal orthodoxy and budgetary retrenchment as the only safe avenues to recovery. The addition of Oklahoma senator Elmer Thomas's amendment to the agriculture bill, though, added more political pressure for the administration to take action.

On April 19 Roosevelt announced that the United States was abandoning the gold standard as a counter to gold raids from Europe and declining domestic prices. This action would also improve the country's position at the upcoming World Economic Conference, a legacy of the Hoover years. Though praised as virtually inevitable by some economic experts, the fiscally orthodox expressed shock. Lewis Douglas said, "This is the end of western civilization," presumably anticipating that economic nationalism would exacerbate lingering antagonisms and lead to another world war. In any event, Roosevelt's acceptance of the congressional drive for inflation and the jettisoning of the gold standard were closely linked policies designed to depreciate the dollar and elevate domestic prices.[12]

In late April Roosevelt's daring monetary policy and the heated congressional discussion of farm relief dominated

Washington news. But as the New Deal's second month came to a close, knowledgeable observers commented on the continued absence of an industrial recovery plan. On April 26 Roosevelt told reporters, "As far as I can tell now, there is only one more major thing going up [to Congress] and that is railroads." Could it be that the special legislative session would end without consideration of industrial inactivity? Actually, Roosevelt had been disingenuous in his April 26 speech, for earlier that month the Senate's passage of Alabama senator Hugo Black's bill mandating 30-hour work weeks ended the administration's inertia. The president had indicated to Congress that he opposed the Black bill, calling it unconstitutional and overly restrictive, but the Senate passed it anyway by a decisive 53–30 vote. To reclaim the initiative and sidetrack a measure he considered seriously flawed, Roosevelt resolved to produce a superior industrial recovery program.[13]

The president ordered Assistant Secretary of State Raymond Moley to coordinate the efforts of the several groups in Washington working on a recovery plan. By May two plans, both emphasizing business-government cooperation, came to the fore—one, by General Hugh Johnson, a former War Industries Board member and a Bernard Baruch associate, provided for business agreements on competitive and labor practices enforced by government licensing powers. The other, created by Senator Robert F. Wagner and Assistant Secretary of Commerce John Dickinson, centered on industrial autonomy through trade associations. On May 10 Roosevelt ordered Johnson, Dickinson, Wagner, Lewis Douglas, Secretary of Labor Frances Perkins, Rexford Tugwell, and labor lawyer Donald Richberg to shut themselves in a room and combine the two versions. On May 14 the bedraggled group emerged from their seclusion, and three days later their product went to Congress with Roosevelt's blessing.

The National Industrial Recovery Act (NIRA), which Congress eventually passed largely in its May 14 form, followed the broad outlines of the Wagner-Dickinson faction but with many specifics reflecting Johnson's views. Title I of the NIRA, "Industrial Recovery," suspended antitrust laws so that industrial codes regulating production, prices, and trade practices could operate. Title I's Section 7(a) guaranteed labor representation in the workplace as well as collective bargaining. Title II, "Public Works and Construction Projects," appropriated 3.3 billion dollars for the

Public Works Administration. Such a remarkable experiment in business-government cooperation represented an undeniable divergence from free enterprise capitalism. As Raymond Moley pointed out to Roosevelt, "You realize then that you're taking an enormous step away from the philosophy of equalitarianism and laissez-faire." The president pointedly replied: "If that philosophy hadn't proved to be bankrupt, Herbert Hoover would be sitting here right now. I never felt surer of anything in my life than I do of the soundness of this passage." Upon signing the NIRA on June 16, Roosevelt prophesied that "history probably will record the National Industrial Recovery Act as the most important and far-reaching legislation ever enacted by the American Congress."[14]

On June 16, the last day of the congressional session, Roosevelt signed three other bills. The Farm Credit Act, establishing the Farm Credit Administration, expanded the amount of credit available to farmers and cooperatives. The Railroad Coordination Act created the federal government position of transportation coordinator. The Glass-Steagall Banking Act separated investment from commercial banking and created the Federal Deposit Insurance Corporation to insure accounts up to twenty-five hundred dollars. Roosevelt's long-standing opposition to government insurance of deposits melted away in the face of popular and congressional pressures. He showed no signs of disappointment when he signed the act, calling it the "second most important banking legislation enacted in the history of the country." Indeed, in later years Roosevelt claimed full credit for passage of the Glass-Steagall Act, including the FDIC provision. And when it emerged as one of the most popular New Deal reforms, Roosevelt willingly accepted the plaudits.[15]

During the Hundred Days, Franklin D. Roosevelt assumed the presidency like a whirlwind. He held press conferences and cabinet meetings twice a week, delivered a dozen speeches, and, most important, guided 15 major laws through Congress. Roosevelt promised the nation "action and action now," and clearly he delivered on that pledge. Whether they approved of or even understood New Deal measures, bystanders admitted that, unlike Hoover, Roosevelt conveyed the impression that he cared about people and would do whatever he could to help them. Peter Norbeck, Republican senator from South Dakota, wrote in May 1933: "I occasionally find myself singing faint praises. Yes, I know he is making a mess of a lot of things, but, My God, he is trying. What is more . . . they are introducing a little humanity into government . . . where it has been outlawed for some time."[16]

Whether or not this melange of legislation would have any impact on depression conditions, the American people took heart at the quickening pace of governmental activity. Political columnist Walter Lippmann observed: "At the end of February we were a congeries of disorderly panic-stricken mobs and factions. In the hundred days from March to June we became again an organized nation confident of our power to provide for our own security and to control our own destiny." Roosevelt refrained from setting unrealistically high expectations and repeatedly emphasized the need to focus on well-intentioned effort rather than results. In a May 7 fireside chat he said: "I do not deny that we may make mistakes of procedure as we carry out the policy. I have no expectation of making a hit every time I come to bat. What I seek is the highest possible batting average, not only for myself but for the team."[17]

At the end of the Hundred Days few Americans seemed willing to evaluate the New Deal innovations; most adopted a wait-and-see attitude, some more warily than others. Both Progressives and conservatives could find things to like and dislike in the legislature's output. Senate Progressives, many of them Republicans from western states, approved wholeheartedly of the TVA and, although they preferred more generous endowments, applauded new public works projects. Fervent supporters of the Black bill, they voted as a bloc against the NIRA (which passed the Senate by only a 46–39 margin). As loyal Brandeisians, many of the liberal insurgents opposed the suspension of antitrust laws and called instead for stricter enforcement of the Sherman and Clayton antitrust acts. They supported Section 7(a) but urged more comprehensive legislation for the workingman. The Emerency Banking and Economy acts troubled them, because of their deflationary aspects as well as their conciliatory approach to big business. As a group Progressives sponsored or supported many amendments and finally voted for laws resignedly as the best that could be achieved. The conservative cast of much of the early New Deal irritated Progressives who hoped for more pointed assaults on concentrated wealth.

Hooverville, with Seattle's skyline in the background. (Bettmann Archive)

The unemployed in New York City line up for meals at reduced prices, 1932. (FDR Library)

Billowing clouds of dirt darken the sky in the Dust Bowl near Spearman, Texas, 1935. (FDR Library)

Franklin D. Roosevelt and Harry Hopkins, June 1942. (FDR Library)

New Dealers Mary McLeod Bethune, Eleanor Roosevelt, and Aubrey Williams in light-hearted conversation. (UPI/Bettmann)

Norris Dam, one of the monumental New Deal public works projects. (FDR Library)

For conservatives the fruit of the Seventy-third Congress seemed a mixed bag as well. The Economy Act and the Emergency Banking Act won high praise as sound fiscal measures. The government-business partnership outlined in the NIRA seemed to favor business, as clearly shown by the tacit acceptance of price-fixing. (Even Robert F. Wagner grudgingly acknowledged the need for it if industrial planning were to have any chance of success.) On the other hand, some measures seemed frighteningly dangerous—particularly the TVA, the Securities Act, and the FDIC. To many conservative financiers, Roosevelt's decision to take the nation off the gold standard seemed an act of unfathomable irresponsibility. Senator Carter Glass of Virginia charged that "Roosevelt is driving this country to destruction faster than it has ever moved before." Glass stood virtually alone, however, in his willingness to condemn the New Deal unequivocally in 1933. Most conservatives, though nettled by some of what they saw, remained at least nominally loyal to the new chief executive.[18]

Onlookers from both ends of the political spectrum—and those in the middle as well—worried about the apparent expansion of executive authority. Horror stories abounded concerning an excessively compliant Congress rubber-stamping whatever Roosevelt sent to Capitol Hill. Tales of the legislature cursorily considering just-finished legislation, the ink still drying on the bills hurriedly rushed by car from the White House to Congress and passed by vocal acclamation with limited or no debate, suggested a complete abdication by one of the government's three branches. Such behavior lasted for only the first few of the Hundred Days, however, and increasingly bitter fights and close votes indicated that by May and June Congress had regained much of its characteristic volubility. Although the new president enjoyed considerable success with Congress in the spring of 1933, his triumphs frequently came grudgingly and at the cost of considerable political capital.

The eagerness of Congress at first to support presidential initiatives owed to several factors. A backlash against Hoover and the Republican party in 1932 left Roosevelt with substantial Democratic majorities, 60–35 in the Senate and 310–117 in the House. With 14 senators and 144 representatives freshmen in 1933 and another huge cohort having been elected in 1930, about half of Congress had been seated since the stock market crash.

Arguably, these newcomers would be especially inclined to support forceful action to combat the depression. The new president's clear mandate and popular pressure for action, combined with emergency economic conditions, undoubtedly influenced legislators to take steps they otherwise might have opposed.

Roosevelt also worked closely and well with Democratic congressional leaders, including Vice-President John Nance Garner. Although some of these finely cultivated relationships would sour in later years and dissident Democrats would desert the New Deal standard, the Seventy-third Congress was remarkably loyal. Roosevelt enjoyed the fealty of several key Democrats, old-timers who placed the highest value on party loyalty. Thus, Senate Majority Leader Joseph Robinson of Arkansas, Speaker of the House Henry Rainey of Illinois, and House Majority Leader Joseph Byrns of Tennessee kept a close rein on Democrats. In both houses of Congress limited floor debate and partisan rulings from the chair kept legislation flowing smoothly.

Along with establishing strong ties with fellow politicians, Roosevelt succeeded in creating a very positive public image. The contrast between the Roosevelt and Hoover White Houses could not have been greater, at least as portrayed in the popular media. The stuffy formality of the Hoover age gave way to a relaxed insouciance that wore well with White House visitors. With or without dinner guests, the Hoovers dined elegantly on gourmet food and expensive wines, apparently as part of the discredited president's plan to keep up appearances. By contrast, Roosevelt dutifully ate bland 19-cent lunches and only slightly more elaborate dinners—all at the insistence of his wife, Eleanor.

It also quickly became apparent that the First Lady would be an invaluable political asset. From the beginning the president intended to send his wife around the country to gain firsthand information about depression conditions. This she did capably while establishing a huge and loyal following of her own. Tireless, caring, and remarkably unpretentious, she proved a priceless ambassador of goodwill from the president to countless Americans throughout the country—so much so, in fact, that the Roosevelt administration seemed almost a matrimonial partnership. After only one year in the White House, Eleanor herself received over three hundred thousand letters.

Roosevelt also enjoyed a protracted honeymoon with the press. Newspaper columnist Heywood Broun admiringly called

Roosevelt "the best newspaperman who has ever been President of the United States," and almost without exception, his relations with the White House press corps were excellent. The reporters' great respect and affection for him resulted from several factors: unlike all of his predecessors since Harding, Roosevelt rejected a "written questions only" policy and fielded verbal queries without limitation at press conferences. Of course, the rapid-fire pace of news generated during the Hundred Days made reporters' jobs easy. Moreover, Roosevelt seemed genuinely to enjoy the company of reporters and treated them affably. He relished the banter and verbal sparring of press conferences and although he would occasionally dodge pointed questions, he would do so with a wink and a grin so that everyone knew his intent. When the United States abandoned the gold standard in 1933, Roosevelt sent a government economist to the White House pressroom to help reporters with the intricacies of the story, a thoughtful gesture that became part of Washington journalism lore. Roosevelt could be overbearing and pedantic at times, and he surely did not take criticism well. Overall, however, reporters gave him high marks for candor and, most of all, for accessibility.[19]

During the Hundred Days Roosevelt held 30 press conferences, and over the course of his 12-year presidency he convened a total of 998—2 per week almost without fail. Although he distrusted editors and columnists and believed that newspaper owners as a group plotted against him, the president maintained cordial relations with correspondents that virtually never wavered. He benefited from a laudatory press—throughout his administration but especially at the outset—so much so that *New York Times* bureau chief Arthur Krock complained that Washington correspondents frequently let the president off too easily.

In the same vein Roosevelt's use of radio proved an effective tool in attracting public support for his policies. In the spring of 1933 he delivered two fireside chats, the first explaining the emergency banking legislation and the second justifying the business-government entente created by the NIRA. Having used radio effectively as New York governor, he delivered 27 radio talks as president. Usually lasting 30 minutes and scheduled between 9:00 and 11:00 P.M. on Sunday nights, the broadcasts reached millions of Americans. Roosevelt often said that he pretended to converse face-to-face with people when he spoke into the microphone, which explained the intimacy and informality that characterized the speeches. Listeners felt that the president spoke directly to them in a friendly, conversational manner; without question, these talks endeared the president to Americans starved for hope and reassurance.

A friendly Congress, an emasculated opposition, a supportive public, and his personal popularity gave Roosevelt great latitude in establishing his programs. Yet the problem persists of identifying exactly what emerged from the Hundred Days. What was the New Deal that took shape during those three months in 1933? Historian Frank Freidel lists the Roosevelt program: "government economy, prohibition repeal, regulation of securities sales, self-sustaining public works, reforestation, a lower tariff, a voluntary crop control program, refinancing of farm and home mortgages, and federal relief." These were, indeed, the essentials, but what unified the various programs? The president set out to rescue the nation's damaged financial institutions and to rekindle industrial activity via a partnership with business. Rejecting a wholesale assault on business concentrations, the federal government opted for regulatory agencies and supervision. Through all of this ran an unprecedented commitment to regional and industrial planning, much of which would be directed by the benign hand of government.[20]

Urgent needs, political concerns, ideological ambivalence, and temporal and financial limitations also served to define the inchoate New Deal. Thus, Roosevelt and his advisors failed to address many concerns in the spring of 1933, including old-age insurance, low-cost housing, unemployment compensation, public utility control, civil rights, income redistribution, tax reform, and tariff adjustment. The decision to ignore so many serious problems owed in large measure to Roosevelt's persistent commitment to economy. His support for the AAA tax scheme and the Economy Act underscored this fiscal conservatism, just as did his rejection of compensatory federal spending. In February 1933, in his testimony before the Senate Finance Committee, future Federal Reserve Board Chairman Marriner Eccles advocated large-scale public works deficit spending. Roosevelt knew of these economic prescriptions later made famous by British economist John Maynard Keynes but did not favor them. Thus, the New Deal was defined as much by what Roosevelt did not attempt as by what he did.

Roosevelt's choices to head newly created government agencies and programs further reflected a cautious approach. Time and again he selected respected conservative figures to guide departments created by controversial legislation. Men like the AAA's George Peek, the NRA's Hugh Johnson, the CCC's Robert Fechner, the RFC's Jesse Jones, and Railroad Coordinator Joseph Eastman shared a reputation for businesslike practicality. Particularly striking was the later appointment of archconservative Joseph P. Kennedy as the SEC's first administrator. Even veteran Progressive Harold L. Ickes was widely thought to be scrupulously honest and tightfisted—a fiscal conservative. Liberal programs tempered by conservative administrators appeared to be the formula upon which the president often relied.

Finally, Roosevelt's fundamental commitment to the American economic system shone through. Later in the decade he remarked, "It is not that the system of free enterprise for profit has failed in this generation, but that it has not yet been tried." In a published reminiscence, Labor Secretary Frances Perkins observed that Roosevelt "took the status quo in our economic system as much for granted as his family." It was unlikely that an aristocratic gentleman farmer from the Hudson Valley would seek to topple the capitalist system, and in this sense Roosevelt behaved as expected. His willingness to cooperate with business, in which he still placed considerable trust, evidenced itself repeatedly in 1933. Disenchantment and alienation with the entrepreneurial class had not yet set in. Rather, Roosevelt remained optimistic that American capitalism could be salvaged and a new business-government harmony established. Evaluation awaited the performance of the New Deal's individual programs, and in Roosevelt's mind no venture held greater import for recovery than the effort to aid agriculture.[21]

CHAPTER THREE

Agricultural Adjustment

In 1931 cotton sold for 5.7 cents per pound, down from a high of 41.7 cents per pound in 1920. Worried planters contemplated financial ruin, as discussion of the cotton crisis raged in southern communities from the Tidewater to the Texas coastal plain. Flamboyant Louisiana Senator Huey P. Long proposed a cotton holiday, a one-year moratorium on production of the staple, to remove the price-depressing glut and restore demand. In August of that year Long's home state enacted a law prohibiting the planting, picking, or ginning of the crop in 1932. Other southern states seemed poised to join the movement until Texas, which produced one-third of the nation's cotton, declined to participate. When the Texas legislature voted down a cotton holiday bill, Long announced that he was giving up the fight for his "drop-a-crop" scheme. Despite the failure of Long's movement, the mass meetings, extensive newspaper coverage, and special legislative sessions throughout the South reflected how seriously desperate cotton growers took his radical-sounding proposal. Such measures as mandatory production limitation and government regulation, unthinkable just years before, became acceptable in the context of the farm crisis and opened the way for the kind of innovative farm policies being discussed in the early 1930s by, among others, New York governor Franklin D. Roosevelt.

The farm problem confronting the new president in 1933 was the culmination of a decade's worsening of conditions, affecting not only southern cotton planters but also farmers in other regions. Although their numbers had been decreasing for years, farmers still composed 30 percent of the labor force in 1933. Moreover, farm acreage and yields had been increasing, along with unsold surpluses. Farmers' share of national income fell from 25 percent in 1919 to 10.4 percent 10 years later. Agricultural indebtedness grew from $8.5 billion in 1920 to $9.1 billion in 1932. Moreover, by the early 1930s the situation was worsening at an accelerated pace: in 1932 farmers received 60 percent less for their crops than they had only 3 years earlier. Farm mortgage foreclosures became epidemic, especially on the Great Plains, where—between 1925 and 1931—state officials in Montana sold for nonpayment of taxes approximately 110 of every 1,000 farms. In neighboring North Dakota, South Dakota, and Idaho the figures were 86, 66, and 68, respectively. The long-cherished American goal of owning a family farm seemed genuinely at risk.

Although most struggling farmers met their fate with a stoicism and resignation forged by a lifetime engaged in a risky, capricious occupation, others reacted more forcefully. Bleak conditions, the threatened loss of home and livelihood, invested some farmers with a fatalism that bred recklessness. In several midwestern states, farmers erected barricades to prevent trucks from getting to market and dumped milk and produce on the roads. Milo Reno's Farmers' Holiday Association captured national attention with the Sioux City milk strike in 1932, and the following year members of the National Guard in Wisconsin attacked striking dairy farmers with tear gas and bayonets. In hundreds of cases armed farmers forestalled evictions by threatening sheriffs, judges, and government officials. Congregating in threatening groups, farmers discouraged participation at foreclosure auctions, submitted low bids, and returned property to relieved neighbors. Such activity impressed upon New Dealers the need for action and, as incidents multiplied, spawned a sense of urgency.

On March 16, 1933, Roosevelt spoke to Congress of the need for quick action on the pending farm bill, saying that "the proposed legislation is necessary now for the simple reason that the spring crops will soon be planted and if we wait for another month or six weeks the effect on the prices of this year's crops will be wholly lost." The Agricultural Adjustment Act did not pass without healthy debate, however, as critics scorned the ideas of reduced productivity, government regimentation, and loss of freedom. Secretary of Agriculture Henry A. Wallace defended production control, likening it to the routine activities of corporations seeking to maximize profits in the free market of supply and demand. "As our economic system works," he adduced, "the greater the surplus of wheat on Nebraska farms, the longer the bread lines in New York." With news of rural violence widespread in the spring of 1933, Congress approved the bill and the creation of the Agricultural Adjustment Administration.[1]

Most independent New Deal agencies enjoyed considerable autonomy and reported directly to the president, but the AAA resided within the Department of Agriculture. This meant that ultimate authority rested with the secretary of agriculture, to whom the head of the agency answered. With Henry A. Wallace and George N. Peek, respectively, filling those positions in 1933, conflict was inevitable. Henry A. Wallace, whose father, Henry C. Wallace, had served as secretary of agriculture in the 1920s, came to Washington in 1933 with the reputation of being both a knowledgeable analyst of farm policy and an impractical dabbler in Eastern religions and mysticism. His personal idiosyncracies notwithstanding, however, his years of editing the family newspaper, *Wallace's Farmer,* had schooled him in crop genetics, farm price fluctuations, and soil science. Despite his unusual avocations, Wallace was a serious and devoted champion of the farmers and held the respect of agricultural experts throughout the country. At the outset of the New Deal, Secretary Wallace wielded considerable influence with the president, and he firmly believed that domestic allotment offered the greatest hope for American farmers.

By 1933 George N. Peek was the nation's most celebrated advocate for the farmer. Peek learned about agriculture as a farm implements executive, first as a vice-president for the John Deere Plow Company and then—after a stint at the War Industries Board during the First World War—as president of the Moline Plow Company. The sorry plight of the farmer concerned him, since, as he remarked, "You can't sell a plow to a busted customer." In 1921 he and a former colleague at the War Industries Board, Hugh Johnson, devised a plan for "equality for agriculture" based on the assurance of cost of production plus profit. In 1924 Peek resigned from the Moline Plow Company and spent much of the rest of the decade lobbying in Congress for the various McNary-Haugen bills embodying his principles. As early as 1931 Peek proclaimed Franklin D. Roosevelt his choice to succeed Hoover in the White House because of the New York governor's commitment to farmers generally rather than his increasing fondness for production control theories. As a member of the new Roosevelt administration, Peek reluctantly agreed to production cutbacks but never accepted the policy as the permanent centerpiece of AAA efforts.[2]

Ironically, Wallace had recommended Peek for secretary of agriculture, but Roosevelt's advisors scotched the idea. In February 1933, Peek testified against production control before a Senate committee and the following month turned down Wallace's offer to administer the new agriculture law. He changed his mind and accepted the job in May, but not before he received a promise of direct access to the president. Wallace agreed to the demand, but insisted that the lines of authority remain clear and that he would make final decisions on all agricultural policy. Given Wallace's commitment to domestic allotment and Peek's preference for marketing agreements and the manipulation of foreign trade, the future of the AAA remained unsettled.

Although Peek held the top spot in the new AAA, advocates of production control occupied important positions throughout the agency as well as in the Department of Agriculture. With few exceptions, these men were social scientists, usually agricultural economists. Brains Truster Rexford G. Tugwell, M. L. Wilson, John D. Black, Howard Tolley, Mordecai Ezekiel, Louis Bean, and Gardiner Means all supported the voluntary domestic allotment plan, as did Secretary Wallace. So, despite the opposition of the AAA's chief administrator, implementation of crop reduction began with a rush in May 1933.

The passage of the AAA bill in May, long after spring planting, presumably necessitated the destruction of a portion of that year's output of corn, cotton, wheat, rice, hogs, and dairy products (the so-called basic agricultural commodities, according to the new law.) A severe drought in the Midwest reduced wheat and corn production to the lowest level of the twentieth century and eliminated the need for action, but planters plowed under ten million acres of cotton and livestock farmers slaughtered six million piglets. Many Americans recoiled at the wholesale destruction of food and fiber at a time when hundreds of thousands went without meals and clothing. The AAA managed to deflect some of the criticism by organizing the Federal Surplus Relief Corporation, which provided over one hundred million pounds of pork to hungry relief recipients. Farmers went along because they received government checks for the portion of their land held out of production as well as the promise of higher prices created by scarcer crops. For hasty implementation the AAA relied upon the county agents of the land-grant colleges' Agricultural Extension Services, a solution that dovetailed nicely with the New Deal's avowed devotion to grass-roots participation. In subsequent months local committees determined acreage restriction, supervised the plow-up, and authenticated farmers' compliance reports. In 1933 county agents signed thousands of farmers to production limitation contracts, and the great plow-up and slaughter campaign commenced. A somber Henry Wallace proclaimed the effort a success, adding that he hoped it would never be necessary again.

The summer of 1933 continued to be a time of great trepidation for farmers, though, since the effectiveness of crop reduction remained very much in doubt. In June Congress passed the Farm Credit Act, which provided more than one hundred million dollars in loans in 1933 to farmers for the refinancing of mortgages. Farm prices shot up in the summer due to speculative buying, but AAA subsidy checks came months late to expectant farmers. By early fall farm prices began to decline, just when the NRA was driving industrial prices up. In spite of AAA efforts, crop yields for 1933 either rose or declined only slightly in comparison with 1932 figures. For example, despite the plow-up of one-fourth of the cotton acreage, unusually favorable weather resulted in a bumper crop. As improvement came more slowly than farmers expected, protest erupted again in the midwestern states. The Farmers' Holiday Association and the Farmers' Union threatened action failing the enactment of a more radical program. But by mid-November the protests quieted down thanks to the tardy arrival of benefit payments, the distribution of agricultural surpluses to the needy, moderate inflation, and crop loans from the newly created Commodity Credit Corporation (CCC). (Originally formed to lend money to cotton growers, the CCC proved so popular that it extended loans to farmers raising other crops.) Looking back over the previous year, farmers could see some improvement.

Overall, 1933 farm prices rose from 50 percent of parity to 68 percent by mid-December. The hog slaughter raised the price of pork approximately 15 percent, and, thanks largely to marketing agreements, the prices of dairy products rose steadily if not spectacularly. By fall 1933 the price of cotton rose to 10 cents per pound, about double the price of 1932. Cash receipts rose most dramatically for flue-cured tobacco, whose average price increased to 15.3 cents per pound in 1933, up from 8.4 cents in 1931. Indeed, price increases indicate that farmers' dissatisfaction with the pace of improvement stemmed from their apparent desire to return to parity immediately. Between the recovery of some lost income and the provision of benefit payments, AAA programs must be judged at least a partial success in their first year of operation.

Early success did not, however, defuse the persistent animosities within the AAA's bureaucracy. And since these conflicts among agricultural specialists involved fundamental differences in policy, their resolution took on added importance for the future of the agency. At the heart of the turmoil remained George Peek, who continued to push hard for marketing agreements and the dumping of surpluses abroad. Wallace rejoined, "We ought to act for the moment as if we were a self-contained agricultural economy." More fundamentally, Peek affirmed his belief that "the sole aim" of AAA "is to raise farm prices." This narrow view contrasted sharply with the goals of Wallace and Tugwell, who sought the development of an agricultural policy as one part of a planned economy.[3]

Peek clashed frequently with the liberal head of AAA's legal division, Jerome Frank, who, coincidentally, had been involved in the liquidation of Peek's former employer, the Moline Plow Company. Frank surrounded himself with young liberal attorneys (including Alger Hiss, Lee Pressman, Adlai Stevenson, Thurman Arnold, Gardner Jackson, Abe Fortas, and Francis Shea) who shared his interest in social reform. Peek and his allies, products of the Farm Bureau, the Extension Service, and the land-grant colleges, held the urban lawyers in contempt for their inexperience in agricultural matters. Their favorite story related how Lee Pressman had said at a contract hearing, "Just tell me this; is this code fair to macaroni growers?" Peek's requests for marketing agreements came under fire in the hostile Legal Division and in the equally unfriendly Consumer Division headed by Frederic Howe. Throughout the summer of 1933 Peek and Frank took turns attacking each other and seeking the support of Secretary Wallace.[4]

The increasingly intolerable situation came to a climax in September in a battle over the flue-cured tobacco contract. The Legal Division reformers sought access to tobacco processors' records and the power to set prices. More sympathetic with businessmen, Peek believed the AAA should limit itself strictly to the concerns of farmers. The disagreement went to the president for resolution, and Roosevelt decided in favor of Peek. He did not, however, support Peek's attempt to remove Frank and his allies. By December, with Peek constantly at loggerheads with Wallace, Frank, and Tugwell, the situation had become untenable. Roosevelt asked Peek to resign, which he did to become special advisor to the president on foreign trade. Peek's replacement at the AAA, Chester Davis, supported domestic allotment, thus confirming the agency's approach and bringing—at least for the moment—peace with Legal Division reformers.

This harmony proved short-lived, for although Chester Davis was less intransigent than his predecessor, he also viewed the AAA as an organization with a limited mandate. Jerome Frank and the urban liberals sought a sweeping readjustment of American farming practices. The inevitable resumption of hostilities came over the question of the AAA's treatment of sharecroppers and tenant farmers in the cotton South. In the 1930s fewer than half of all southerners owned the land they farmed, and tenant labor operated nearly three-fourths of the region's cotton farms. The South contained nearly two million tenant farmers in 1935, about 63 percent of the nation's total. Seventy percent of Mississippi farmers were tenants. In 1936 the President's Commission on Farm Tenancy reported that as many as one-fourth of the nation's farmers lived in wretched poverty and suffered from chronic malnutrition, pellagra, malaria, and hookworm, and that southern tenants suffered disproportionately. Here, thought the urban liberals, the AAA could institute agrarian reforms for the betterment of a substantial portion of American society.

The 1933 cotton contract drafted by the AAA paid scant attention to tenants or sharecroppers. Landowners signed the agreements and made their own arrangements with tenants. The AAA instructed landowners to share their production limitation payments "according to the interest each tenant held in the crops," but the absence of enforcement provisions meant that landowners had no reason to comply. Planters also customarily deducted old debts from the settlement when they tallied tenants' accounts, resulting frequently in no payments being made. In high-tenancy counties of Virginia, for example, AAA officials reported that most tenants received no benefits at all. Even worse, with less land in cultivation and a reduced need for labor, landlords released many of their tenants. A sizable landless work force roamed the countryside, some crowding the highways in certain counties of cotton country and others settling in the cities to seek relief. In any event, an uprooted peasantry, landless and powerless, threatened to emerge as an unintended by-product of AAA policy.[5]

Several sound reasons existed for the AAA to work through landlords instead of bypassing them to distribute benefit payments directly to sharecroppers and tenants. Ignoring landlords would challenge traditional southern practices and the existing social order (which, of course, appealed to the liberal reformers). Such a tack would alienate the landlords, without whose support the cotton program would be sorely jeopardized. Also, southern planters made the key decisions about cotton in the AAA; Cully Cobb, head of the agency's cotton section, owned a Mississippi plantation, and AAA finance officer Oscar Johnston managed a plantation, reputedly the nation's largest, that employed over one thousand sharecroppers. Moreover, the chairmen of both the House and Senate agriculture committees were southerners with strong ties to cotton interests. In short, political and economic power in the South rested firmly with the landlords and not with the landless laborers.

Tenants inveighed bitterly against their worsening circumstances. In keeping with its penchant for decentralization, the AAA's grievance mechanism provided for the submission of complaints to committees of county agents. These screening committees, when not actually composed of planters, invariably contained members of the local gentry who sympathized with their landholding peers. Not surprisingly, tenants found no satisfaction within formal channels. The plight of the forlorn sharecroppers began to gain national attention, particularly when several of them in southeastern Arkansas formed a labor union, the Southern Tenant Farmers Union (STFU), in July 1934. Advised by prominent Socialist Norman Thomas, the fledgling organization boasted fourteen hundred members in five Arkansas counties within a few months. With many of the STFU leaders being preachers, union meetings took on the air of religious revivals. Because its avowed biracialism threatened regional mores, planters and area townspeople had another reason to oppose the union. Landlords shot at and brutally beat union organizers, who often fled armed bands of vigilantes across the Mississippi River into the safety of Memphis, Tennessee. Such terrorism discredited the landlords in the national media and did nothing to silence the malcontents. By the end of 1935 STFU membership reached thirty thousand in several states, and the AAA could not continue to ignore the problem. Legal Division liberals, in particular, showed acute interest.

In the preparation of the 1934–35 cotton contracts Alger Hiss lobbied avidly for sharecroppers and tenant farmers but found arrayed against him the combined influence of Chester Davis, Cully Cobb, and Oscar Johnston. The resultant contract encouraged landlords to share equitably with their tenants but again avoided specific requirements and included no enforcement provisions. Secretary Wallace and AAA officials recognized the inequities and regretted them but could see no viable alternatives. At the request of the agency, Duke University Professor Calvin B. Hoover conducted a study on the effects of cotton acreage reduction on southern tenants. He criticized the AAA for inadequate enforcement and supported the STFU's claims of landlords' unfair treatment of their workers but concluded that, on balance, the cotton program had benefited the South. Secretary Wallace maintained that the Department of Agriculture would do what it could for tenants but warned that the forces of change would not be deflected. One-third of American farmers produced cotton, he noted, and with a shrinking world market not all of them could continue to raise the staple indefinitely.

The AAA liberals remained unconvinced. News of increased terrorism against the STFU in 1934 stiffened the liberals' resolve to combat the widespread eviction of tenants. In February 1935 the AAA's Legal Division challenged the policy outlined in the new contract that landlords had to employ the same number of tenants but not necessarily the same individuals. Believing that landlords fired tenants for joining the STFU, the Legal Division, principally Alger Hiss and Francis Shea, prepared a 36-page opinion arguing that landlords must retain the identical tenants.

Bowing to pressure from southern congressmen, Wallace sided with Chester Davis to negate the Hiss-Shea opinion. On February 5, 1935, Wallace fired Frank, Pressman, Shea, and Jackson; Hiss resigned shortly thereafter. The "purge" of the liberals ensured that AAA officials would speak with one voice on the cotton tenancy question. Having no desire to reform the landownership system of southern agriculture entrenched since Reconstruction, the AAA bowed to expediency and political pressure. The New Deal agency invested in the cotton planters the authority to administer the program, thus ensuring that these landlords would be the principal beneficiaries. The removal of masses of nonlandowning farm workers—releasing what Wallace called a "damming up on the farms of millions of people who normally would have been taken care of elsewhere"—came faster because of New Deal programs. And because of the suddenness, the tenants and croppers suffered horribly.[6]

In a limited and certainly inadequate fashion, the New Deal tried to help the rural poor. Beginning in 1933 the Federal Emergency Relief Administration (FERA) spent a small part of its allocation on a host of programs including rural rehabilitation, resettlement of farmers, and land-use planning. An obscure section of the National Industrial Recovery Act (NIRA) allocated twenty-five million dollars for the creation of subsistence homesteads. Thus, in the first two years of the New Deal several modest programs existed in different agencies—outside of the Department of Agriculture—to aid poor farmers, but increasingly concerned bureaucrats like Rexford Tugwell called for consolidation into one unit. Fearing congressional opposition, Roosevelt created the Resettlement Administration (RA) by executive order on April 30, 1935. Funded by relief appropriations the RA absorbed the agriculture-related programs of the FERA, NIRA's Subsistence Homesteads Division, and the Farm Credit Administration. Rexford Tugwell became the RA's administrator while remaining assistant secretary of agriculture. From the outset, Tugwell sought to make land reform the focus of Resettlement Administration activities.

The RA sought to educate farmers about better land-use practices. In the Appalachian hills, the cotton South, and the soil-depleted southern Great Plains especially, the RA hoped that improved farming would salvage land neglected and abused for generations. At the same time the agency bought submarginal land and helped to resettle its prior occupants on better land or in government-created suburbs. From the beginning, however, elements of planning and collectivization in the RA created problems. The political powerlessness of its supporters, paltry appropriations from Congress, and negative publicity hamstrung the RA. A frustrated Tugwell, whose grandiose plans for rural rehabilitation never came close to realization, resigned his government posts after Roosevelt's 1936 reelection. His successor at the RA, Will Alexander, continued to head an agency beset by problems, not the least of which was President Roosevelt's tepid support.

On February 13, 1937, the President's Special Committee on Farm Tenancy, which included such noted social scientists as Tugwell, M. L. Wilson, Mordecai Ezekiel, Charles S. Johnson, and Howard Odum, submitted its report calling for an expansion of RA programs. In conjunction with Congress's passage of the Bankhead-Jones Farm Tenant Act in July 1937, the Farm Security Administration (FSA) assumed the responsibilities of the RA but within the Department of Agriculture. Largely because of necessary concessions to congressional critics, the new agency abandoned Tugwell's emphasis on resettlement. Under Will Alexander the FSA emphasized the creation and protection of the small family farm, not the transplanting of farmers to better land. The FSA lent money to tenants so that they could purchase land and offered grants to embattled small landowners for improvements and debt repayment. Although the emphasis on preserving the family farm rather than subsistence homesteads engendered less controversy, the FSA enjoyed no greater success at procuring funds from a tightfisted Congress. In its first two years of operation the FSA filled the loan requests of only 6,180 of 146,000 applicants. By 1940 the agency could make fewer than ten thousand loans annually, and the coming of the Second World War brought new priorities for federal spending and fewer dollars for struggling farmers and farm workers.

The programs of the Farm Security Administration, despite the succor they provided to a relatively small number of recipients, fell far short of ameliorating the conditions of the rural poor. No panaceas existed, and inadequate resources doomed the effort from the start. Perhaps the FSA's greatest contribution rested with its exposure of rural poverty. First through the RA and later, more extensively, through the FSA, a talented group of photographers under the direction of Roy Stryker recorded the lasting images of America's rural proletariat. Walker Evans, Arthur Rothstein, Dorothea Lange, Ben Shahn, Margaret Bourke-White, Marion Post Walcott, Gordon Parks, and Russell Lee snapped more than 270,000 pictures of America's suffering farmers. Pare Lorentz produced two documentary films, "The Plow That Broke the Plains" in 1936 and "The River" in 1937, that played in hundreds of theaters nationwide. Whatever awareness of America's farming crisis developed in the 1930s and after no doubt owed to the remarkable images preserved by the FSA's Photographic Section.

New Dealers also tried to ameliorate the suffering of another group of struggling farmers, the American Indians. Given unlimited authority as commissioner of Indian affairs by Interior Secretary Ickes, John Collier endeavored to revoke the nation's policy of assimilation established in the 1887 Dawes Severalty Act. By the time of the depression, reservation life had degenerated to a condition of perpetual penury with astronomical rates of crime and alcoholism. Under the Indian Reorganization Act of 1934, Collier hoped to resuscitate the Indian economy through a multimillion-dollar credit fund. At the same time, he sought to preserve traditional Indian culture and install tribal self-government.

Collier's efforts produced some salutary changes, including the addition of seven million acres of land to the Indian domain, the improvement of medical care, and the reform of the notoriously venal Bureau of Indian Affairs, but few lasting economic changes resulted. He encountered fierce opposition from entrenched government bureaucrats and from the Indians themselves, many of whom preferred greater assimilation to a "return to the blanket." Indians resisted sweeping land-use changes and herd reductions, while the amount of financial aid Collier promised never materialized. As the New Deal sputtered in the late 1930s, the plight of the American Indian remained as bleak as ever. Plagued by unusually high rates of poverty, disease, and unemployment, Indians remained dependent wards of the federal government.

While the New Deal aided the landless poor to a limited extent, most farmers enjoyed improved conditions in the mid-1930s. The AAA continued to propose voluntary crop restrictions, but initial successes led many farmers to demand mandatory participation. Grass-roots pressure convinced Congress to pass in 1934 the Bankhead Cotton Control Act and the Kerr-Smith Tobacco Control Act, both of which employed the taxing power to ensure compliance. Pending approval by referendum of at least two-thirds of all farmers, the Bankhead Act levied a tax of 50 percent of the value of cotton ginned for every farmer exceeding his allotment. The Kerr-Smith Act assessed a tax of 25 to 35 percent on the sale of tobacco in excess of production quotas. In 1933 and 1934 the AAA rice section principally utilized marketing agreements, in 1935 a processing tax; in both instances prices remained high. By the end of 1935 agricultural commodities brought 88 percent of pre–World War I prices. Additionally, farmers received almost two billion dollars in benefit payments. Whereas the NRA could claim little success in the struggle for industrial recovery by 1935, the AAA performed much better. In 1935, wheat, corn, tobacco, and cotton farmers all voted overwhelmingly in referenda to continue AAA programs and subsequently reacted negatively when the courts intervened to dismantle the agency.

In January 1936, the U.S. Supreme Court ruled on the constitutionality of the AAA in *U.S.* v. *Butler.* Following the *Schechter* decision's destruction of the NRA, over eleven hundred processors filed suit against the AAA. Anticipating a favorable decision, the plaintiffs withheld payment of approximately one hundred million dollars in processing taxes. The Court held the AAA processing tax an improper exercise of the federal government's power because it forced farmers to regulate agricultural production. This, Justice Owen Roberts intoned, speaking for the majority, impinged upon the reserved powers of the states. Congress reacted quickly, repealing the Bankhead and Kerr-Smith acts and passing the Soil Conservation and Domestic Allotment Act. This new law abandoned processing taxes and acreage quotas, instead seeking limited production of certain soil-depleting crops through soil conservation. (It also provided for the mailing of benefit checks directly to tenants and sharecroppers.) Withdrawing land from cultivation, introducing enriching grasses and legumes, combating erosion, and rotating crops, the federal government continued to pursue the same goal of agricultural practices adjustment but in alternative ways.

Unquestionably a much needed reform, soil conservation unfortunately exacerbated the problem of overproduction. With the elimination of the worst land from cultivation and the introduction of sturdier crops, existing acreage produced more bountiful harvests. In 1937, for example, a record cotton crop of 18,946,000 bales resulted in a price drop to 8.4 cents per pound. Suffering farmers satiated the Commodity Credit Corporation's resources for loans, and a staggering surplus of cotton clogged the market for the remainder of the decade. Southern congressmen and the Farm Bureau Federation, as well as cotton planters, called for a return to compulsory production controls. In 1938 Congress passed a second Agricultural Adjustment Act, one that avoided processing taxes and made soil conservation payments dependent upon voluntary acreage restriction. It also established the ever-normal granary plan long propounded by Henry Wallace, whereby crops were stored until farm prices rose to acceptable levels, and created crop insurance for wheat and, later, for corn.

By the end of the decade the efforts of the two AAAs to restore income had met with some success. Total farm income, down to $39 billion in 1933 from a high of $79 billion in 1929, rebounded to $66 billion by 1939. The New Deal failed to retire land from cultivation rapidly enough to offset good weather, better farming practices, and record harvests. But even though efforts to control production and restore parity prices fell short, numerous other policies had a dramatic effect on farmers. Discounting George Peek's view that only the raising of agricultural prices mattered, the introduction of path-breaking methods in the 1930s remade the business of farming.

The New Deal's campaign for soil conservation took on great importance especially in those areas of the nation where decades of abuse had leeched soils of their fertility. In the South protracted reliance on such crops as cotton and tobacco, coupled with heavy rainfall and perpetual neglect, resulted in massive erosion of the landscape. Department of Agriculture soils specialist Hugh Hammond Bennett, a native of North Carolina and advocate for conservation since 1903, had been a tireless but unsuccessful proselytizer for the cause of government action. The huge dust storms rolling out of the Great Plains in mid-decade, however, provided the needed impetus. (One of these dust storms dramatically clouded the skies in the nation's capital at the exact time Bennett testified before a congressional committee on the urgency of legislative action.) Years of indifference to gradual deterioration in the South gave way to the undeniable evidence of soil erosion provided by the storms.

Rain fell plentifully on the Great Plains in the 1920s, producing bountiful wheat crops where farmers had plowed up grazing land but masking a potential problem that awaited an absence of moisture. Too many years of cultivation had destroyed the precious grass—grass that kept the topsoil from blowing away and retained moisture in the soil. Gusting westerly winds lifted the unanchored dirt and carried it hundreds of miles, blackening the sky, choking farmers, and leaving a thin residue of grit in its wake. Throughout the Midwest city officials closed schools and turned on streetlights in the afternoon. Farmers stuffed newspapers and rags under doors, around windows, and in cracks, but the dust nonetheless sifted into houses. Those who ventured outside at the worst moments held wet handkerchiefs over their noses and mouths just to be able to breathe. When the wind subsided, the dust piled high in drifts and the absence of vegetation gave ample testimony to the land's worthlessness. Moreover, when ruined farmers vacated their homesteads, the abandoned land offered no check to wind erosion and the problem grew apace.

With the Soil Conservation Act of 1935 the federal government assumed responsibility for addressing the problem. The Soil Conservation Service (SCS), originally situated in the Department of Interior but moved to the Department of Agriculture, appropriated several million dollars for the construction of water storage facilities. The service was dedicated to educating farmers in the adoption of rain conservation programs; contour plowing and the erection of earthen terraces abutting crop rows would allow rainwater to accumulate. The SCS also inaugurated programs for crop rotation, the introduction of new grasses and crops, terracing, drainage, and strip-cropping that rejuvenated previously lifeless land.

In attempting to counter wind erosion the Forest Service used WPA and CCC labor in the erection of a shelterbelt that extended from the Dakotas to Texas. North-south strips of trees sometimes extending for miles and varying in width created a wall against windstorms. By 1940 the federal government had planted over forty million trees in shelterbelts extending twenty-five hundred miles long, and after 1937 it provided trees to farmers for creation of their own windbreaks. Programs to alleviate soil and wind erosion merely constituted a palliative, however, returning much threatened land to production while encouraging the cultivation of semiarid areas. As the worst conditions in the dust bowl abated, farmers often disregarded the cruel lessons of the "dirty thirties" and fell back into careless practices. Instituting no basic economic changes, the New Deal left open the possibility of another erosion crisis.

Throughout the West the Bureau of Reclamation, situated in the Department of Agriculture, attacked the problem of scarce water. Because the bureau's irrigation projects did not involve basic foodstuffs and most affected crops were consumed locally, no conflict existed with the AAA's production limitation program. In California, for example, several New Deal agencies cooperated to complete the All-American Canal, which irrigated the Imperial and Coachella valleys with water from the Colorado River. Begun in 1937 and completed 10 years later, the Central Valley Project irrigated two million acres at a cost of $2.3 billion. By the end of the 1930s the New Deal irrigated twenty million acres in the densely populated rural areas west of the 100th meridian and made agriculture possible where previously it had been impractical.

Western grazing and ranching industries were also affected by New Deal policies. The Taylor Grazing Act assailed the decades-old open range policy in the public domain, in favor of government-imposed management and restricted access. The Department of Interior began issuing grazing permits and charging stockmen fees for use of specified preserves. A 1936 amendment to the Taylor Act increased the grazing range from 80 million to 142 million acres, and within four years eleven million cattle, sheep, goats, and horses roamed federal ranges. Increasing the number of acres designated for livestock pasture had the additional benefit of retiring land from wheat farming.

Extraordinary conditions in the 1930s—depression, drought, and dust—made the western states especially receptive to New Deal incursions into what traditionally had been a bastion of rugged individualism and the free market. Westerners needed solutions to massive water and soil erosion problems, and the Departments of Interior and Agriculture provided sensible solutions involving resource management and planning. The New Deal recommended the extension of pasture in place of one-crop farming and the enlargement of farms where possible for greater efficiency. The Resettlement Administration proferred loans and grants to farmers who increased their landholding and changed from wheat cultivation to raising fodder. As the dust storms eased and the outbreak of the Second World War increased the demand for American farm exports, farmers planted "fence post to fence post" and pursued profit with renewed zeal. New Deal conservation and education programs carried less weight with farmers, and the permanent solution to the loss of topsoil went unrealized. Nonetheless, breakthroughs in irrigation and the management of scarce water resources constituted a signal contribution to agriculture in the West.

In that region as well as other remote areas of the country where isolation and low population density characterized farming, the New Deal engineered a breakthrough by making electricity widely available for the first time. In 1930 only 1 of 10 farmers enjoyed the benefits of electrical power, in Mississippi fewer than 1 in 100. The prohibitive cost of extending power lines to reach a relatively few isolated customers (usually two to five dwellings per mile in the country) kept private power companies from venturing far away from profitable urban markets. By the 1930s, city life included street lighting, trolleys and subways, elevators, electric fans, radios, and motion pictures. The absence of electricity in rural areas, however, precluded the use of such modern amenities as indoor plumbing, refrigerators, washing machines, freezers, sewing machines, and electric lighting for the home and such labor-saving devices as chicken brooders, feed grinders, and milking machines for farm work. Kerosene lamps provided light, women did laundry and bathed their children outdoors, and men relied on mules and human energy for power. Without electricity and with the cost of windmills prohibitive for most farmers, water had to be carried by hand from the nearest streams or wells. With the average farm family of five using an estimated two hundred gallons of water daily for various purposes, hauling buckets back and forth consumed hours every day. The majority of American farmers continued to function in the "dark" ages.

Franklin D. Roosevelt developed an interest in public power when he discovered in 1924 that his electricity charges in Hyde Park, New York, totaled one-fourth the rates he paid at his Warm Springs, Georgia, home. The pressure for rural electrification increased during his presidency, coming not only from the Farm

Bureau Federation and the National Grange but also from southern politicians. Morris L. Cooke, a trustee appointed by Roosevelt in 1931 to the New York Power Authority, led the crusade for public power nationally, and in 1935 the president created the Rural Electrification Administration (REA) as a temporary agency with Cooke as its first chief. Originally inclined to work closely with private power interests, Cooke found that the furor created by the Wheeler-Rayburn Bill (mandating dissolution of public utility holding companies) made that unrealistic. Therefore, he chose to use farmer cooperatives. Popular in Europe and Canada where the vast majority of farms had electricity, cooperatives existed on a small scale in the United States (about 50 operated by 1935). The REA encouraged prospective borrowers to apply for federal loans and charged low interest rates with 25-year amortization periods. In 1936 the REA became a permanent agency and in 1939 moved into the Department of Agriculture. By that year 417 REA cooperatives served 268,000 households, reaching approximately one-fourth of all farms in the United States. After World War II the pace quickened, and within 15 years approximately 78 percent of American farms enjoyed electricity.

Contrary to the hopes of many of its boosters, rural electrification failed to reclaim a bucolic way of life, to halt the movement of country folk to the cities, or to save the vanishing small family farm. It did, however, significantly modernize the occupation of farmer, eliminate much of the drudgery of rural housewifery, and improve the quality of life for all rural inhabitants. Electricity narrowed the social and cultural gap between city and country as did no other development, with the exception of the automobile. For farmers who lived through the change, it was a veritable revolution.

In many other ways, however, New Deal policies and programs had a less than revolutionary impact. Certainly, the AAA and other federal agencies made no attempt to redistribute income or to alter existing social and economic hierarchies. The largest land units took the most acreage out of cultivation and received the fattest benefit checks. (In 1933, for example, Oscar Johnston's Delta and Pine Land Company, the nation's largest plantation, received $114,840 for crop reductions.) Cotton planters in the South could hardly have asked for more, receiving substantial government subsidies, cheap financing for new machinery, and a powerless labor force for planting and harvesting. Along Tobacco Road the warehouseman maintained his critical—and lucrative—role as middleman between grower and buyer. Local administration of AAA programs fell to county agents who worked closely with large landowners, not with sharecroppers, tenant farmers, and blacks. Keenly aware of political realities, New Dealers worked with powerful and influential spokesmen for farmers from the national to the local level.

Similarly, the agricultural establishment formed a powerful force with which all New Deal agencies had to contend. New Deal administrators largely ignored STFU protests out of deference to Senate Majority Leader Joe Robinson of Arkansas. The Extension Service, the land-grant colleges, and, most important, the American Farm Bureau Federation composed a formidable alliance in support of the respectable commercial farmer. In 1933 the Farm Bureau had approximately 150,000 members, in 1940 nearly 450,000. By the mid-1940s the Farm Bureau, working in tandem with congressional conservatives, emasculated the Farm Security Administration and the Department of Agriculture's Bureau of Agricultural Economics, an agency populated with reform-minded social scientists. Led by Alabama planter Ed O'Neal, the Farm Bureau kept the pressure on Secretary Wallace to temper the AAA's concern with the rural poor and to keep its focus on more traditional targets for aid. By the late 1930s Wallace's rising political ambitions, specifically aiming at the nomination for president in 1940, made him increasingly desirous of support from the agricultural establishment.

Not surprisingly, tenant purchase and resettlement schemes never received top priority from New Deal officials. Limited appropriations consigned to failure Rexford Tugwell's vision of a massively resituated agrarian work force. Widespread views of such programs as "collectivistic" and "socialistic" made them controversial and politically explosive. The Farm Security Administration extended loans to only 46 tenant farmers in the entire state of Virginia; at that rate, noted one cynic, landownership would be achieved in the commonwealth within four hundred years. RA and FSA rehabilitation loans went to those who had the best chance of repaying them; thus, the most destitute farmers infrequently received government aid. The Bankhead-Jones Act, the Farm Security Administration, crop insurance, and the ever-normal granary all were getting established at the end of the decade just as the New Deal entered its decline. The rise of political conservatism and the intrusion of wartime concerns slowed whatever momentum had been achieved for the rural poor.

In the long run, the New Deal accelerated the process of moving much of the rural poor off the land. In the comparatively restricted rice and tobacco growing areas, the displacement of labor occurred less frequently than it did elsewhere so conspicuously, and nowhere was displacement more clearly evident than in the Cotton Kingdom. In the South the wholesale eviction of sharecroppers increased as the 1930s advanced, as did the hiring of wage laborers to replace them. Tenancy evaporated rapidly after 1935; the number of hired workers equaled the number of tenants by the early 1950s, and there were twice as many hired hands by 1960. But even as wage earners replaced tenants, their numbers dwindled—increasingly replaced by cotton harvesters, tractors, and combines. Ultimately, tenants gave way to machinery.

Throughout the nation farmers began buying tractors in the 1920s, but on a small scale. Low farm prices in the 1920s and early 1930s, the unavailability of capital and credit, and the abundance of cheap labor kept most farmers from investing in machinery. New Deal lending agencies provided the funds for capital purchases, and thousands of farmers spent their AAA benefit checks on equipment. According to agriculture historian Gilbert C. Fite, "as the cost of credit declined in relation to the cost of labor, farmers turned to machines." In 1930 only 13.5 percent of the nation's farmers owned tractors; 10 years later the figure had grown to 23.1 percent, and the acquisitions came with increasing frequency thereafter. Landowning farmers with ready access to capital took advantage of these opportunities; agricultural laborers and small landowners did not.[7]

The mechanization of agriculture went hand-in-hand with the consolidation of farmland. In the 1930s and after, the declining number of farms and the increase in the size of those remaining constituted a kind of enclosure movement abetted by New Deal programs. Consolidation also involved changes in land use, as New Deal planners and conservationists urged. Throughout the more fertile southern flatlands and the prairies of the Great Plains, farmers turned to beef cattle production, dairying, and new crops such as hay, sorghum, soybeans, and improved grasses. The modern farmer cultivated more acres with a greater array of crops, used more expensive machinery, depended less on human labor, applied more scientific knowledge, and relied more than ever before on government.

When Henry A. Wallace defended AAA policies in 1933, he urged American farmers to behave more like businessmen. The subsequent rise of larger units of production, increased capitalization, and heightened efficiency—at the cost of considerable human suffering—indicates that farmers took the path the secretary recommended. The widespread acceptance of subsidy payments and the concept of parity reflected the expanded role of government in American agriculture commonplace after the 1930s. Many of these developments, admittedly initiated before the Great Depression, could not be credited solely to the New Deal. Nevertheless, the efforts of the Roosevelt administration ushered along at a much quicker pace these seminal changes in American agriculture. As historian Theodore Saloutos concluded, "With all its limitations and frustrations, the New Deal by making operational the ideas and plans that had been long on the minds of agricultural researchers and thinkers, constituted the greatest innovative epoch in the history of American agriculture."[8]

CHAPTER FOUR

The Blue Eagle

The National Industrial Recovery Act (NIRA) initiated an unprecedented experiment in business-government cooperation, whereby President Roosevelt established a code system for industrial production and an emergency public works program to restore economic prosperity. The NIRA suspended antitrust laws for two years and provided for the drafting of industrial codes regulating production, prices, and labor policies. A welter of contradictions, the NIRA exempted codes from antitrust violations yet prohibited agreements "to permit monopolies or monopolistic practices, or to eliminate, oppress, or discriminate against small enterprises." So that no administrator would wield too much power, Roosevelt put General Hugh Johnson in charge of the National Recovery Administration (NRA) and Secretary of the Interior Harold L. Ickes in charge of the Public Works Administration (PWA). Whatever its virtues, this division of authority resulted in bureaucratic and personal rivalries, balkanizing arms of the federal government that should have worked in tandem. Skeptics questioned the plausibility of business-government cooperation and worried that labor's position in the partnership would prove too vulnerable. Old-line congressional Progressives like William Borah feared that the NRA would destroy the competitive economic system and open the door to the spread of monopolies. But despite the uncertainties and apparent anomalies, support for the new program came from many quarters. American Federation of Labor president William Green described Section 7(a) as a

"Magna Charta" for the worker, and John L. Lewis of the United Mine Workers called it another Emancipation Proclamation. H. I. Harriman, chairman of the National Chamber of Commerce, predicted that the NRA would launch a new era of "constructive cooperation" in the economy, while eliminating the "industrial buccaneer," the "exploiter of labor," and the "unscrupulous price-cutter." Whatever their reservations, many people felt compelled to support the president's program out of desperation as much as loyalty.[1]

Almost immediately, however, the NRA encountered serious difficulties. Within two years the U.S. Supreme Court found the NIRA unconstitutional, and few people mourned its passing. It had failed to bring economic recovery, had alienated many original supporters, and had become a genuine political liability for Roosevelt and the Democrats. Personnel problems, noncompliance, bureaucratic snafus, and negative publicity had all plagued the starstruck agency at various times from 1933 to 1935. Moreover, the NRA's failure doomed the attempt at business-government cooperation and exposed the New Deal's inability to forge a coherent policy regarding economic concentration. Although some positive developments can be traced to the NRA—the abolition of child labor and the eventual strengthening of unions, for example—its immediate impact on the economy was, at best, negligible and, at worst, damaging. For Franklin D. Roosevelt and everyone else associated with the agency, the NRA became a highly visible and embarrassing failure.

From its inception the NRA came to be associated by the American people with its grandiloquent leader, General Hugh S. Johnson. Born in Kansas, Johnson grew up in frontier Oklahoma and became the first Oklahoman to graduate from West Point. During World War I he helped develop the Selective Service System and acted as the army's representative on the War Industries Board (WIB). After the war he resigned his commission and went into business with two associates from the WIB; first he teamed up with George Peek to operate the Moline Plow Company (and draft the McNary-Haugen bills) and later served as financial advisor to Bernard Baruch. In 1932 Johnson and Baruch worked behind the scenes at the Democratic National Convention to deny Roosevelt the presidential nomination. When that failed Baruch made amends with a hefty financial contribution to the Roosevelt campaign, and Johnson became

"Baruch's man" on the Brains Trust. Johnson participated in the drafting of the NIRA, and the president never really considered anyone else to head the new agency. Seeking to appease Baruch, Roosevelt appointed Johnson to the NRA and Peek to the AAA. Baruch actually considered Johnson ill-suited for the position, as he explained to Secretary of Labor Frances Perkins, because of the general's obstreperousness, instability, and alcoholism. His misgivings proved prescient.

In the early days of the New Deal, Hugh Johnson captured the fancy of the reporters covering Washington with his salty language and quickness to offer an opinion—no matter how impolitic—on any subject. Crude, truculent, and strong willed, Old Iron Pants Johnson recognized his own proclivity for the controversial and predicted that his appointment to head the NRA would lead to conflict. "It will be red fire at first," he said, "and dead cats afterward." Always inclined to see issues in blacks and whites, he gave himself wholeheartedly to the recovery program and charged that "only fools and crooks could find flaws in the NRA." A man of excesses, he spoke in hyperbole, excoriated his opponents with unceasing invective, drank alcohol in awesome binges, and worked for days without rest. He brought this great drive to the NRA, inaugurating the program with a remarkable flurry of activity that kept his and the agency's names on the front pages day after day.[2]

But despite Johnson's infectious energy, the summer months of 1933 slipped away without the completion of many industrial codes. Johnson decided to concentrate initially on drafting agreements in the critical steel, petroleum, automobile, textile, lumber, and coal industries. He turned first to the cotton textiles code, and his experiences there presaged in microcosm the kinds of difficulties NRA administrators would encounter elsewhere. Excessive competition, unsold surpluses, and low profits had ravaged the textile industry, leaving its leaders eager to rationalize production exempt from antitrust prosecution. Easily achieving consensus, a code-drafting committee composed of mill owners approved a 40–40 plan limiting workers to 40-hour weeks with machines operating no more than 80 hours per week. They approved minimum weekly wages of $10 in the South and $11 in the North and accepted NIRA's Section 7(a), which guaranteed workers the right to organize and bargain collectively. On June 27–30 Johnson presided over the public hearing on the code that drew considerable fire from labor critics. Regardless of the owners' landmark decision to eradicate child labor in the mills, American Federation of Labor president Green and Alabama senator Hugo Black criticized as excessive the 40-hour week and as inadequate the $10–$11 minimum wages. The textile industry raised wages by $2 to $12 and $13, and Johnson approved the amended code despite continued objections by unions. Further, he acceded to the industrialists' demand that, to counter rising labor costs, they be allowed to limit production.

Roosevelt approved the textile code but with several changes, the most important of which limited the agreement to a four-month trial period and opened up the possibility of substantial revision thereafter. Determined to demonstrate the government's good faith to the mill owners, Johnson insisted that the four-month trial be dropped and Roosevelt, still intent on securing business cooperation and eager to announce finally the adoption of a code, agreed. As many fearful observers noted, the resultant code conceded to the mill owners on all points of contention. In eliminating the trial provision, Johnson helped preserve business's position in its partnership with government by limiting presidential prerogatives. At the same time he gave short shrift to labor's concerns and virtually no attention to consumers. Thus, one of the recurring criticisms of Johnson's performance—his preferential treatment of business—surfaced with the very first code.

The success with cotton textiles, though it seemed at the time the result of protracted and delicate negotiations, turned out to be remarkably easy in comparison with the efforts expended in the other major industries. Iron and steel manufacturers refused to relinquish the open shop and resisted the raising of wages and lowering of hours to what they termed unrealistic levels. Even Johnson admitted that the code finally hammered out after weeks of contentious bargaining was "not altogether satisfactory," in that the industry maintained the right to set prices and divide markets. More important, although the steel interests agreed to remove an explicit reference to open shops in the code, they continued to insist that Section 7(a) had no impact on their traditional labor policy.[3]

In the beleaguered petroleum industry, where prices had fallen from $2.28 a barrel in 1928 to 10 cents a barrel in 1933, opinion was divided between the major companies and the independent producers on the desirability of federal intervention. The former favored state controls while the latter supported the Marland-Capper Bill, which empowered the federal government to determine production and fix prices. Congress failed to pass the bill, but in Section 9(c) of the NIRA it did authorize the president to stop the interstate shipment of "hot" oil (produced in violation of state laws). Meetings to draft an oil code proved unsuccessful when major companies and independents could not agree on production quotas and prices. Johnson and Harold Ickes presented their own oil codes to Roosevelt, who ultimately approved the general's. It included provisions for production quotas and price-fixing by the federal government but limited Washington's involvement to "recommendations," in deference to the larger companies. Further muddying the waters, Roosevelt then named Ickes petroleum administrator.

Johnson found progress just as grudging in the other major industries. Unlike petroleum and textiles, the automobile industry had not suffered from overproduction or disastrously low prices and had already created an effective trade association, the National Automobile Chamber of Commerce. As a result, the leading auto companies saw no reason for codification, particularly since Henry Ford indicated that he would not participate, and the other firms feared that he would outproduce and underprice them. Johnson attempted to compose a code for the bituminous coal industry, where increased competition from European mines, oil, and natural gas, along with technological advances, combined to produce huge surpluses. In the Kentucky coal belt hundreds of children died of malnutrition and related diseases, as John L. Lewis's United Mine Workers (UMW) fought pitched battles to organize workers in the coalfields. Mine owners agreed to higher wages and safer working conditions but balked at signing codes that recognized union representation. Eventually, Johnson managed to secure codes in all the major industries but only after prolonged and bitter negotiations.

By July 1933, the NRA had only the textile code to show for its efforts. Many businesses apparently refused to participate, hoping to obtain a competitive edge over those companies that agreed to sign codes. During the early summer months the nation's economy showed renewed life; industrial production rose from an index figure of 56 in March to 101 in July, and stocks doubled in value. This boomlet, however, stemmed largely from businessmen increasing productivity and accumulating large inventories before NRA codes took effect. At the PWA Harold Ickes's cautious approval of public works projects meant that months, even years, would pass before such initiative invigorated the economy. With the initial optimism fading and the NRA scoring few successes, Johnson concluded by the first week in July that dramatic action was needed to break the codification logjam.

On July 19 Roosevelt endorsed Johnson's idea of a blanket code, the President's Reemployment Agreement, to operate from August 1 to December 31, 1933, or until specific industrial codes were completed. The NRA urged all employees to subscribe voluntarily to the blanket code, which eliminated child labor, established a $12–$15 weekly minimum wage, and set maximums of 35 hours per week for industrial laborers and 44 hours for white-collar workers. Doubting the constitutionality of the NRA's licensing powers and his ability to enforce code provisions, Johnson opted for moral suasion and peer pressure to encourage participation. On August 1, he launched a prodigious public relations campaign to saturate the nation with information about the NRA. Johnson chose a symbol (a blue eagle modeled on an Indian thunderbird) and a slogan (We Do Our Part) to represent compliance with governmental initiatives. The suddenly ubiquitous blue eagle appeared in newspapers and shop windows, on billboards and pennants. Moviegoers viewed short features touting NRA successes and urging consumers to buy only from businesses displaying the new emblem. In New York, Miss Liberty and Miss Nira (an acronym for National Industrial Recovery Act), bedecked in red, white, and blue costumes, appealed to the patriotism of the citizenry. In city after city government officials organized massive parades to underscore the community's fealty to the recovery program: in Memphis fifty thousand marched in the annual Christmas parade, and one hundred twenty-five thousand spectators cheered Santa Claus mounted atop a blue eagle. In New York City a quarter of a million people marched down Fifth Avenue while an estimated two million looked on. From the motorcades, bandstands, radios, and podiums came General Johnson's ceaseless appeal for patriotism, cooperation, and selflessness, and to a great extent Americans responded to the NRA's entreaties and signed the blanket code.

Meanwhile, code making for separate industries proceeded apace, with the task largely completed by the end of 1933. In all, the NRA approved 541 industrial codes and 185 supplemental codes. In most cases, a representative from an industrywide group or trade association submitted a code proposal. The NRA then sponsored preliminary conferences, at which representatives from the agency's Industrial Advisory Board (representing business), Labor Advisory Board, and Consumers Advisory Board, along with the NRA's Legal and Planning divisions, could propose modifications. Next the agency held public hearings and, following additional changes, the proposals reverted to the code committee for further refinements. Finally, the NRA administrator advised the president to accept, reject, or alter the code. The Industrial Advisory Board and Labor Advisory Board were appointed by the secretaries of commerce and labor, respectively, but Johnson chose the members of the Consumers Advisory Board. Lacking the support of any unified, formal constituency, the consumers board never exercised much influence. Indeed, Johnson frequently ignored its views altogether and on one occasion screamed, "Who the hell cares what your board thinks?" Because the labor and consumers boards took a back seat to the industrial board, code making became little more than an accord between businessmen outside and inside government.[4]

The NRA's antilabor bias became increasingly evident as the codes took shape. Johnson candidly offered his view that the primary task of the NRA was "to get industry back at making a profit." Addressing the American Federation of Labor's annual convention in October 1933, he asserted that unions were obsolete and the creation of a new arbitration machinery within the NRA obviated the need for strikes. To automobile manufacturers concerned about their loss of autonomy due to Section 7(a), the general responded, "The fact that you bargain with the men doesn't mean you have to agree." NRA general counsel Donald Richberg, a Chicago lawyer with close ties to the railroad workers unions, initially had been chosen as labor's spokesman. Almost immediately, however, Richberg joined Johnson in denying that union representatives could speak for all workers in a shop and in refuting labor's assertion that Section 7(a) precluded company unions. In the steel industry, as a result, the number of company unions increased from seven in 1932 to nearly one hundred in 1934. Early on, it became apparent that both Richberg and Johnson supported management's limited view of the scope of Section 7(a).[5]

Labor discontent, mirrored in the multitude of strikes involving over three hundred thousand workers in the summer months of 1933 alone, led Roosevelt to consider creating a mechanism for settling grievances. In August he created the National Labor Board (NLB) to adjudicate disputes between management and workers over interpretations of the President's Reemployment Agreement. Chaired by New York Senator Robert F. Wagner and composed of three representatives from labor and three from industry, the NLB possessed no enforcement powers; it could only punish delinquent employers by commandeering their blue eagle emblems. Spearheaded by the National Association of Manufacturers' campaign against the NLB, employers by the hundreds denied its jurisdiction and ignored its rulings. In a March 1934 showdown between the NLB and the automobile industry, Roosevelt sided with the latter and obliterated whatever credibility the former still retained. Senator Wagner introduced in Congress a new labor disputes bill, abrogating the NLB in favor of a National Labor Relations Board (NLRB) independent of the NRA. The president signed a watered-down version of Wagner's original bill on June 19 that gave the NLRB no more authority than its predecessor. Counseled by Richberg and Johnson, Roosevelt stopped short of truly empowering labor for fear of the negative impact on the NRA.

The favoritism toward business—at the expense of the other partners in code making, labor and consumers—effectively allowed industries to form cartels with the government's imprimatur. It also resulted in higher prices, wages that lagged behind, and, therefore, reduced purchasing power. Critics charged by the fall of 1933 that the NRA under Johnson's leadership was an impediment to economic recovery and, through the relaxation of antitrust laws, a patron of monopolies. Although the codes contained the mandatory references to labor and a few concessions to competition, as a group they fostered industrial self-government. Veteran lobbyists for well-established trade associations effectively represented the interests of big business, whereas labor unions and consumers suffered for want of experience in pressure group politics. Code authorities charged with administering the agreements, empowered to interpret and grant exemptions, were almost exclusively businessmen; labor representatives made up less than 10 percent of the authorities, consumer advocates less than 1 percent. Nor did Johnson act against code violators. He occasionally denounced chiselers who ignored their obligations, but he never risked alienating big business, whose support he deemed critical to the recovery effort. Businessmen may not have received carte blanche in the NRA, but they undeniably cemented their position as the strongest of the competing elements in the American economy.

Mounting criticism of the NRA led Roosevelt in November 1933 to send Hugh Johnson and Henry Wallace on a goodwill tour of the western states. Instead of conciliating small businessmen, farmers, and politicians, the pugnacious NRA administrator gave bellicose speeches and thereby alienated even more people. Meanwhile, Roosevelt sought in a series of highly publicized meetings with North Dakota senator Gerald P. Nye to forestall a congressional investigation of the NRA's nurturing of monopolies. He finally succeeded only by agreeing to create the National Recovery Review Board, charged with a thorough inquiry into NRA practices. Johnson concurred and, in what he later called a "moment of total aberration," agreed to the selection of famed trial lawyer Clarence Darrow to chair the committee. On March 7, 1934, Roosevelt formed the National Recovery Review Board and announced that it would report directly to him, not to the NRA.[6]

On May 1, 1934, the Darrow Board sent the first of its three reports to the White House. The 155-page document, much like the two that followed, excoriated the NRA for supporting monopolies at the expense of small businesses. A firmly grounded belief in small units of production and unfettered competition caused the members of the Darrow Board to find very little good to say about Johnson's approach to recovery. The board recommended reenforcement of the antitrust laws and the removal of price controls. The NRA promptly released a 157-page response, berating the board's report for methodological errors, selective use of evidence, and ideological biases. In a letter to Roosevelt, Johnson called the report the "most superficial, intemperate and inaccurate document" he had ever seen.

Although Johnson was correct in many of his criticisms, the controversy surrounding the report's publication lent credence to the increasingly popular opinion that the NRA favored big business over the little man. Further, the developing feud between Darrow and Johnson, played out in a series of charges and countercharges exchanged in the press, kept the contretemps alive. Clearly, as one editor noted, the blue eagle "lost some feathers from the discharge of the Board of Review's shotgun."[7]

Long at the center of controversy, Hugh Johnson's behavior became more and more erratic. Throughout his tenure he occasionally vanished without warning for days at a time to recover from drinking bouts, leaving no one in charge and throwing the NRA's national office into chaos. By spring 1934, his alcoholism and intemperate public actions had become a liability the president could no longer ignore. Johnson clashed openly and often with Frances Perkins and Donald Richberg, both of whom should have been allies. The ambitious Richberg, motivated in part by his own designs on Johnson's office, led a campaign within the administration to oust his superior. Notorious for his reluctance to fire subordinates, Roosevelt temporized for months but finally enlisted the aid of Bernard Baruch to convince Johnson to resign. On September 24, 1934, the general left the New Deal.

Hugh Johnson's 16 months at the helm of the NRA could hardly be judged successful. His shortcomings as an administrator—inattentiveness to detail, obduracy, and alcoholism—exacerbated his flawed view of business-government cooperation. He devoted an inordinate amount of time and resources to codemaking. Although he unabashedly favored business over labor and consumer interests, by 1934 even industry chafed under his mercurial direction. Even so, the reasons for the NRA's failure ran deeper than one man's failed leadership. It seems doubtful whether any individual could have made the New Deal's recovery program a success, as evidenced by the fate of the NRA after Johnson's stormy exit.

On September 27, 1934, Roosevelt announced the creation of the National Industrial Recovery Board (NIRB) to assume Johnson's administrative duties. The president chose S. Clay Williams, former president of the R. J. Reynolds Tobacco Company, as chairman; the board contained four other members who represented business, labor, and consumers. The next month the president announced yet another reorganization for the NRA, placing the NIRB and all recovery agencies under the aegis of a new National Emergency Council headed by Donald Richberg. Noting that Richberg wielded power equal to if not exceeding Hugh Johnson's, newspapermen began referring to the NRA's new chief as the assistant president. Allied with the archconservative Williams, Richberg continued the NRA's earlier approach of favoring business. He hailed the virtues of industrial self-government and urged that the NRA codes be made permanent. Organizational alterations aside, the NRA under Richberg clearly pursued the same policies as it had under Johnson.

By early 1935 the belief became widespread that no amount of administrative reshuffling could resuscitate the NRA. Richberg had proved incapable of managing the agency's sprawling bureaucracy. (In August 1933, the agency's staff of four hundred spent $393,000 per month, but by February 1935, the NRA employed forty-five hundred with a $1,054,000 monthly expenditure.) Nor had Richberg patched over the differences between the NRA and either labor or government personnel. Admittedly less confrontational than Johnson, Richberg appeared every bit as inflexible. Most damaging, the NRA's Research and Planning Division announced that real wages in January 1935 showed no increase during the previous year. Since the adoption of industrial codes, the increase in retail prices had actually exceeded wage gains. A study of the NRA released by the prestigious Brookings Institute further discredited the embattled agency. In painstaking detail the Brookings economists, many of whom had worked for the NRA, enumerated its many shortcomings, including haphazard conceptualization, faulty economic theory, and poor administration, and noted that its net effect had been to encourage profiteering and monopolization.

Still unwilling to repudiate the experiment, Roosevelt asked Congress for a two-year extension of a modified NRA when it expired in June 1935. Congressional hearings dragged on for weeks as supporters like Hugh Johnson and opponents like Clarence Darrow offered starkly opposing evaluations of the NRA's effectiveness. The House of Representatives seemed to be headed for a favorable recommendation, but the Senate approved a bill that emasculated the remnants of the recovery agency. When a frustrated S. Clay Williams resigned, Roosevelt appointed Richberg chairman of the NIRB. Richberg refused to assess policy questions until Congress reached a decision on the fate of the NIRA. He also sought a clarification from the judiciary, submitting a test case on the NIRA's constitutionality to the U.S. Supreme Court. Before the two houses of Congress could reach agreement, the Court decided the NRA's fate.

In *United States* v. *A.L.A. Schechter Poultry Corporation*, the U.S. Supreme Court put the blue eagle permanently to rest. In October 1934, a federal district court found the four Schechter brothers, suppliers of kosher poultry to Jewish customers in Brooklyn, New York, guilty of selling uninspected products and violating NRA wage and hour regulations. When a circuit court sustained the verdict in April 1935, the defendants appealed to the Supreme Court. On May 27, Chief Justice Charles Evans Hughes announced the Court's unanimous verdict in favor of the Schechter brothers. The justices ruled that what the Schechter brothers did—purchase chickens raised in other states but slaughter and sell them in New York—was not true interstate commerce and not subject to the commerce power of Congress. (President Roosevelt would subsequently term this a horse-and-buggy definition of interstate commerce.) Also, the Court abrogated NIRA's Title I as an unconstitutional delegation of legislative power to the executive. The decision rendered the NRA codes illegal and for all practical purposes invalidated the act. Congress quickly passed extension legislation, allowing the NRA to dissolve gradually. In its last months the agency attempted to develop voluntary codes for business cooperation but achieved no success. In later years, "little NRAs" persisted or resurfaced in a few sick industries such as coal, oil, and textiles, but the idea of nationwide economic planning perished in 1935.

By the time of the Supreme Court's decision, many Americans thought the NRA a hopeless failure. Most New Dealers, including the president, breathed a sigh of relief when Chief Justice Hughes resolved the nagging question of what to do with a seemingly insoluble problem. Progressive critics urged legislative action to preserve some of the NIRA's better innovations, such as minimum wages, maximum hours, the abolition of child labor, and Section 7(a). The NRA reported wholesale wage cutting as businesses jockeyed for position in an economy suddenly devoid of centralized controls. Some firms acquiesced to the government's call for voluntary retention of wage and price agreements, but not for long. Ironically, the merchants who had complained vigorously of government regimentation and the threat to free enterprise suddenly inveighed against the resurfacing of unscrupulous, cutthroat business practices.

Its abrupt, unceremonious demise—and the obvious sense of relief with which it was greeted by the administration—left the NRA few advocates in the summer of 1935. In retrospect, the obviously flawed agency engendered some positive changes, a few of which took years to surface. Although the NRA did relatively little for labor and at times appeared downright hostile to unions, the NIRA established a foundation of support for the workingman upon which later achievements were constructed. Section 7(a) asserted labor's right to organize and bargain collectively, principles at the heart of later union gains. The NIRA established a tradition of wages-and-hours legislation and ended child labor. Largely an economic failure, the NRA could claim a measure of financial success in the summer of 1933; between June and October of that year some 2.5 million previously unemployed workers found jobs. Because most codes imposed 35–40 hours per week maximums for workers, the NRA spread employment out to more people; the Brookings Institute estimated that the employment rate increased by approximately 7 percent because of shortened hours. Thus, it could be argued that the NRA provided a holding action, however brief, in the generally desolate economic climate of the 1930s.

Furthermore, as economic historian Gavin Wright has shown, the NRA significantly narrowed the wage differentials between North and South. Since NRA codes especially affected low-wage industries, the relatively impoverished southern workers gained the most. Beginning with the NIRA, and reinforced by work-relief programs and the Fair Labor Standards Act, federal policies drove southern wage rates up in the 1930s while northern rates remained relatively steady. At least in part, the drive to raise southern wages came from the desire of northern manufacturers to keep their southern counterparts from slashing costs of production and prices. By blocking the growth of low-wage industrial expansion in Dixie, New Deal policies preserved northern manufacturing competitiveness and, coincidentally, benefited southern labor.[8]

Despite these laudatory developments, the NRA fell short of its primary goal, economic recovery. If the codes had any effect at all, they restricted production, permitted higher prices, and reduced purchasing power, none of which enhanced the possibility of invigorating the economy. The reasons for this outcome abounded. First, the NRA tried to accomplish too much and spread itself too thin. Instead of limiting codes to a few basic industries and doing a thorough job with them, the agency drafted hundreds of agreements involving, among others, the hog ring industry, the horsehair dressing industry, and even burlesque. Columnist Walter Lippmann concluded that "the sensible thing was to concentrate on the steel code and a few other important codes, revising them to insure competition and a genuine system of collective bargaining." Unfortunately, the NRA not only spent months drafting 541 codes but also issued 11,000 administrative orders interpreting the codes. The result, as critics quickly pointed out, was a bureaucratic nightmare.[9]

Administration of the NIRA proved a problem, as well. Arguably, Roosevelt undercut Hugh Johnson's position at the outset by assigning the operation of Title II to another arm of the bureaucracy. Johnson chafed at Harold Ickes's glacial approval of public works, arguing the necessity of stimulating heavy industry to increase spending. In 1933 the nation's lifeless economy needed a massive creation of jobs to increase purchasing power. With hindsight many historians have lamented the fact that Johnson and Ickes had not had their administrative roles reversed. Johnson's boundless energy unleashed in the PWA would doubtless have resulted in the kind of immediate building boom recovery demanded. Similarly, Ickes's excruciating caution would have limited the number of codes, just as the old Progressive's innate distrust of big business and penchant for minute scrutiny would have led him to police more thoroughly the nearly autonomous trade associations dominating the NRA. Unfortunately, Ickes and the PWA played a very limited role in increasing consumer spending.

Another knotty problem—noncompliance—plagued the NRA throughout its existence, worsening as time went on. Johnson maintained that agreements could not be enforced until all codes had been drafted, thereby establishing a policy of benign neglect. In September 1933, with codification proceeding more satisfactorily, he announced his readiness to "start disciplining these people." Scathing rhetoric aside, however, Johnson initiated very little action against a huge and expanding list of enterprises violating the codes. Some businesses displayed the blue eagle emblem despite not subscribing to the industry's code, and some refused to remove the emblem even after an unfavorable compliance ruling. Others, like the New Orleans Steamship Association, proudly advertised their refusal to sign a code. Johnson found that small businesses that lost their blue eagles frequently saw an increase in sales because customers anticipated that a removal of restriction would lead to price cuts. Convinced that the NRA disdained consumers' concerns, the public felt fully justified in ignoring blue eagles and seeking the best available bargains. The NRA's most publicized noncompliance case involved a Jersey City tailor who charged 35 cents for a pressed suit instead of the 40 cents required by the Tailoring Industry Code. Sentenced to 30 days' imprisonment and fined one hundred dollars for the violation, the tailor spent only 3 days in jail before being released. In the meantime, his case attracted national attention and more opprobrium for the embattled NRA.[10]

Nothing undermined the NRA's drive for compliance more than the celebrated case of the Ford Motor Company. Henry Ford refused to sign the automobile agreement because of the expansion of government authority and the increased power of unions. Although he observed the auto code's wages and hours provisions throughout the life of the NRA, he did not adhere to Section 7(a) and adamantly refused to sign the code. Because Ford's highly publicized holdout alarmed the other auto companies and emboldened other recalcitrants to flaunt their independence, the NRA saw him as the major test of its authority. The federal government refused to award contracts to the Ford Motor Company and conducted a spirited propaganda campaign urging the public to boycott its cars. The dearth of government orders hurt a bit, but Ford turned a substantial profit in 1934 and maintained its share of the domestic auto market. The inability to discipline America's premier individualist further damaged the NRA's credibility.

By the time of the *Schechter* decision, dissatisfaction had resulted in virtually total noncompliance in many industries and spotty compliance in others. The growing legion of critics, who sarcastically charged that NRA stood for "No Recovery Allowed," "National Run-Around," and other unflattering nicknames, complained most often about the lack of economic progress and bureaucratic inefficiency. Progressives of both political parties, however, felt most dismayed by the NRA's support for monopolies. Always the defenders of small business, they blanched at the favoritism shown large corporations, particularly their dominant role in the creation of industrial codes and the apparent impunity they enjoyed while ignoring Section 7(a). The passage of the NIRA clearly charted an economic course in favor of government-supported cartels rather than enforcing competition and, therefore, the neo-Brandeisians grieved not at all when the NRA foundered. Feeling fully vindicated, they heartily endorsed the Brookings Institute's assessment of the NRA. "The propriety of attempting to administer a new body of law through agencies made up of representatives of the private interests to which the law applies is very questionable."[11]

The explosion of the idea of a business commonwealth rejuvenated the spirits of the antitrusters, who intensified their lobbying for action against monopolies. For the balance of the decade the disciples of Louis Brandeis and Felix Frankfurter tried to get Franklin Roosevelt to take a firm position on the problem of economic concentration, but despite the NRA fiasco and his souring relations with big business the president continued to straddle the fence. Emphasizing his lack of ideology and the need for flexibility, Roosevelt never embraced the antitrust position. From 1939 to 1941 Thurman Arnold, the recently appointed head of the Justice Department's moribund Antitrust Division, breathed new life into the battle against monopolies. Arnold filed 180 suits in those two years, nearly half of the proceedings initiated under the Sherman Antitrust Act, and registered some notable victories against industrial behemoths. Like so many other programs, however, the antitrust campaign ended abruptly with the coming of the Second World War, a casualty of the need for large-scale planning and centralized control. Even before the war Arnold's campaign failed to promote recovery, for it lacked the political or legal support to dismantle corporations on a scale sufficient to restore competition. Neither the NRA nor the belated antitrust movement provided for the New Deal an effective stimulus for the enervated economy; recovery came only with the war.

Both during and after the NRA's stormy existence, the New Deal's principal relief agency proved to be the Reconstruction Finance Corporation (RFC). Under Roosevelt the RFC bore faint resemblance to the modest organization it had been under Hoover. In 1933 it softened collateral requirements and lowered the interest rate on loans by 0.5 percent. Within months the RFC was parceling out loans to banks, building and loan associations, railroads, credit unions, commercial businesses, insurance companies, school districts, federal land banks, farmers, farm cooperatives, livestock credit corporations, and other New Deal agencies. (When Congress created the Works Progress Administration in 1935, for example, the RFC appropriated start-up funds of one billion dollars to launch the program.) In short, the RFC acted as the New Deal's primary source of capital, lending more than ten billion dollars by 1940. Roosevelt relied on the RFC repeatedly, because its huge cash reserves and independence from congressional supervision gave him considerable latitude in dispensing funds. And Jesse Jones, the RFC's administrator until 1939, possessed the conservative credentials to mollify potential congressional critics.

Jesse Jones came to Washington from Texas as a successful entrepreneur, the multimillionaire president of the Texas Commerce Bank, an original stockholder in the Humble Oil Company, and owner of the Houston *Chronicle*. A fervent devotee of capitalism, he refused to make the RFC the center of a planned economy and used the agency solely as a source of funds for capital-starved investors. Imbued with a Populist hatred for the conservative Wall Street establishment, Jones instituted a generous credit policy favoring speculative interests in the South and West. He erroneously assumed that a shortage of investment capital forestalled recovery, but the economy's most severe problem continued to be inadequate purchasing power. The RFC helped revive ailing money markets but did little to encourage investment or pry money loose from chary bankers who preferred government securities to commercial credit. Jesse Jones made the RFC the largest single investor in the nation's economy, but recovery continued to elude the New Deal.

No government program implemented during the 1930s brought the country out of the depression, and as the linchpin of the recovery effort the NRA was the most conspicuous disappointment. Forging a sincere business-government cooperative effort, especially with repeated deference to industry that shortchanged other supposedly coequal partners, proved impossible. The NRA ended up satisfying no one—not labor or the consumer and, finally, not even business. One wag succinctly summarized the reasons for its failure as "too many codes, too many bureaucrats, too little muscle, and too little trust." For millions of Americans, the New Deal's inability to right the economy meant continued unemployment and the need for assistance. If the New Deal could not provide recovery, it could at least bring some relief.[12]

CHAPTER FIVE

Relief and Social Welfare

When the Great Depression struck, the United States stood less prepared than any other industrialized nation to cope with widespread suffering. With the exception of providing veterans' benefits, the federal government played no role in public welfare. Unlike many Western nations that had followed the lead of Germany and England, the U.S. government recognized no responsibility for the care of the aged, unemployed, or infirm; it provided no social insurance, retirement stipends, or health benefits. States acknowledged responsibility in a limited fashion and with great variation. By 1931 only 12 states had passed pension laws; among these states only 3 (New York, California, and Wyoming) made them mandatory, and in the other 9 states only 13 percent of the counties chose to participate. In 1933 only 10 states had old-age assistance laws, and in 8 states resided more than half the families receiving unemployment benefits, more than one-third of them in just 4 states (New York, Pennsylvania, Ohio, and Illinois). In most instances, local governments bore the brunt of the relief burden in a tradition emanating from the English Poor Law of 1601. This and subsequent English laws recognized a community's obligation to care for the "deserving" or "worthy" poor, but insisted that healthy persons be left to fend for themselves and their dependents. Invariably, the unemployable received aid in the form of food and other necessities—not money—so that extravagances could be eliminated. Private charity efforts supplemented government aid but proved wholly inadequate during the periodic economic downturns that punctuated the industrial America of the nineteenth and twentieth centuries. A firm commitment to rugged individualism minimized relief and kept officials watchful to guard against the receipt of benefits by the "unworthy" poor.

For all his reticence to deviate from the American tradition of hardy self-reliance, Herbert Hoover met the challenge of the Great Depression with unprecedented government forays into social welfare activity. The president provided information and ideas to state, local, and private charitable agencies and urged them to expand relief programs. He encouraged large business concerns and influential entrepreneurs to increase their involvement in welfare activities, and in the waning months of his administration finally assented to providing federal funds for employment on construction projects. Yet Hoover stopped short of countenancing federal spending to distribute food, clothing, or money to the unemployed. Such activities, he maintained, must remain the responsibility of private charity and local government.

As governor of New York from 1929 to 1933, Franklin D. Roosevelt forged a record that contrasted sharply with Hoover's. In principle, Roosevelt also favored a decentralized approach to relief provision and questioned the desirability of expanded roles for the state and federal governments. But concluding that traditional approaches had proved inadequate, he affirmed the need to experiment with nontraditional sources of aid. In 1931 he established the Temporary Emergency Relief Administration (TERA) to administer twenty million dollars in state funds for care of the needy. Underscoring the "temporary" and "emergency" nature of this departure, Roosevelt still maintained to the state legislature that "aid must be extended by government, not as a matter of charity but as a matter of social duty." Several years later he asserted, "Better the occasional faults of a government that lives in a spirit of charity than the consistent omissions of a government frozen in the ice of its own indifference." Such rhetoric and the path-breaking TERA established the New York governor by 1932 as a humane, innovative executive who offered hope to the suffering masses and an alternative to the unpopular Hoover.[1]

At the time of Roosevelt's inauguration, roughly eighteen million Americans required relief of some kind. At least one-fourth and perhaps as much as one-third of the population could not support themselves because of unemployment, inadequate wages, or physical infirmity. During the Hundred Days Roosevelt signed into law a bill creating the Federal Emergency Relief Administration (FERA), which could distribute five hundred million dollars in outright grants—not loans—to the states to augment relief efforts and fund temporary employment. Obviously patterned after New York's TERA, the FERA would deal directly with public agencies run by the states, not with private or local organizations. States would receive a portion of the grant corresponding to their own relief expenditures, thus encouraging increased spending by the states, but the FERA administrator would also retain discretionary funds to target allocations where he perceived the gravest need. To initiate such a prodigious undertaking, Roosevelt chose the only person with comparable experience—the head of New York's TERA, Harry Hopkins.

The son of an Iowa harness maker, Harry Hopkins grew up in the rural Midwest and studied the social sciences at Grinnell College. He encountered grinding poverty and wretched social conditions only after he moved to New York City in 1912. Prior to his tenure at the TERA, Hopkins served as a social worker, Red Cross administrator, and director of various health agencies. As head of New York's TERA he developed the reputation of being a superb administrator who abhorred red tape. Impatient, informal, and hard working, Hopkins drove himself and subordinates at a frantic pace and ignored protocol to get results. His small-town innocence long since tempered by the imposing task of ministering to New York City's teeming masses of poor people, he appeared sarcastic, even "hard-boiled," to newspapermen who interviewed him. His life-style seemed a far cry from that of the stereotypic social worker, as evidenced by his passion for horse track gambling and penchant for hobnobbing with millionaires at their estates. Nevertheless, no one questioned his commitment to the poor, in whose behalf he labored long and hard throughout the depression.

On May 19, 1933, Hopkins accepted Roosevelt's offer to direct FERA activities, and the following day the Senate confirmed his appointment. On May 21, finding his new office in the RFC Building unfinished, he began work at a desk in the hallway and in just two hours disbursed five million dollars. Determined to dispatch desperately needed funds to the states without delay, he notified governors that they could telegram their requests to him and file formal applications later. Not wanting to be constrained by technicalities, Hopkins initially refused to hire a lawyer for the FERA. (Later, he invited Lee Pressman of the AAA Legal Division to become the agency's counsel.) He surrounded himself with a staff of social workers, engineers, economists, and accountants who shared his commitment to helping the needy and worked assiduously to get relief to state administrators. Hopkins preferred cash relief to grocery orders and commissaries, saying, "It is a man's business how he spends it," and under the FERA unrestricted monetary awards became customary. The FERA did, though, require relief applicants to submit to a means test.[2]

From 1933 to 1935 the FERA composed an impressive record. Millions of dollars went to the unemployable in the form of cash, clothing made by FERA labor, and surplus food. Utilizing commissaries, home deliveries, and cooperating grocery stores, the Federal Surplus Relief Corporation, a private organization that functioned essentially as a FERA subsidiary, distributed AAA surpluses to millions of indigents. Increasingly, the agency devoted its resources to work relief with the greatest emphasis on construction projects. FERA workers constructed 240,000 miles of roads and five thousand public buildings, laid thousands of miles of sewer lines and storm drainage systems, and built hundreds of bridges. Other agency projects allowed workers to utilize skills they already possessed or to develop new ones in specialized areas. Thus, FERA medical workers administered over one million vaccinations, and teachers conducted literacy classes for over one-half-million people. Other white-collar projects, admittedly on a small scale, provided work for jobless writers, musicians, doctors, and artists. For millions of suffering Americans FERA relief was a godsend.

Yet for all the FERA's impressive achievements, the American people never benefited as fully from federal assistance as they might have—or as much as Hopkins and other New Dealers knew they should have. President Roosevelt intended the matching-grant provision to induce the states to increase their relief contributions, but their refusal to do so resulted in the direct grants becoming dominant. Hopkins was unequivocal in his support for Roosevelt's goal, telling FERA state administrators, "Every department of government that has any taxing power left has a direct responsibility to help those in distress." Throughout the life of the FERA, and later under the CWA and the WPA, Hopkins fought a recurring battle with state and local governments intent on minimizing their contributions to relief while avidly accepting all the federal largess they could attract.[3]

The contentiousness of state and local governments owed to several causes. Strapped for funds, many governments simply could not produce any more resources for relief without incurring huge budget deficits. Some ideologues feared the damage the acceptance of relief would do to the hallowed principle of self-reliance. In some cases, governors and legislators resented federal intrusions and feared the loss of autonomy. All too often, however, Hopkins felt that home rule and states' rights became convenient excuses for politicians tapping federal resources while safeguarding their own funds. Accordingly, many state and local governments accepted FERA aid and, rather than increase their own assistance budgets, cut relief rolls by the number of clients added by the federal funds. More frequently, state authorities simply restricted the amount of relief available to their constituents by refusing to apply for matching grants. As Hopkins clashed with obdurate state and local officials, potential relief recipients suffered for lack of action.

Confronted with highly publicized recalcitrance on the part of rebellious officials, Hopkins federalized relief in several states by establishing new FERA offices, selecting new administrators, and channeling all federal funds directly from the comptroller general of the United States. As a result, delinquent governors, mayors, and other public officials wielded no authority at all in the relief process. In Oklahoma, Governor "Alfalfa Bill" Murray agreed to accept federal relief funds only if exempted from FERA regulations. Although some counties in the eastern portion of the state had 70 percent of their families eligible for relief, Murray and his successors, Ernest W. Marland and Leon Phillips, reduced state budgets and kept taxes on oil and natural gas ridiculously low. In 1934 Hopkins assumed control of relief in Oklahoma but never could force the state to contribute more funds for care of the indigent. Ohio governor Martin Davey fired the state's FERA administrator for insisting on keeping politics out of relief, and North Dakota governor William Langer similarly attempted to use federal relief for patronage. Hopkins federalized both states.

In Georgia, Governor Eugene Talmadge emerged as one of Roosevelt's most bitter critics. He termed the New Deal "a combination of wet-nursin', frenzied finance, downright communism, and plain damn-foolishness." In a thoroughly tasteless jab at Roosevelt's physical handicap, he said that "the next President who goes to the White House will be a man who knows what it is to work in the sun fourteen hours a day. . . . That man will be able to walk a two-by-four plank, too." The governor insisted that farmers desperately needed help, but city dwellers were "bums" and "chiselers." The best way to deal with relief applicants would be to "line them up against a wall and give them a dose of castor oil." When Talmadge steadfastly refused to award relief in minimal quantities set by the FERA, Hopkins removed all the governor's cronies on the Georgia Relief Commission and appointed Gay Shepperson relief administrator for the state. Talmadge harassed Shepperson and vetoed legislation intended to raise money for increased relief. In 1936 avowed New Dealer E. D. Rivers replaced Talmadge, but a tightfisted legislature undermined the new governor's blueprint for a "Little New Deal." By 1938 the state's refusal to provide matching grants led President Roosevelt to terminate all WPA and PWA funds.[4]

Huey Long's tempestuous career had an equally deleterious effect on federal relief provision in Louisiana. Senator Long ruled the state as if it were a fiefdom and demanded subservience from all Louisiana officials. When New Orleans mayor T. Semmes Walmsley balked, Long cut off all state relief funds to the city. Hopkins reorganized the Louisiana Emergency Relief Administration, removing Long loyalists and importing a new state relief administrator from Alabama. When the new administrator subsequently allied with the Kingfish, Hopkins replaced him and federalized the Louisiana relief structure. PWA chief Harold Ickes threatened to cancel all programs in the state, prompting Long to respond that Ickes could "go slap damn to hell." In July 1935 the administrator announced that no more applications would be accepted from Louisiana and only projects 95 percent completed would not be terminated. By the end of 1936 only 18.5 percent of the funds authorized for New Orleans by WPA and PWA had been spent (compared to a national average of 65.6%). The situation in Louisiana improved only after Long's assassination in 1935; the successors to his entrenched political machine,

Governor Richard Leche and Lieutenant Governor Earl Long, worked with dispatch to mend fences with the Roosevelt administration, and the flow of federal relief dollars resumed.[5]

Although Hopkins took the drastic step of federalizing relief offices in only six states, he spent an inordinate amount of time laboring to force governors and legislatures to shoulder their share of the relief burden. Idaho governor C. Ben Ross reflected the beliefs of many of his peers. "The states can do but little through their legislative bodies to increase the income of our people. But what they can do is to ECONOMIZE!" For months Ross dismissed Hopkins's demands that he call a special legislative session to provide more relief funds. Hopkins became so frustrated with the delaying tactics of Kentucky governor Ruby Laffoon that he personally addressed the state legislature to argue for increased state appropriations. The legislators responded by passing a small tax on beer and liquor, but within months the state coffers stood empty again. When Hopkins indicated that the federal government would absorb 75 percent of the cost of relief in North Carolina, Governor John Ehringhaus refused, saying the state could not manage the remaining 25 percent. When he left office in 1937, the penurious Ehringhaus left the state a hefty five-million-dollar surplus. During its two-year existence, the FERA provided over 90 percent of Virginia's relief funds, yet state officials, especially powerful U.S. senators Harry Byrd and Carter Glass, complained continuously about the New Deal's spendthrift policies and federal intrusiveness. Defending its tiny relief allotments, the commonwealth's welfare director noted that "it takes people a long time to starve." Hopkins's incessant haggling, coupled with threats to terminate all federal money, usually forced incremental increases in state support, but never enough to suit the FERA in Washington and far too much for New Deal opponents.[6]

Miserly state and local relief support exacerbated an already inadequate amount of federal funds, as both Roosevelt and Hopkins clearly understood. By the fall of 1933 they also realized that the inability to create new jobs was impeding economic recovery and that conditions would worsen for the unemployed with the arrival of harsh winter weather. Hopkins and FERA field representative Aubrey Williams, both of whom viewed relief as a temporary expedient and favored work relief, formulated a plan for the hiring of four million unemployed for the winter months. On November 9, 1933, Roosevelt issued an executive order diverting four hundred million dollars from the PWA to create the Civil Works Administration (CWA). Concerned only with putting people to work as quickly as possible, CWA officials did not administer means tests and hired as many of the unemployed as their budgets allowed. Roosevelt appointed Hopkins to administer the program, which would fund light construction public works projects until the coming of spring. Hopkins would also continue to supervise FERA relief payments, especially to transients and drought victims. Working at his usual frenetic pace, Hopkins cut bureaucratic corners and managed to employ two million idle workers within three weeks and the full four million by February 1934. As early as mid-January, Hopkins began cutting back appropriations in preparation for the CWA's termination. In February Congress provided some additional funds for demobilization, and the final discharge of work crews came on Easter weekend. True to the administration's pledge, the CWA's brief existence spanned but 4.5 months.

The haste with which the CWA took shape caused logistical problems. Assigning too many workers to a project site left some men leaning on their shovels with nothing to do. Some projects lacked adequate supervision; others, poorly conceived, were of questionable value. Although Hopkins policed the projects avidly, some graft and corruption crept into CWA affairs. Suppliers of materials and equipment sometimes charged exorbitant rates, and local politicians attempted to use CWA labor as patronage. New Deal critics among the media highlighted every depredation and condemned the program as a costly boondoggle. Although millions of Americans profited significantly from not having to endure another winter like the previous one, the plethora of negative publicity left American public opinion about the CWA divided.

In a very brief time the CWA established an impressive record of achievement. With the states contributing 10 percent of the project's total cost, the CWA spent $933 million, approximately 80 percent for wages. This made possible the construction or improvement of 500,000 miles of roads; 40,000 schools; 3,500 parks, playgrounds, and athletic fields; and 1,000 small airports. Assigning 10 percent of its jobs to white-collar and professional occupations, the CWA employed roughly 50,000 teachers and 3,000 artists and writers. Indeed, the CWA provided so much aid for the unemployed that many New Dealers—including Harry Hopkins—pleaded with the president to retain it. Already concerned that the CWA far exceeded original cost estimates, Roosevelt insisted on the project's liquidation on schedule. If nothing else, the agency's experience solidified Hopkins's commitment to work relief, and as the FERA prepared to assume again the full responsibility for all federal relief programs he placed greater emphasis on the works division. The FERA completed numerous unfinished CWA projects and prepared to initiate many more of the same.

By 1935 Hopkins and Roosevelt had both concluded that, insofar as the stagnant economy continued to sputter and some form of relief remained necessary, the federal government should stop issuing cash relief and attempt to secure work for the unemployed. As Hopkins said: "Give a man a dole, and you save his body and destroy his spirit. Give him a job and pay him an assured wage and you save both the body and the spirit." Announcing the dissolution of the FERA that year, Roosevelt said: "The lessons of history, confirmed by the evidence immediately before me, show conclusively that continued dependence upon relief induces a spiritual and moral disintegration fundamentally destructive to the national fibre. To dole out relief in this way is to administer a narcotic, a subtle destroyer of the human spirit." Averring that "the Federal Government must and shall quit this business of relief," the president announced the return of responsibility for "unemployables" to state and local officials and the commitment of the federal government to find work for the "able-bodied but destitute workers." The dole would be cheaper than work relief, but Roosevelt noted that "most Americans want to give something for what they get."[7]

In 1935 Congress passed the Emergency Relief Appropriation Act with an initial outlay of $4.8 billion for federal works projects. To direct the new Works Progress Administration (WPA), Roosevelt had to choose between PWA administrator Harold L. Ickes, who argued for the financing of massive construction projects built with efficiency and economy, and Harry Hopkins, who favored spending the bulk of federal money on wages, rather than materials, for smaller-scale projects that could be initiated more quickly. Given the exigencies of the time, Roosevelt understandably sided with Hopkins—with greater flexibility and the promise of a quicker stimulus to purchasing power. The WPA would pay a security wage in excess of the relief stipend but less than prevailing wage rates. By limiting wages and hours and, therefore, total earnings, the WPA sought to avoid competition with private enterprise; the unemployed should work rather than accept a dole and leave WPA rolls whenever possible for regular employment. The WPA bureaucracy would operate separately from the states, unlike the FERA, and funds would be awarded to local project sponsors (who would sometimes have to contribute a portion of the cost) by the national office. Like the FERA, but not the CWA, the WPA mandated a means test for job applicants.

The allocation of billions of dollars to local sponsors required diligent supervision to guard against fraud and misuse of public funds. Hopkins had established an unassailable record regarding such matters with the FERA and the CWA, but with such huge sums of WPA money involved the task became more difficult. And, as anti–New Dealers quickly pointed out, the ability to award relief to millions of Americans created the potential for the WPA to become a political machine for the Democratic party—a very real possibility, Republicans feared, when Hopkins was quoted as saying, "spend and spend, tax and tax, elect and elect." To keep politics out of the WPA bureaucracy Congress required after 1936 that all government appointees earning in excess of five thousand dollars be confirmed by the Senate. Hopkins was especially sensitive to charges of electioneering by WPA officials and meted out harsh penalties to agency employees guilty of electoral irregularities. He increased WPA enrollments just before fall elections in 1936 and 1938 but not to help Democratic candidates—in 1936 because of drought conditions and in 1938 due to economic recession. In the latter year the WPA reduced aid to Michigan, where avid New Deal governor Frank Murphy was fighting a losing battle for reelection. If anything, protested disgruntled Democrats, Hopkins and his subordinates appointed too many Republicans when they should have been taking better care of the party faithful.[8]

Even so, Hopkins admitted that he had long since ceased being a disinterested social worker. "I thought at first I could be completely non-political. Then they told me I had to be part non-political and part political. I found that was impossible, at least for me. I finally realized there was nothing for it but to be all-political." This did not mean sacrificing all propriety for partisan gain, nor would Hopkins manipulate relief awards at the expense of the poor. He maintained his professional standards but also adopted a more realistic view of how government and politics commingled. He understood that WPA appropriations depended upon Congress and knew that he could not afford to alienate powerful legislators who held the purse strings. Similarly, he found life much easier working with empathetic state and local leaders and naturally tended to favor those elected officials who cooperated with him. Hopkins suffered much criticism for his chummy relations with such big-city Democratic bosses as Chicago mayor Ed Kelly and Kansas City's Tom Pendergast, but Hopkins argued that their cities could not be ignored and found their cooperation essential for getting relief to the needy. As his biographer noted, Hopkins "was willing to accommodate sympathetic politicians by appointing their political supporters, but not if it meant sacrificing professional standards." By all accounts he pulled off that delicate balancing act quite successfully. Considering the potential for scandal and the intense scrutiny by administration foes, the record of the WPA was remarkably good.[9]

As with the FERA, Hopkins encountered strong resistance from states when he sought contributions for WPA projects. If anything, attitudes seemed to have hardened after two years of providing aid to the unemployed. Oregon governor Charles Martin, a self-professed Hoover Democrat, publicly informed Hopkins that the WPA administrator could "keep his money out of Oregon." In January 1936, Baltimore Emergency Relief Commission administrator Howard Beck reported 25 cases of "actual starvation," but Mayor Howard Jackson persisted in denouncing federal intervention while cutting the relief rolls. In Newark, New Jersey, Mayor Meyer Ellenstein's plan for a new water system foundered as a coterie of local businessmen successfully opposed capital expenditures. The WPA provided the funds to employ seventy thousand people in Philadelphia, but Mayor J. Hampton Moore approved projects for only half that number. When Moore refused to cooperate further, Hopkins arranged for trains to carry jobless Philadelphians to work in the suburbs; by December 1935, over twelve thousand of them worked in collar counties. Undaunted, Hopkins maintained the same position, saying, "Lots of people don't like the idea of taking care of their unemployables, but there is no state in the union that hasn't the power to take care of their unemployed."[10]

The Works Progress Administration, renamed the Work Projects Administration in 1939, survived until 1943, although drastic cuts in appropriations by the end of the decade limited its importance. In its eight-year existence the WPA spent slightly over $11 billion, of which $8.8 billion went toward construction and engineering costs. It constructed 40,000 buildings and repaired another 85,000; improved 572,000 miles of rural roads; erected 78,000 new bridges; paved 67,000 miles of city streets and 24,000 miles of sidewalks; built 350 airports; landscaped 8,000 new parks; and created a variety of sewerage systems, water treatment plants, and drainage facilities.

Indeed, one could hardly go to any community in the nation and not find highly visible evidence of the WPA's presence in an improved infrastructure—whether through the repair of existing streets, bridges, and parks or the provision of new viaducts, culverts, buildings, and sidewalks. A list of notable WPA projects would include New York City's LaGuardia Airport, Boston's Huntington Avenue Subway, Lake Shore Drive in Chicago, and the San Antonio Zoo, among many others. In the South the lining of miles of ditches with concrete veritably eliminated malaria as a serious health problem and in that notably backward region, according to one federal administrator, physical improvements came 30 years earlier than they otherwise would have. As with the CWA, there may have been some aimless "leaf raking," but overall the WPA fulfilled Roosevelt's pledge that relief work would serve a useful purpose.

Although the WPA spent 78 percent of its money on bricks-and-mortar projects, Roosevelt and Hopkins also sought to elevate morale and allow the unemployed to cultivate unique talents through a variety of community service programs. The WPA employed the jobless to stuff mattresses, count livestock, survey land, write books in braille, and care for children. WPA workers toiled not only on construction sites but also in offices, hospitals, museums, schools, libraries, and parks. One arm of the WPA, the Historical Records Survey, had as its primary objective the inventory and preservation of county records in each state. To a lesser degree, the survey dealt with such private collections as manuscripts, church records, and personal correspondence. The Women's Division of the WPA hired women in greatest numbers for work in sewing rooms and canneries, although some prepared school lunches, received housework training, or actually served as domestics.

In November 1934, Aubrey Williams devised a program to aid the nation's young people, and in June 1935, President Roosevelt created by executive order as part of the WPA the National Youth Administration (NYA). Under Williams's guidance the NYA performed two functions: First, the agency provided grants for college and high school students whose lack of money jeopardized their chances of remaining in school. The NYA enabled the students to complete their education and kept them out of the already crowded labor market. Second, the NYA sought to help young people not attending school and unable to find a job through vocational training and temporary financial aid. The NYA gained considerable notoriety because of its special attention to the needs of black youth. An outspoken champion of racial justice, Williams appointed famed black educator Mary McLeod Bethune to the NYA's Advisory Committee to serve as an advocate for her race. By the time of its abolition in 1943 the NYA had assisted more than two million young people, allowing many to complete their educations, providing relief for others, and becoming one of the most popular New Deal programs.

Perhaps the most innovative WPA undertaking was Federal Project One, composed of agencies to employ artists, actors, musicians, and writers who met the criteria for relief. The Federal Arts Project (FAP) supported young artists like Jackson Pollock, Stuart Davis, and Yasuo Kuniyoshi, as well as less talented painters, sculptors, photographers, and art teachers. It left a lasting impression through the 2,566 murals and 17,794 pieces of sculpture decorating public buildings and the dozens of community art centers that remained long after the depression. The Federal Writers Project (FWP) launched the careers of such noted novelists as Saul Bellow, Richard Wright, Ralph Ellison, John Cheever, Nelson Ahlgren, and Eudora Welty, but generally concentrated on the production of nonfiction. It published the American Guide Series, a comprehensive set of state histories, and the 150-title Life in America Series on a host of diverse topics. The FWP also collected American folklore and recorded the recollections of more than 2,000 ex-slaves. The Federal Music Project (FMP) employed hundreds of musicians who gave free public concerts and, according to FMP director Nikolai Sokoloff, performed the music of 14,000 American composers. The Federal Theatre Project (FTP) entertained at its peak a weekly audience of 350,000, performing a wide variety of plays ranging from *Pinocchio* to Shakespearean tragedies. Many Americans remembered most the FTP's *Living Newspaper,* dramatizations of current issues on stage.

The federal arts projects attracted much attention in the 1930s, not all of it laudatory. Critics questioned the appropriateness of supporting struggling young painters, actors, and the like, but Harry Hopkins never wavered, saying, "Hell, they've got to eat just like other people." Anticommunists thought they detected evidence of "Red romance," especially in the controversial Federal Theatre Project. FTP director Hallie Flanagan, a former Grinnell College classmate of Hopkins and head of the Vassar College Experimental Theatre, believed strongly in staging socially relevant plays, and a good number of FTP workers openly admitted to being political radicals. As the historian of the FTP concluded, the federal theatre "acquired for itself . . . a reputation for radicalism which a renewed emphasis on historical pageants, classical drama, and children's plays could never fully erase." In 1939 conservative congressmen on the House Committee on Un-American Activities and the House Subcommittee on Appropriations managed to terminate the project; the less volatile music, art, and writers' projects suffered severe budget cuts at that time but survived in modest fashion until the WPA's demise in 1943. Idealists who hoped federal support for the arts would result in a "cultural democracy," greater accessibility of art for the masses, and a new national art were inevitably disappointed. They could applaud, however, the New Deal's success in keeping struggling artists employed and establishing a precedent for public patronage of the arts.[11]

Through its many-faceted employment programs the WPA provided jobs for 8.5 million people, as many as 3 million at a time. For some of the millions of unemployables, the federal government provided additional aid with Social Security. As governor of New York, Roosevelt had signed into law an old-age retirement bill based on states and localities sharing cost that became a prototype of its kind. Nevertheless, in the early days of his presidency he gave scant attention to discussion of a national bill, preferring to wait for a more propitious economic climate. In addition, legal and philosophical issues divided Americans, and even the proponents of some kind of comprehensive social welfare legislation differed on substantive matters.

The rising public clamor over the plight of the elderly finally brought action. In 1930 only about one-third of men and about one-twelfth of women over the age of 65 still had gainful employment, and neither public nor private resources came close to providing care for old-age dependents. Industrial retirement plans served about 15 percent of the aged, and only 10 percent of these programs required employers to honor their commitments to retired persons. In the Great Depression many companies reneged on retirement payments, using pension funds for more pressing needs; bankrupt companies, of course, had no choice but to default. Only 18 states had old-age assistance laws, paying one dollar a day on the average in benefits to the few who qualified. In such a dire situation, the blandishments of Dr. Francis E. Townsend, a retired Long Beach, California, physician, found a willing audience. Townsend's panacea called for a pension of two hundred dollars a month for all retired persons over 60, providing they spent their allotment by the end of each month. Although financial experts dismissed the Townsend Plan as wholly unrealistic, the doctor's huge following put additional pressure on Roosevelt to confront the issue of care for the aged. So did Minnesota congressman Ernest Lundeen's proposal to allow elected committees of workers to distribute benefits from federal income tax revenues.

In 1934 Roosevelt created the Committee on Economic Security, chaired by Secretary of Labor Frances Perkins. Cognizant of rising medical costs and the fact that only 6 percent of Americans possessed health insurance, the committee considered the inclusion of medical benefits. Fearful that the already intense opposition from the American Medical Association would threaten passage of the entire measure, however, Perkins argued for postponement of the issue. The rest of the committee concurred, and the Social Security Act contained no provision for national health insurance. In January 1935, the committee presented to the president its recommendations, which became the substance of a bill forwarded to Congress. After months of debate and revision, both houses approved the Social Security Act, which Roosevelt signed on August 14, 1935. Title I provided for a compulsory old-age insurance program funded by employer and employee contributions. Unlike the many European old-age programs, in which the national governments funded at least part of the retirement benefits, Roosevelt felt it more politic for the federal government to make no contribution. "We put those payroll contributions there so as to give the contributors a legal, moral, and political right to collect their pensions and unemployment benefits. With those taxes in there, no damn politician can ever scrap my social security program." The exemption of farmers, domestic servants, and government workers from the pension program excluded approximately 9.4 million workers.[12]

Because of the intense interest in old-age pensions, drafters of the Social Security Act listed the retirement plan as Title I. Other portions of the law actually generated more controversy, and lengthy discussion of their merits explained the amount of time Congress took to pass the bill. One measure provided for a federal-state unemployment compensation program, and other titles provided federal grants to states for categorical assistance (the care of mothers, dependent children, and the blind, as well as for public health services). The sweeping reforms initiated by the omnibus bill brought almost immediate constitutional challenges in the courts, and in 1937 the U.S. Supreme Court upheld Congress's right to address economic issues affecting residents of all the states. Its future assured, amendments to the Social Security Act in 1939 extended coverage to include benefits for dependents of retired workers and their survivors.

Roosevelt lauded the Social Security Act for giving "at least some measure of protection to the average citizen and to his family against the loss of a job and against poverty-ridden old age." Esteemed economist and longtime champion of social insurance Paul Douglas praised the new law as a landmark breakthrough in the struggle to bring the United States up to the level of achievement of most European nations, but he noted its shortcomings as well and called it "merely a first step which must soon be followed by others." Conservatives condemned the further expansion of government initiative and decried the mandatory employer contributions to retirement benefits. Fears of creeping socialism in the New Deal seemed to conservatives eminently justified. For state governments having to deal with decreased federal relief programs after 1935, however, the passage of the Social Security Act promised additional aid for unemployment insurance and categorical assistance.[13]

In 1935 Roosevelt estimated that, independent of the WPA and Social Security, the states would still have to care for 1.5 million "unemployables." Unfortunately, the actual number turned out to be 4.7 million. Mindful of the problem many states were having as the FERA was being dismantled and as the WPA suffered the inevitable foul-ups and false starts of a new program, Roosevelt extended the date for termination of relief funds by six months. Even so, a November 1935 survey revealed that only 2 states possessed fully functioning relief operations and 23 states were totally unprepared. By the summer of 1937, 4 states (Kentucky, Maryland, Mississippi, and South Dakota) had abdicated all responsibility for relief to local governments. Nine states (Florida, Georgia, Indiana, Kansas, Massachusetts, Nevada, North Carolina, South Carolina, and Vermont) contributed nothing for relief but paid some administrative costs. New Jersey and Missouri stopped funding relief for a time but later reconsidered and provided nominal assistance. The remaining states assumed some degree of responsibility, although they frequently kept expenditures small by reducing amounts of relief payments, tightening eligibility requirements, and generally reverting to pre–New Deal practices. Until the return of prosperity state and local governments remained unable—or unwilling—to care for the still sizable stable of unemployed.

The spotty record of the states calls into question what lasting impact—if any—New Deal relief programs had on American social welfare policies. On the one hand, the New Deal forced state and local governments to create public welfare agencies as preconditions to receiving federal aid—something rarely done prior to the 1930s—and these newly created bureaucracies became permanent fixtures long after the depression ended. Certainly, Social Security constituted a major breakthrough in the creation of a limited welfare state. Although Franklin Roosevelt spoke of "cradle to the grave" security, the 1935 legislation eschewed national health insurance and limited benefits to only about 60 percent of the work force. Moreover, unemployment compensation and various forms of categorical assistance relied upon state conditions, usually funded by regressive sales taxes, with the result of significant variations in the generosity of benefits. In 1937, for example, Mississippi old-age pensions of $3.84 per month paled in comparison with California's $37.95. Aid to dependent children ranged from $8.10 monthly in Arkansas to $61.07 in Massachusetts in 1939, by which time 10 states had not yet chosen to participate. Like most Americans, Roosevelt and Hopkins thought smaller units of government should continue to play a large role in the selection and payment of relief recipients. The decision to vary WPA maximum payments by region (and sometimes by race) reflected this esteem for different local circumstances and a desire to avoid inflexible national standards.

The reluctance to tamper with existing social welfare customs appeared most clearly in the South. FERA average monthly stipends per family in that region ranged from $3.96 in Mississippi to $13.89 in Louisiana, at a time when the national average exceeded $15.00. When Hopkins insisted that Mississippi increase its benefits, 27 of the state's 82 counties withdrew from the FERA in protest. (They all returned within three months.) In 1935 the monthly pay rates for the WPA's southeastern region—$14 to $30 for unskilled workers and $35 to $68 for skilled laborers—were the lowest of its four regions. Certainly relief stipends fell short of desirable levels nationwide, but southern public workers suffered most, receiving from 33 to 65 percent of the national average "emergency standard of living expense" identified by federal authorities.

Southern spokesmen defended such discrepancies with reference to traditionally low wages in Dixie, the purported lower standard of living, and race. Indeed, many southerners thought the WPA wages paid to blacks excessive, even at those modest levels, particularly in light of the scant remuneration imposed under slavery and sharecropping. A North Carolina landlord lamented that "ever since federal relief . . . came in you can't hire a nigger to do anything for you. High wages is ruinin' 'em." Southern cotton magnates protested that the WPA drained the countryside of unskilled labor and voiced their outrage at WPA workers' refusal to relinquish their "make work" to pick cotton. In 1936 Hopkins instituted a practice of deleting reliefers from WPA rolls during cotton-picking season and requiring them to work temporarily in the fields. In such ways, the federal relief program accommodated itself to regional idiosyncracies.[14]

The American distaste for relief and suspicion of those who accepted it, the insistence on maintaining a distinction between the "worthy" and "unworthy" poor, persisted even in the midst of the worst economic calamity in the nation's history. The intense resistance Hopkins encountered from state and local authorities when he sought greater relief contributions showed the degree to which traditional attitudes persisted. Although such exceptions as Michigan's Frank Murphy and New York's Herbert Lehman existed, most governors thought balanced budgets more important than expanded relief rolls. Judging by their records, most state legislatures concurred. At best, "Little New Deals" operated in four states—Georgia, New York, Michigan, and Pennsylvania. Independent Progressive governors Floyd Olson in Minnesota and Philip LaFollete in Wisconsin disclaimed that title, but their enlightened welfare policies arguably brought the total to six. Americans recognized the need for more government action in the extraordinary conditions of the 1930s, but a strong sense of ambivalence remained. In 1939 people polled across the country chose the WPA most often when asked to name both the New Deal's "greatest accomplishment" and the "worst thing" it had done.

Government officials at all levels acted rationally in mirroring the apparent attitudes on social welfare shown by their constituents. As early as 1935, polls reported that 60 percent of the population (including 36% of the Democrats) opposed the level of government spending on relief. To be sure, unemployed councils, frequently dominated by Communists and Socialists, staged demonstrations to protest inadequate care for the unemployed. But radical groups calling for the end of the capitalist system attracted a small following, and even those apolitical unemployed demanding increased relief spending constituted only about 5 percent of the population. More commonly, politicians were pressured by advocates of property tax reduction and prudent government spending. Resistance to relief spending came from farmers' groups and such business organizations as the National Economy League, the Chamber of Commerce, and the National Association of Manufacturers. Furthermore, in city after city voters defeated bond proposals necessary to fund public improvement projects more often than they approved them.

Opposition to "excessive" social welfare provision resulted in a comparatively modest New Deal commitment. Harry Hopkins admitted that "we have never given adequate relief." At its peak the WPA supported approximately 39 percent of the able-bodied unemployed, more often around 30 percent. The number of certified relief workers left unassigned to federal work projects varied from 600,000 to 1.3 million a month after 1935. That year under the FERA the average monthly wage for workers and dependents amounted to less than $30, roughly the equivalent weekly earnings of a predepression industrial worker and far less than the $100 a month designated as a minimum subsistence wage. The WPA usually paid more, as much as $55 per month, but in some communities workers received as little as $21 monthly. Severe means tests, seldom altered for the unemployed who suddenly lost their jobs, disqualified applicants who owned homes, automobiles, or life insurance policies. By 1936 comparatively high wages fell when congressional appropriations dwindled. From March 1936 to September 1937, as economic conditions improved, the WPA cut the number of persons on its rolls from 2.9 to 1.5 million. During the 1938 recession the number soared to 3 million, but it fell dramatically the following year when Congress mandated the removal of all workers who had received WPA benefits for more than 18 consecutive months. The meager, often inadequate, pay and the uncertainty of employment underscored the limited nature of New Deal relief.[15]

American attitudes and traditions shaped the social welfare program the New Deal bequeathed the nation. Roosevelt's administration broke new ground in aiding the impoverished, and if it failed to do as much as it might have, the New Deal still provided succor for a substantial number of Americans who would otherwise have suffered terribly. Roosevelt saw New Deal relief as a temporary emergency measure, whereby work took precedence over the dole and, as much as possible, state and local responsibility predominated. By providing work relief for millions (about one-third of the idle), the WPA significantly enlarged the role of public institutions in caring for the poor. Nevertheless, misgivings about the value of excessive beneficence limited the scope of New Deal action. The social welfare system emerging from the 1930s, despite its new programs and larger budget, relied on contributory social insurance and continued to exhibit an aversion to relief. For all that it did, the New Deal could have done much more. As historian Robert H.

Bremner concluded, "In social welfare, as in other fields, the New Deal followed a middle course abominated by traditionalists, scorned by radicals, and not entirely satisfactory to the more forward looking of the President's own supporters."[16]

CHAPTER SIX

The Politics of Preemption, 1934–1936

In 1933 FERA administrator Harry Hopkins sent 16 newspaper reporters around the country to assess conditions among the American people. Hopkins chose Lorena Hickok, a veteran newspaperwoman and close friend of Eleanor Roosevelt, as chief investigator. Hickok sent Hopkins dozens of letters throughout the second half of 1933 and all of 1934, relaying her observations on the economic circumstances and attitudes of all varieties of people—community leaders, wealthy businessmen, relief recipients, indigents, and politicians. She wrote repeatedly about the "tremendous popularity" of President Roosevelt, detailing how those receiving FERA benefits—and even those unable to qualify for relief—praised Roosevelt unstintingly. In addition, she noted, people had begun to ignore state and local government, instead focusing their expectations and demands on New Deal agencies in Washington. Hickok warned, "All this, it seems to me, puts the President, the Federal Emergency Relief Administration, and the Federal Government as a whole in a pretty difficult and serious dilemma." As long as the New Deal induced recovery and Americans believed that the vastly expanded federal bureaucracy would lead the way out of the depression, Franklin Roosevelt's popularity would be assured. But how long would relief be accepted as a temporary measure and when would regular employment by private industry replace the FERA, the CWA, and the CCC? Was the New Deal the slickly marketed failure its critics decried? And what of Roosevelt, did his innovations amount to anything more substantive than Hoover's more limited actions?[1]

The state of the economy offered decidedly mixed signals. During the first year of the Democratic administration, conditions improved noticeably. National income rose by 25 percent, and approximately two million unemployed went back to work. Productivity in many industries increased, but often it was temporary, as in the summer 1933 spurt anticipating NRA production limitations. The NRA's lack of success became increasingly evident as the months passed, and indicators of business activity showed little cause for optimism. Millions remained jobless. A dispirited Lorena Hickok wrote Hopkins in April 1934: "Oddly, I think most of the farmers and businessmen I've talked to these last few weeks would accept anything the President wanted to put over, if they felt he had the power to FORCE them to do it. I think they actually WANT a dictator. I think they'd rather anything in the world would happen than that Congress should get the whip hand. Oh, why did this year have to be an election year?"[2]

Republicans and other New Deal opponents eagerly awaited the 1934 congressional elections, believing that stalled recovery would render Democratic candidates especially vulnerable. Although Roosevelt spoke optimistically of the Democrats' chances in the fall contest, doubters noted that without exception in American history the party in power lost congressional seats in off-year elections. But if the political experts were correct in calling the 1934 contest the first full-fledged public referendum on Roosevelt and his programs, then the president had more than good reason for celebration. Democrats increased their lead over Republicans in the Senate by 10 to 69–25 and in the House from 314–117 to 322–103. Not only had the Democrats become the first party ever to increase its control of both houses of Congress in an off-year election, but the emasculated Republican party could claim only 26 percent of Senate seats and 24 percent of the House. The election outcome removed all doubts of Roosevelt's popularity, causing journalist William Allen White to observe admiringly, "He has been all but crowned by the people."[3]

The outcome of the 1934 election reflected more than just support for the president. Voters denied reelection to several prominent anti–New Dealers, while sending to Washington a group of outspoken liberals that included Vito Marcantonio of New York, Maury Maverick of Texas, Ernest Lundeen of Minnesota, and Tom Amlie of Wisconsin. The *New York Times* claimed that the election outcome "literally destroyed the right wing of the Republican Party." The message the voters sent to Washington seemed to provide a mandate for the New Deal and then some. If Roosevelt's efforts disappointed so far, the electorate wanted not a return to the cautious approach of the preceding Republican administration but the use of bolder policies by the federal government. The new Congress that Roosevelt assayed in early 1935 was more than just a partisan Democratic body; its composition invited the executive branch to take the New Deal farther to the left.[4]

In 1934–35 numerous other factors pressured Roosevelt into more liberal departures. The striking success of parties and politicians to the left of the president revealed a significant undercurrent of radical sentiment in the nation. No single organization posed a threat, electoral or otherwise, to Roosevelt and the Democrats, but collectively they represented a considerable presence on the left of the political spectrum. The Farmer-Labor Political Federation and its successor, the American Commonwealth Political Federation, thrived in the upper Midwest, and the National Farm Holiday Association's annual convention attracted ten thousand delegates in 1935. The American Communist Party (CPUSA) commanded probably no more than eighty thousand members and exerted the most influence when allying with organized labor, black organizations, and other liberal groups. Under the leadership of Norman Thomas, the Socialist Party of America (SPA) saw its membership peak at an estimated twenty-one thousand in 1934; just two years earlier presidential candidate Thomas received over eight hundred thousand votes. To many Americans searching frantically for solutions to the nation's protracted economic problems, support for such radical groups became a decidedly more respectable alternative in the 1930s.

In California Socialist Upton Sinclair, famed author of *The Jungle* and two-time unsuccessful candidate for governor, registered as a Democrat in 1933 and sought the party's gubernatorial nomination the following year. He published a pamphlet, *I, Governor of California,* outlining his End Poverty in California (EPIC) program, whereby capitalism would be replaced by a network of cooperatives managed by the unemployed. A massive grass-roots campaign resulted in the establishment of almost two thousand EPIC clubs throughout the state and, most remarkably, a victory for Sinclair in the Democratic primary. Originally laudatory of the Democratic candidate, Roosevelt backed away when a coalition of business interests and Republicans falsely labeled Sinclair an atheist, Communist, and an immoral practitioner of free love. Conservative Hollywood movie moguls produced fabricated newsreels in which actors affected Russian accents to praise Sinclair. In the November 1934 election Sinclair received 879,000 votes but lost to Republican Frank Merriam. Nevertheless, EPIC candidates won 30 seats in the California legislature, and public opinion forced archconservative Merriam to endorse the New Deal.

In Wisconsin the sons of Senator Robert M. LaFollette kept their father's brand of progressivism alive in the state's Republican party after his death in 1925. In 1934 Bob LaFollette, Jr., and his brother, Philip, formed the Wisconsin Progressive party. Roosevelt endorsed the former for reelection to the Senate but opposed the latter's bid for governor and supported the Democratic candidate. Both LaFollettes won in 1934, and Phil especially sounded more radical thereafter. The newly elected governor asserted: "We are not liberals! Liberalism is nothing but a sort of milk-and-water tolerance. . . . I believe in a fundamental and basic change." Ignoring the advice of political advisor Jim Farley, Roosevelt remained publicly friendly with the LaFollettes, who urged the president to inject more thoroughgoing reform into the New Deal. Wisconsin voters continued to support Roosevelt in the years 1934–36 but, as one historian noted, "their enthusiasm for the 'radical' LaFollettes leaves little question about which direction they wanted FDR to take."[5]

In Minnesota, another traditional hotbed of progressivism, a coalition between agrarian radicals and urban laborers gave birth to the Minnesota Farmer-Labor party in the 1920s. In 1930 Farmer-Laborite Floyd Olson was elected governor and established a reputation for radicalism, observing that capitalism was "steeped in the most dismal stupidity." When conservatives in the state legislature tried to block relief appropriations, Olson used the threat of martial law to force action. Like the LaFollettes, Olson remained friendly with Roosevelt but criticized the president's moderation. What the country really needed, the governor suggested, was "not just a new deal, but also a new deck." He contemplated running for president on a third-party ticket in 1936 but died of cancer earlier that year. The Minnesota Farmer-Labor party continued to thrive after Olson's death, electing yet another governor (Elmer Benson), a U.S. senator (Ernest Lundeen), five U.S. representatives, and the vast majority of state officeholders.[6]

The striking success of such left-of-center groups in Minnesota, Wisconsin, and California, coupled with the Communist and Socialist parties' appeal to certain elements in American society, presented a fragmented and apparently isolated threat. Of more immediate concern, three national movements attracted great popular attention and financial support. Huey Long, Father Charles E. Coughlin, and Dr. Francis Townsend elicited wildly varying responses from Americans. Some viewed them as irresponsible demagogues, others as comical charlatans. Some saw the three messiahs as descendants of populism, others as forerunners of fascism. Whatever they were, collectively or individually, they amassed huge and loyal followings among depression-era Americans. Moreover, Franklin Roosevelt took them seriously as political rivals.

Father Charles E. Coughlin, the famed radio priest from Royal Oak, Michigan, started out as an enthusiastic supporter of Roosevelt and the New Deal. Broadcasting a weekly radio program that CBS syndicated nationally, the Roman Catholic priest enjoyed an audience of forty million at the height of his popularity. Originally confined to religious topics, his programs turned to political commentary as economic conditions deteriorated in the early 1930s. He excoriated simultaneously communism and capitalism, blaming the depression on an international banking conspiracy. Although he once called the New Deal Christ's Deal, Coughlin grew impatient with Roosevelt's unwillingness to destroy the banking community. In 1935 he formed the National Union for Social Justice, a loosely knit organization devoted to forwarding Coughlin's economic panaceas and electing sympathetic candidates to national office. The increasing virulence of his attacks on Roosevelt, his outrageous charges of Communist infiltration in Washington, a sickening anti-Semitism, and his unbridled megalomania drove many followers away and eventually led to orders from the church hierarchy to end all political activities. Public humiliation and censure came later in the decade, however, and in the New Deal's early years Coughlin's indictment of Wall Street and demand for sweeping economic change found an appreciative national audience.

Exceedingly popular and much more respectable, retired physician Dr. Francis E. Townsend rose to prominence on the strength of his retirement plan for the aged. The Townsend Plan centered on two-hundred-dollar monthly pensions for all unemployed Americans over the age of 60, provided that they spend the money within 30 days. The pensions would be funded by a 2-percent sales tax he vaguely called a transaction tax. Although the vast majority of the 3.5 million dues-paying members of Townsend Clubs were retired persons, the doctor claimed that his plan would benefit all Americans by removing old people from the labor market and stimulating the economy through the increased purchases made by the elderly. The soaring popularity of the scheme belied several critical problems: consumer prices would need to increase 80 percent to raise the necessary funds, the sum of which equaled one-half of the 1934 national income. Based on a regressive sales tax, the plan would simply have taken from one disadvantaged group (working-class consumers) and given to another (the aged). Widely credited with having forced the Roosevelt administration to consider the plight of the elderly poor, Townsend expressed dissatisfaction with the Social Security Act and continued his crusade after its passage in 1935.

Unlike Coughlin and Townsend, Louisiana senator Huey P. Long harbored aspirations for higher political office and made no attempt to disguise his designs on the presidency. Raised in the poor hill country of northern Louisiana, the Kingfish (as he liked to be called) abandoned the practice of law for a career in politics. Always emphasizing his humble origins and affinity for the common folk, Long parlayed his experience on the Louisiana Public Service Commission and with Populist rhetoric into his election as governor in 1928. While publicly clashing with the state's powerful planter elite and oil interests, he built roads, improved public education, extended the reach of public health, and reformed egregiously unfair tax codes. At the same time, he created a powerful political machine and used force—sometimes illegally—to rule the state in dictatorial fashion. Elected to the U.S. Senate in 1930, Long refused to take his seat for two years and remained governor until 1932, when he installed a surrogate in the statehouse to mind the store back home. He became a nationally prominent figure because of his Share Our Wealth Plan, a call for steeply graduated taxes, the limitation of income to one million dollars per year, and the redistribution of wealth to provide all families a guaranteed annual income of twenty-five hundred dollars. The Kingfish counseled farmers to grow as much as they could and, when they produced a normal year's yield, to put away their plows and work on government-funded projects. Although as flawed as the Townsend Plan, Long's schemes attracted a huge following in the South and a growing one elsewhere by mid-decade.

In 1932 Long supported Roosevelt early and assiduously, playing a leading role in keeping the New Yorker's disparate supporters together during the Democratic National Convention. Within a few months, however, Long broke with the administration over policy and patronage matters and began to lay the groundwork for his own presidential candidacy in 1936. He openly consorted with Coughlin and Townsend and flayed Roosevelt and the New Deal incessantly from the Senate rostrum. The president, who labeled Long "one of the two most dangerous men in America" (General Douglas MacArthur, the other), publicly sought to discredit Long and privately plotted against him; federal officials aided Long's enemies in Louisiana and conducted investigations of the senator's income taxes hoping to discover criminal offenses. Concern mounted when a secret poll taken by the Democratic National Committee in 1935 uncovered a shocking amount of support for Long as a third-party candidate; as many as four million Americans inclined to vote for him. Such a result could well have diminished the Democratic vote enough to elect a Republican, and administration officials, many of whom had long dismissed the Kingfish as a minor irritant, began to take his widespread appeal seriously. Long's assassination in September 1935 removed the immediate threat of his candidacy, but concerns about the depth of his support and the feasibility of attracting his supporters back into the Democratic fold remained.[7]

The impulse to preempt challengers from the political left by initiating additional reforms received reinforcement from the wave of worker unrest that swept the country in 1934. The rights guaranteed labor by Section 7(a) of the NIRA raised workers' morale, but the NRA's indifferent support of the unions dashed their hopes. It quickly became apparent that industry had no intention of voluntarily forfeiting any of its cherished prerogatives. In 1934 alone, about 1.5 million workers participated in nearly two thousand strikes. In September the United Textile Workers (UTW), an American Federation of Labor affiliate, called a general strike idling 376,000 laborers in Georgia, North Carolina, Alabama, Mississippi, South Carolina, Tennessee, Virginia, Rhode Island, Pennsylvania, Massachusetts, New Hampshire, and Maine. After three weeks of violence, the Board of Inquiry for the Textile Industry found the UTW's request for recognition "not feasible" and asked the union to end the strike. President Roosevelt, who had appointed the independent investigatory commission, endorsed its recommendation and asked workers to return to the job. The decade's largest strike ended in failure for labor and called into question Roosevelt's commitment to the goals outlined in Section 7(a).

Not all labor upheavals that year ended so dismally, as evidenced by the triumphant general strike staged in Minneapolis. The Minneapolis Central Union lent its support to the efforts of a local union of the International Brotherhood of Teamsters, which battled an employer's organization, the Citizen's Alliance, as well as the city police. Thousands of relief workers and unemployed citizens joined the vast majority of the city's union members in support of the truckers during the 36-day strike. In one clash, the list of strikers' casualties included 50 wounded and 2 dead; subsequently, strikers killed 2 members of a strikebreaking force assembled by management. With Governor Floyd Olson sympathetic to the strikers and denying employers their customary support from state militia, the truckers captured a favorable settlement that included union recognition and higher wages.

Another success for labor occurred in San Francisco, beginning with a walkout staged by the city's militant longshoremen. On July 5, 1934, the entire San Francisco police force joined strikebreakers in a pitched battle against thousands of workers for control of the waterfront. Driven back by bullets and tear gas, the strikers finally retreated, leaving behind two dead and dozens wounded. Bay area workers struck in nearly unanimous support of the longshoremen, paralyzing the metropolitan area for several days. The remarkable shutdown of city services forced management to accept arbitration, and the strikers received a favorable decision from the National Longshoremen's Board. As in Minneapolis, workers took great risks—against the advice of timid local labor leaders—and won exhilarating victories. In these and other labor confrontations that year, the meaning seemed clear: the New Deal had energized a slumbering labor movement, which then prepared to move ahead with or without administrative support.

Sensitive to criticism from liberals and concerned that a restless electorate might be influenced by individuals and organizations committed to more forceful action, Roosevelt also found a move to the left more congenial because of continued assaults from the right. Despite promulgating measures clearly designed to aid business recovery, Roosevelt suffered a growing business hostility that he found impossible to explain. As late as November 1934, he lamented, "One of my principal tasks is to prevent bankers and businessmen from committing suicide." Souring on NRA-style planning and resistant to such New Deal measures as capital market regulation and currency inflation, the aroused business community began to question the president's programs. They also rued an apparent changing of the guard among New Deal advisors, in which the engineers of the Hundred Days (Moley and Berle, principally) gave way to the disciples of Louis Brandeis and the New Freedom (Benjamin Cohen and Thomas Corcoran). Especially bitter because of the Roosevelt family's lofty social standing, they called the president a "traitor to his class." Not content to mold the National Chamber of Commerce and the National Association of Manufacturers into antiadministration lobbies, a group of the nation's wealthiest businessmen felt the New Deal so threatening that they resolved to create a new organization to mobilize the political opposition.[8]

Founded on August 22, 1934, the American Liberty League professed nonpartisanship but immediately became the hub of conservative opposition to Roosevelt and the New Deal. The Liberty League could truly claim bipartisanship, for it drew its leadership from both parties. Prominent charter members included Republicans Nathan Miller (director of U.S. Steel and former governor of New York) and Irenee duPont; and Democrats Jouett Shouse (former party Executive Committee chairman), John J. Raskob (former director of General Motors and chairman of the party's National Committee), and former presidential candidates John W. Davis and Al Smith. The league claimed 125,000 members by the summer of 1936, and although its officials insisted that the vast majority were not rich, the leaders certainly were. The organization's funding came from the wealthy. In 1936, when the league spent $518,000 to unseat Roosevelt, two-thirds of the total came from just 30 men and one-fourth from the duPont family. Clearly, the American Liberty League, as the public believed, responded to the desires of the plutocrats who founded and endowed it.

The Liberty League conducted an extensive campaign to discredit the New Deal, distributing pamphlets, mailing a monthly newsletter, and advertising on radio. Its principal aim was to restore to business the freedom it had enjoyed before excessive government regulation despoiled the nation. As the league's leading spokesman, Al Smith accused Roosevelt of fomenting class hatred and subverting the Constitution, the judiciary, and the federal system through the expansion of executive power. The league maintained that New Deal policies not only inhibited economic recovery but did so intentionally to sustain the crisis and maintain the Democrats in power. An unofficial whispering campaign charged Roosevelt with being a syphilitic, an alcoholic, a dictator, a dupe of blacks and Jews, and a pathological liar. Such innuendos did the organization no credit, and it failed to attract a widespread popularity principally because few Americans shared its point of view. To the general public Franklin Roosevelt was not the problem; rather, he was trying—however successfully—to find solutions. If anything, the class unrest Al Smith blamed the president for inciting constituted the cause, not the product, of Roosevelt's turn to the left.

Thus by 1935, with his reelection only a year away, Roosevelt feared the dissolution of his political coalition. The breach with business seemed beyond repair, and opposition on the left appeared to be increasing daily. Court decisions threatened measures critical to the administration's program—the Supreme Court would later abrogate the NRA and AAA—and the fate of much of the legislation passed during the Hundred Days seemed uncertain. Perhaps most unsettling, after two years of effort recovery measures had produced few notable successes. Always open to experimentation, by the spring of 1935 Roosevelt began to discuss the need for a "second hundred days." A May 14

White House dinner with five prominent Senate Progressives, arranged by Felix Frankfurter, confirmed the president's inclination to exert bold leadership once again. Determined to seize the initiative, Roosevelt busied administration draftsmen to prepare a new package of bills for Congress.

The ensuing burst of legislative activity, what historians have called the Second New Deal, provided reformers with yet another chance to improve American society. Ironically, the opportunity for a Second New Deal arose out of frustration and failure, but that did not deter the liberal New Dealers hoping to obtain reform along with relief and recovery. When Roosevelt had begun to explore such possibilities with his advisors after the 1934 elections, an enthusiastic Harry Hopkins said to his staff: "Boys, this is our hour. We've got to get everything we want—a works program, social security, wages and hours, everything—now or never. Get your minds to work on developing a complete ticket to provide security for all the folks of this country up and down and across the board."[9]

Roosevelt began the Second New Deal with the Emergency Relief Appropriations Act, which allocated $4.8 billion (the largest amount ever allocated in peacetime) for the WPA. A flabbergasted Arthur H. Vandenburg, conservative Republican senator from Michigan, criticized the bill for spending an unprecedented amount of the taxpayers' money. Congressional liberals had no qualms about the cost of relief, arguing instead that the bill did not go far enough for the relief worker. Senators Robert F. Wagner, George Norris, and Robert LaFollette criticized the intention to pay WPA workers less than they would be earning in private industry, and the Senate added a "prevailing wage" amendment before approving the bill. With one eye on an already bulging budget, Roosevelt threatened a veto and demanded reconsideration of the amendment. Fearing that the wage issue could block the bill's passage, Wagner accepted a compromise amendment that still allowed the president to pay WPA workers less than their counterparts in private industry. The rift between Roosevelt and his liberal supporters in Congress healed, the Emergency Relief Appropriations Act became law and extended work relief opportunities for more of the unemployed.[10]

Much of the spring 1935 congressional session slipped by with little further evidence of activity from the White House, but shortly after the Supreme Court sundered the NRA on Black Monday (May 27), Roosevelt suddenly announced a package of "must" legislation. These five new bills included Social Security, a substantial tax increase, a banking act, a public utilities measure, and a labor bill to replace the NIRA's Section 7(a). The first of these to capture Congress's attention in the sweltering Washington summer, the National Labor Relations Act (NLRA), appeared in many ways the most problematic. In 1934 Robert F. Wagner had introduced a labor bill, but Roosevelt, apprehensive about the midterm elections and not yet ready to break with business, intervened to block a vote for the measure on the Senate floor. In 1935 the president promised a neutral stance, and Wagner proceeded with a bill substantially different from the previous year's version. The new law granted more authority to the National Labor Relations Board (NLRB), empowering it to safeguard labor's right to organize and bargain collectively. Unlike earlier incarnations, this NLRB would act as a powerful, independent tribunal of labor-management relations and not just an arbiter of disputes.

Wagner employed great tactical skill in guiding the NLRA quickly through to a vote in the Senate after only two days of debate, keeping its many enemies from mounting an effective countercampaign. On May 15 Roosevelt blithely responded to a newsman's question about the fate of the NLRA by saying he had not given it any thought one way or the other. The next day the Senate passed the bill by an eye-opening 63–12 vote. Following the advice of Felix Frankfurter and Louis Brandeis, who argued for the exercise of bold leadership and an end to the appeasement of business, Roosevelt belatedly endorsed the NLRA on May 24. In June the House of Representatives passed the bill by voice vote, and the president signed it on July 5. Secretary of Labor Frances Perkins later noted that Roosevelt contributed nothing to the NLRA's passage and only jumped on the bandwagon when it became evident Congress would approve the measure. Again, the leader scrambled to get out in front of his impatient followers.[11]

As one of the principal architects of the Social Security Act and the man who introduced the bill in the Senate, Robert Wagner again urged more liberal legislation than the president wanted. Roosevelt had delayed action on social insurance legislation by appointing an ad hoc committee under Perkins in 1934 to formulate proposals, but by the spring of 1935 he assented to consideration of a bill. As much opposition arose from liberals deriding the Social Security Act's limitations as from conservatives denouncing the nation's drift toward socialism, but eventually it passed both houses of Congress without much difficulty. Less than totally satisfied supporters recognized that, for all its shortcomings, Social Security did more for society's dependents than had anything else in America's history. And it added another brush stroke to the developing picture of the New Deal looking out for society's unfortunates.

Along with attention to the "forgotten man," another developing theme of the Second New Deal was opposition to big business. Beginning tentatively, Roosevelt first targeted the hated utility companies. When he became president, 13 holding companies controlled three-fourths of the nation's private power concerns. These holding companies performed no function other than to issue stock and inflate prices, while producing enormous profits and charging consumers exorbitant amounts for electricity. New Dealers Benjamin Cohen and Thomas Corcoran drafted a bill most notable for its death sentence, a provision empowering the Securities and Exchange Commission to liquefy any holding companies unable to demonstrate that they served a useful economic purpose. The utilities industry responded with an unprecedented million-dollar lobbying campaign on Capitol Hill, whereby congressmen found themselves outnumbered by lobbyists. The strategy worked. The Senate passed the Wheeler-Rayburn Bill by a single vote, but the House defeated the bill by a hefty margin. Forced to compromise, Roosevelt agreed to the elimination of the death sentence; instead, the version of the bill approved by Congress eliminated all holding companies beyond the second generation and mandated that those beyond the first generation justify their existence or suffer the same fate. By the end of the decade most of the gigantic utility conglomerates had been dissolved, and Roosevelt appeared to have won another great victory over the privileged upper class.

The decision to challenge the rich inevitably raised the possibility of redistributing wealth through taxation. In the 1930s less than 5 percent of Americans paid income taxes, and a small group of them carried most of the load. From 1933 to 1935 New Deal taxation policy featured substantial levies on alcohol, AAA processing taxes, and regressive excise taxes extended from the Hoover years, none of which could be called progressive. Nor did Social Security payroll taxes redistribute wealth for the benefit of the nation's poor. But the undeniable popularity of Huey Long's "soak the rich" tax scheme compelled the president to act. In a message to Congress, Roosevelt excoriated the "unjust concentration of wealth and economic power," while calling for a graduated tax on corporations, federal inheritance and gift taxes, and an increase in the maximum income tax rate from 63 to 79 percent.[12]

As historian Mark Leff has shown, Roosevelt's support of the Wealth Tax Act in 1935 owed more to political considerations than to any genuine effort at economic reform. Radical oratory aside, the president gave only sporadic support to the bill. He agreed to congressional adjournment without a vote on the bill, and Treasury Secretary Henry Morgenthau called Roosevelt's tax message "more or less of a campaign document laying down the principles as to where he stands." The Revenue Act of 1935 enacted a small estate tax, a token corporate tax, and no inheritance tax. Income tax increases came entirely at the expense of the very rich, sparing those of slightly smaller fortunes, and, due to the few people affected, generated very little additional revenue to be redistributed. (For three years after the law's enactment, only John D. Rockefeller occupied the top tax bracket.) The new law merely "skimmed the top," a politically popular tactic but not economically meaningful. In short, the Wealth Tax Act redistributed little wealth but assumed great symbolic importance as another affront to Wall Street and a link between the New Deal and the vulnerable masses.[13]

The last bill on Roosevelt's must list, the Banking Act of 1935, also appeared to threaten the power and influence of the wealthy. The creation of Federal Reserve Board governor Marriner Eccles, the Banking Act sought to curtail the role of private bankers and create a truly centralized banking system controlled by the Federal Reserve Board. Plotting strategy with powerful New York banking interests, conservative senator Carter Glass fought to stave off the most stringent centralizing features of the bill. Glass rewrote much of Eccles's draft before Congress approved, and Roosevelt willingly accepted the compromises. The bill that survived stopped far short of the changes liberals sought but adopted enough of them to roil the banking community. In place of the existing Federal Reserve Board, a new Board of Governors, appointed by the president subject to confirmation by the Senate, could veto decisions made by regional Federal Reserve Banks. To a greater extent than ever before, the 1935 law established government control of credit and currency.

The legislative harvest of 1935—the Second New Deal—produced some of the most important and long-lasting achievements of the Roosevelt administration. The common thread running through the Wagner Act, the Social Security Act, the Wheeler-Rayburn Bill, and the taxation and banking laws was an antibusiness animus. Economic recovery remained important, but the reform of American institutions loomed larger as a goal in 1935 than it had two years earlier. And that reform, a response to disillusionment with conservative business interests and what political scientist James MacGregor Burns called "thunder on the left," aimed to protect the working class and the disadvantaged. Although Roosevelt's Second New Deal delivered less than his rousing antibusiness rhetoric promised, the changes engendered were substantial even after the obligatory political compromises. Moreover, Roosevelt's move to the left in 1935 had a colossal political impact, which, of course, had always been a vital consideration. The ensuing 1936 congressional session produced little of note—a modest undistributed profits tax and the Soil Conservation and Domestic Allotment Act were the principal achievements—and reflected Roosevelt's acknowledgment of the need for a "breathing spell." The incumbent would face the voters on the strength of the earlier legislation.[14]

In his speech accepting the nomination at the 1936 Democratic National Convention in Philadelphia, Roosevelt served notice that his appeal to class interests would continue unabated in the campaign. He denounced the "economic royalists" and "new dynasties" seeking to impose "economic tyranny" on the American people. The American economic system had become "privileged enterprise, not free enterprise." In the following months he continued to invite the criticism of Wall Street interests, casting the national election as a struggle between the haves and have-nots. To an appreciative Madison Square Garden crowd on the eve of the election he said: "Never before in all our history have these forces been so united against one candidate as they stand today. They are unanimous in their hate for me—and I welcome their hatred. I should like to have it said of my first Administration that in it the forces of selfishness and of lust for power met their match. I should like to have it said of my second Administration that in it these forces met their master."[15]

Intent on discrediting the image of their party as an appendage of eastern financial interests, Republican leaders rejected the candidacy of the available Herbert Hoover. The man they chose, Kansas governor Alf Landon, had the distinction of being both the party's only governor west of the Mississippi and the only Republican chief executive elected in 1932 and retained by the voters in the 1934 Democratic landslide. No doctrinaire conservative, Governor Landon had eliminated the state's poll tax, supported increased utilities regulation, and defended the civil liberties of college professors against red-baiters. Moreover, he had endorsed much of the New Deal. He was, however, a fiscal conservative who lambasted the Roosevelt administration for its improvident ways. As the campaign wore on, Landon's criticisms grew more trenchant; he called Social Security "unjust, unworkable, stupidly drafted and wastefully financed" and constantly inveighed against the inefficiency of big government. The Republican's campaign never seemed to engage the masses, however, in large part because of his own ambivalence toward Roosevelt's policies. Never disagreeing fundamentally with the New Deal, he could only offer to do it better.[16]

The American Liberty League supported the Republican candidate—much to Landon's chagrin. At first the league tried to block Roosevelt's nomination at the Democratic National Convention, even going so far as to support the candidacy of Georgia's reactionary Eugene Talmadge, but had no success at all. Next the league diverted its considerable financial resources to the Landon campaign and thereby provided the Democrats with more ammunition for their depiction of the Republican party as the tool of big business. The Liberty League's wretched popular image—one critic said the organization thought the American Revolution "was fought to make Long Island safe for polo players"—undoubtedly harmed more than helped the Landon candidacy.[17]

Another electoral threat to the president came from the Union party, the concoction of Father Coughlin, Dr. Townsend, and Huey Long's successor in the Share Our Wealth movement, the Reverend Gerald L. K. Smith. Long's death and the Second New

Deal stole much of the thunder from these demagogues, but Democrats still worried about the possible loss of votes to the new party. Financing came largely from the secret contributions of wealthy Republicans who assumed that whatever votes the Union party attracted would likely come from disaffected Democrats. For president, the party put forth William "Liberty Bill" Lemke, congressman from North Dakota and coauthor of the radical Frazier-Lemke bills to refinance farm mortgages. Roosevelt's refusal to support the last of these measures led Lemke to break with the New Deal. Dissension among the leaders and the concomitant lack of organizational cohesion dissipated whatever potential strength the Union party might have marshaled. By October, the Reverend Mr. Smith had been expelled for his open embrace of fascism, and the Roman Catholic church had censured Coughlin. Lemke campaigned energetically but could poll only 892,000 votes (2% of the total) in November. Acknowledging that the results fell far short of the 9 million votes he had promised earlier that year, Coughlin admitted that the disintegrating Union party had been "thoroughly discredited."[18]

Despite the apparent liabilities of Roosevelt's opposition, the outcome remained in doubt until election day. Most public opinion polls, including those by George Gallup and Elmo Roper, predicted a Roosevelt triumph, but others forecast a narrow victory for Landon. The *Literary Digest* poll, uncannily accurate in every presidential election since 1920, predicted a 370–161 win for the Republican in the electoral college. The election produced, instead, a spectacular victory for the incumbent. Roosevelt won the popular vote, 27,751,841 to 16,679,491, garnering 60.8 percent of the ballots cast. The margin was even more lopsided in the electoral college, 523–8. Landon carried only two states (Maine and Vermont), prompting Jim Farley to revise the old political chestnut, "As Maine goes, so goes the nation" to "As Maine goes, so goes Vermont." Other Democrats did well also; in the House the Democrats increased their numbers from 322 to 331 and in the Senate from 69 to 76. The president's party controlled two-thirds of the seats in both chambers of Congress, an advantage no chief executive has enjoyed since.[19]

How could the previously inerrant *Literary Digest* have been so wrong? How could it have misjudged so severely the temper of the American electorate? In large part, because its sample came from lists of automobile owners and telephone directories, thereby ignoring the millions of voters unlikely to own automobiles or telephones. The developments of 1934–35 made Roosevelt extremely popular with these lower classes, who saw the president as their champion. Likewise, the policies that favored the disadvantaged alienated the privileged classes. In 1936 bankers and brokers gave only 4 percent of contributions over one thousand dollars to the Democrats (as opposed to 24% in 1932), and the Republicans outspent their rivals, fourteen million to nine million. But in an electoral contest between the rich and the poor, many more of the latter existed in depression America.

The president's sweeping victory in 1936 has been called the Roosevelt Revolution and has been credited with making the Democrats the majority party. In 1932 the electorate voted against Hoover but four years later cast their ballots for Roosevelt. The vast army of voters that returned the incumbent to office in 1936, the so-called Roosevelt coalition, consisted of several groups bound together by the New Deal commitment to the common man. To the old-time Democratic party of the solid South and the big city political machines, the New Deal brought a new group of voters. The Roosevelt revolution occurred not because the Democrats lured away great numbers of Republicans but because they captured large segments of the previously nonvoting population. These new Democrats came largely from the industrial cities of the Northeast and Midwest—working class first- and second-generation immigrants from the southern and eastern portions of Europe, many Roman Catholics and Jews, most lower income. In the maelstrom of the depression they lost jobs and suffered the most, and they had the most to gain from government beneficence. They were the same people who fueled the growth of the unions, another important component of the Roosevelt coalition. In 1936 American Federation of Labor president William Green stopped just short of a formal endorsement of FDR, but no one doubted whom organized labor favored. The unions offset much of the loss of business contributions, donating $770,000 to the Democrats in 1936. That year another disadvantaged group, blacks, began to vote for Roosevelt and for the same reasons—not in overwhelming numbers but cementing a commitment that would be critically important in later years.

The Roosevelt revolution produced a Democratic party with a broader base and more extensive appeal. Although the South remained an important part of the Roosevelt coalition, its influence in the Democratic party was declining. In 1918 the South claimed 26 of the 37 Democratic Senate seats; in 1936, 26 of 76. In 1920, southerners occupied 107 of the 131 Democratic seats in the House; in 1936, just 116 of 333. Roosevelt's solid ties to Dixie and deference to the many powerful southerners entrenched in key congressional committee chairmanships kept the South solid for the Democratic party during the early years of his administration. By the late 1930s, however, New Deal liberalism was beginning to strain the South's historic ties to the Democrats, and the consequent ideological divisions started a gradual defection of southerners to the increasingly alluring Republican party.

Roosevelt's decision to broaden the Democratic party's appeal conflicted with the desires of many Progressives at that time and many liberal critics thereafter. They hoped that the president, capitalizing on his overwhelming popularity and the receptiveness of the people to sweeping reform, would purge the party of conservative elements and make it a truly liberal confederation. Political scientist James MacGregor Burns, in particular, has castigated Roosevelt for his failure to achieve ideological purity within a party clearly leaning toward liberalism and for "his eternal desire to keep open alternative lines of action, including a line of retreat." What the liberals demanded, however, was that Roosevelt tamper for the sake of ideology with the powerful coalition he had just assembled, to threaten immediately the party's huge majorities in Congress and to repudiate the election that had just given him the most overwhelming presidential victory in history. This the master politician from Hyde Park understandably had no intention of doing. In the aftermath of the 1936 election the president, whose popularity had been overwhelmingly ratified by the American people, could look forward to doing business with a solidly Democratic Congress. The future of the New Deal appeared bright indeed in the last days of 1936.[20]

The New Deal in Eclipse, 1937–1939

Buoyed by a landslide reelection and favored with substantial majorities in both houses of Congress, Franklin D. Roosevelt looked forward to his second term as the opportunity to bring the New Deal full circle. Armed with an electoral mandate, the president surveyed the country and found recovery from the depression only partially complete. Much had been accomplished, but more remained to be done. This was the note Roosevelt sounded in the most eloquent and memorable passage of his second inaugural address:

> In this nation I see tens of millions of its citizens—a substantial part of its whole population—who at this very moment are denied the greater part of what the lowest standards of today call the necessities of life. I see millions of families trying to live on incomes so meager that the pall of family disaster hangs over them day by day. I see millions whose daily lives in city and on farm continue under conditions labeled indecent by a so-called polite society half a century ago. I see millions denied education, recreation, and the opportunity to better their lot and the lot of their children. I see millions lacking the means to buy the products of farm and factory and by their poverty denying work and productiveness to many other millions. I see one-third of a nation ill-housed, ill-clad, ill-nourished. It is not in despair that I paint you this picture. I paint it for you in hope—because the Nation, seeing and understanding the injustice in it, proposes to paint it out. . . . The test of our progress is not whether we add more to the abundance of those who have much; it is whether we provide enough for those who have too little.[1]

As the first session of the Seventy-fifth Congress convened in January 1937, Roosevelt turned his attention to the judiciary. The Supreme Court, to which he had made no appointments in the previous four years, had become the great enemy of the New Deal. The Court's three liberals (Louis Brandeis, Benjamin Cardozo, and Harlan Fiske Stone) frequently clashed with the four conservatives (James C. McReynolds, Pierce Butler, Willis J. Van Devanter, and George Sutherland), while Chief Justice Charles Evans Hughes and Owen Roberts forged majorities by voting with one side or the other. In the early years of the Roosevelt presidency no discernible pattern emerged from the Court, but by 1935 Roberts and Hughes began to join the conservatives with increasing regularity. As a result, the Supreme Court had invalidated such key New Deal measures as the National Industrial Recovery Act (NIRA), the Agricultural Adjustment Act (AAA), and the Guffey Coal Act. In early 1936 the Court struck down a New York State minimum-wage law in a decision so contrived it even drew the ire of Herbert Hoover. With the Court preparing to rule on the constitutionality of the Social Security and Wagner acts, Roosevelt felt a special urgency to act in the early months of 1937. New Dealers complained that the Supreme Court was abusing the power of judicial review to thwart the will of the people and their elected representatives in the executive and legislative branches. As Alabama senator Hugo Black complained, "A majority of our judges should not amend the Constitution every time they decide a case."[2]

Initially Roosevelt considered reform of the Supreme Court by constitutional amendment but concluded that ratification by three-fourths of the states would take too much time. Instead, he and Attorney General Homer S. Cummings devised a plan to "pack" the Supreme Court by adding as many as six new justices for every member over the age of 70 who refused to retire. Having kept news of the plan from all but a handful of advisors, Roosevelt presented the bill to Congress on February 5, 1937. Rather than attacking the Court's decisions forthrightly, Roosevelt disingenuously referred to the backlog of cases left unattended by the "aged, overworked justices." While members of the Senate listened to the bill being read, Vice-President Garner mimed his displeasure, holding his nose and turning thumbs down. Almost immediately a groundswell of opposition arose, reflecting an aversion to any undermining of judicial independence. Fears of runaway executive power and anger at

Roosevelt's transparent machinations surfaced among Democrats and Republicans, supporters and enemies. Most important, Americans revered the Supreme Court and, regardless of its questionable recent performance, believed that the institution should be preserved absolutely intact. Blinded by his obvious personal popularity, the president grievously underestimated the resistance his court-packing plan engendered.[3]

Roosevelt's assault on the Supreme Court proved especially damaging, because it revitalized conservative adversaries long humbled by New Deal successes at the polls. Frank Gannett, owner of the nation's third-largest newspaper chain, and socially prominent New York lawyer Amos Pinchot organized the National Committee to Uphold Constitutional Government as an immediate response to the court-packing proposal. Composed of liberals and Democrats primarily, the committee used Roosevelt's action as a springboard to criticism of his administration's budget deficits, progressive taxation, and support for unions. Long after the furor over court packing subsided, the organization remained active and sought to forge a bipartisan anti–New Deal alliance; its sophisticated letter-writing campaigns marshaled public opinion against executive reorganization as well as other presidential initiatives in 1937–39.

Most harmful to the president, the proposal enflamed congressional passions. Roosevelt made a serious error in formulating the plan without consulting with key Democrats on Capitol Hill. A few minutes before telling the press, he briefed six congressional leaders in the White House and requested their support. Vice-President Garner and the other five Democrats received the news in stunned silence, then left without comment. As they drove back to the Capitol, House Judiciary Committee Chairman Hatton Sumners said at last, "Boys, here's where I cash in." Sumners subsequently opposed the plan, but the other members of the Democratic leadership—including Garner, Senate Majority Leader Joe Robinson, and Speaker of the House William Bankhead—set aside their misgivings and publicly supported the president. Robinson worked avidly for court reform in part because of party loyalty, but also because the creation of six new justiceships would bring him closer to the appointment on the Supreme Court he believed Roosevelt had all but promised him.[4]

While the Democratic congressional leadership remained at

least nominally loyal, however, a bipartisan alliance developed in opposition to court reform. The Republicans, led by Senator Charles McNary, wisely remained quiet while lending moral support to the rapidly growing number of dissident Democrats deserting the president. Southern Democratic senators Carter Glass and Harry Byrd of Virginia and Josiah Bailey of North Carolina, long-time vocal opponents of the New Deal, found new converts to their cause in such previously reliable administration stalwarts as Senators Thomas Connally of Texas and Burton K. Wheeler of Montana. Liberals critical of the Supreme Court and open to some kind of action joined conservatives in repudiating what Wheeler called "a sham and a fake liberal proposal." Only a few months before, an embittered Carter Glass had groused, "Why, if the President asked Congress to commit suicide tomorrow, they'd do it." This was no longer the case and as Roosevelt refused to compromise, the opposition grew steadily stronger.[5]

In various ways the Supreme Court undercut Roosevelt's proposal. Chief Justice Hughes composed a letter, which Wheeler triumphantly presented to the Senate Judiciary Committee, citing facts and figures to discredit charges of the Court's inefficiency. At the same time, the Court reversed its earlier decision and approved a Washington State minimum-wage law; within a few weeks it approved the Social Security and Wagner acts as well. Suddenly, Justices Hughes and Roberts had adopted more liberal postures. On May 18 Justice Van Devanter (who had been born during the presidency of James Buchanan) announced his impending retirement, providing Roosevelt his first opportunity to make a Supreme Court appointment. The New Deal no longer seemed in jeopardy, and in June Roosevelt agreed to the substitution of a compromise bill. On July 14, Senator Robinson died, and all hope of a peaceful resolution expired with him. Many congressmen who had supported the president out of personal ties to the majority leader no longer felt a sense of obligation. The end came after 168 days of rancor as the Senate voted 70–30 to recommit the bill to the Judiciary Committee. A massively revised bill passed later that year that modified lower court procedures but dealt not at all with the Supreme Court.

Roosevelt later boasted that he may have lost the battle but won the war, a reference to the compliance the Supreme Court exhibited toward administrative actions thereafter. Moreover, by

1941 a series of resignations allowed the president to appoint a majority of the Court's members. But, as historian James T. Patterson has noted, although the Court shifted in the late 1930s, it is not at all clear that the court-packing scheme was the reason; Roosevelt's 1936 victory may have been the cause. More important, his impetuosity alienated many congressmen, who then formed a conservative coalition sufficiently powerful to block much of the New Deal's remaining domestic program. Opposition to court packing united western Progressives, Republicans, and some moderate Democrats with the already disaffected Democratic conservatives. Once the legislative branch had reasserted its independence, emboldened congressmen looked to challenge the president with greater hope of success. As Patterson succinctly put it, "The President had gained a court but had begun to lose part of his Congress."[6]

The president's relations with Democratic senators deteriorated further in the summer of 1937 over the selection of a new majority leader to replace Joe Robinson. By virtue of seniority and reputation among his colleagues, Mississippi senator Pat Harrison quickly emerged as Robinson's likely successor. Harrison had clashed with Roosevelt over the 1935 tax bill but overall had supported the New Deal out of party loyalty. Nevertheless, the president wanted a reliable majority leader and indicated to the Senate that he preferred the more liberal Alben Barkley of Kentucky. Bristling at what they deemed unseemly interference in the Senate's family business, many lawmakers criticized Roosevelt bitterly. Working behind the scenes, White House agents lobbied for Barkley even as Roosevelt disclaimed any interference. On July 22 the Senate chose Barkley by the slimmest of margins, 38–37. With his machinations Roosevelt made a powerful enemy in Harrison, who no longer felt any loyalty to the administration. Many other senators reacted negatively to the president's heavy-handedness as well, much to the delight of conservative Democrats yearning to exploit Roosevelt's growing vulnerability.

Apart from Roosevelt's insensitivity to congressional prerogatives, many legislators felt alienated from what they perceived to be the new directions taken by the Democratic party. A thorough analysis of the 1936 presidential vote, revealing the great support the president received from northern urban areas, led many old-line Democrats to suspect that traditional policies were being altered to reward new members of the Roosevelt coalition. Thus, southern Democrats feared that the court-packing plan would lay the foundation for the appointment of liberal justices whose rulings would disrupt southern racial customs. Administrative requests for relief payments would similarly benefit northern blacks in particular, so southern congressmen began opposing WPA extension bills. And the rise of organized labor, seemingly abetted by New Deal legislation, aroused additional fears of unwanted change.

By 1937 the labor issue came to center around a new tactic employed by the unions, the sit-down strike. Struggling for recognition, the newly created Congress of Industrial Organizations (CIO) chafed at the vulnerability of picketing strikers to attacks by strikebreakers and law enforcement authorities. Therefore, strikers ensured work stoppages by barricading themselves in factories and holding out against sieges. The sit-down produced a remarkable breakthrough in negotiations with industrial giant General Motors at its Flint, Michigan factory because empathetic governor Frank Murphy refused to dispatch state police against the strikers. Conservatives railed at the illegal occupation of private property and blamed Roosevelt in part for his failure to enforce the law. Calling his refusal to evict the strikers "neutrality," the president understood the importance of not alienating his growing support among the unions. So did the conservatives, who clearly saw his inaction as a form of benign neglect damaging to their interests.

On April 1, 1937, South Carolina senator James F. Byrnes, one of Congress's most outspoken critics of labor unions, offered an amendment to the Guffey coal bill prohibiting sit-down strikes in that industry. Debate over Byrnes's amendment raged for days in the Senate, as long-silent foes of labor vented their wrath in a series of impassioned speeches. Beseeched by administration spokesmen, Byrnes refused to withdraw the amendment and instead changed its language to condemn sit-downs in all industries. The Senate defeated the amendment but only after Roosevelt agreed to a separate consideration of the issue. Later the Senate passed a nonbinding resolution calling sit-downs illegal but also affirming collective bargaining. The neutral resolution constituted no clear-cut victory for the conservatives, but the episode revealed both the growing sentiment in Congress that the New Deal had gone far enough and the newfound boldness of a no longer pliant legislature.

Congressional independence flared repeatedly during 1937, as New Dealers found their liberal measures voted down or passed in drastically altered form. Roosevelt's proposal of six new regional development authorities (little TVAs) met immediate resistance and had to be abandoned. Senator Robert F. Wagner's housing bill ran into determined opposition from legislators representing predominantly rural interests in the South and West. Led by Senators Harry F. Byrd of Virginia and Millard Tydings of Maryland, the conservative bloc succeeded in severely limiting the amount of housing constructed overall and the amount built in any given state (a clear impediment to the heavily urbanized states of the North). A fair labor standards bill mandating minimum wages and maximum hours passed in the Senate, despite bitter opposition from Harrison, Byrnes, and Garner, but lost in the House. Senator Wagner's introduction of an antilynching bill sparked an immediate filibuster by southerners and had to be withdrawn. At the end of the legislative session Roosevelt nominated Hugo L. Black to fill the vacant Supreme Court seat, a blatant affront to the Alabaman's many detractors in the Senate. Liberal, acerbic, and aloof, Black exasperated conservatives in both parties enough that the Senate rejected the customary practice of waiving confirmation hearings for one of its own members. After a tempestuous debate, the Senate confirmed Black's appointment, but conservatives rightly perceived his nomination as Roosevelt's deliberate attempt to bait his foes. Herbert Hoover groused that the Supreme Court was now "one-ninth packed."[7]

As relations with Congress deteriorated, the Roosevelt administration suffered another telling blow in the collapse of the nation's economy. Although 14 percent of the labor force remained unemployed by the summer of 1937, Democrats could claim genuine improvement since the horrific days of 1933. Economic expansion during that time arguably resulted from New Deal policies and, therefore, redounded to Roosevelt's credit. In August 1937, however, production and income began to decline as five million workers lost their jobs and the unemployment rate reached 20 percent. The resultant recession, which lasted until June 1938, was as severe as any in the nation's past. In the 6 months from August 1937 to January 1938, industrial output declined as sharply as in the 13 months following the stock market crash in 1929; production dropped 70 percent in steel, 50 percent in automobiles, and 40 percent in rubber. The downturn became known as the Roosevelt recession, since the president's decision in 1937 to cut federal spending programs and balance the budget precipitated the crisis. Convinced that the nation had settled safely onto the road to recovery and eager to demonstrate his commitment to sound fiscal policies, the president slashed federal spending from 10.3 billion dollars in 1936 to 9.6 billion dollars in 1937. Impervious to the fact that whatever recovery accrued under the New Deal resulted from deficit spending, Roosevelt's belt-tightening indeed led to economic reversal.

For months Roosevelt temporized, clearly baffled at the unexpected economic collapse that seemed to be worsening daily. He received contradictory advice, some New Dealers like Federal Reserve Board chairman Marriner Eccles calling for a resumption of deficit spending and others like Treasury Secretary Morgenthau urging him to weather the storm. Suspecting that Wall Street investors manufactured the crisis as part of the business community's plan to discredit the New Deal, Roosevelt instructed the FBI to investigate possible criminal conspiracies. The inquiry turned up no evidence, and the controversy subsided. Months passed before the weary president finally opted for a return to pump priming, and by June 1938 recovery resumed. The recession added significantly to Roosevelt's problems, vitiating the New Deal's claims of economic success, further reducing his popularity, and giving more hope to conservatives disabused of the myth of Rooseveltian invincibility.

In November 1937 the president called a special legislative session of Congress to consider wages-and-hours legislation, a new farm program, executive reorganization, and regional planning programs patterned after the TVA. Irritated at being summoned to the capital to act on bills they had shown no inclination to pass a short time before (and which seemingly had little to do with the worsening recession), disgruntled legislators greeted Roosevelt's welcoming address with polite tolerance. In subsequent weeks Congress muddled through hearings, reports, and debates but passed no bills. When the special session dissolved just before Christmas, everyone agreed it had accomplished nothing. Especially disappointing, it had provided no ameliorative measures for the recession.

In the absence of any other newsworthy developments, anti–New Deal legislators captured the headlines during the special session with the production of a "conservative manifesto." By 1937 North Carolina senator Josiah Bailey believed that Roosevelt intended to run for a third term in 1940 at the head of a new liberal party underwritten by the CIO. Accordingly, Bailey took the lead in drafting a document that affirmed the principles of the "traditional" Democratic party. Joined by Democratic senators Royal Copeland of New York, Edward Burke of Nebraska, Harry F. Byrd of Virginia, Millard Tydings of Maryland, and Republican senators Arthur Vandenburg of Michigan and Warren Austin of Vermont, he drew up a 10-point program to restore prosperity through budget balancing and a check on "unnecessary" spending. Working quietly behind the scenes, the conservatives combed the halls and cloakrooms of the Senate looking for others willing to sign the manifesto. The conspirators hoped to secure at least 30 signatures before going public, but the *New York Times* published the complete text on December 16. For several days no one admitted involvement, but finally Bailey and the others came forward and read the document to the Senate. Forced to acknowledge their secret plotting prematurely, Bailey and his cohorts continued to seek more cosigners but with mixed success. Many senators sympathized with the sentiments expressed in the protest but hesitated to commit their signatures to paper. Although they harbored numerous grievances, influential party leaders like Byrnes and Harrison had no desire to break openly with the administration; they guarded their right to remain loyal generally but to dissent in individual cases. If the conservative manifesto did not launch the full-scale rebellion its creators sought, it did expose a significant opposition to New Deal liberalism latent in the upper house. And if party loyalty still precluded a genuine bipartisan conservative coalition, the huge Democratic majorities in Congress seemed less daunting than ever before.[8]

In 1938 the president and Congress remained at loggerheads with both sides able to claim some victories. By April conservative forces dealt Roosevelt two stunning setbacks, rejecting for the third time an executive reorganization proposal and securing a revision of the undistributed profits tax. Roosevelt had long viewed reorganization of the executive branch as one of his top priorities, not just to save money but to provide better management. In 1936 he appointed a three-member committee of public administration experts (Louis Brownlow, Charles Merriam, and Luther Gulick) to study the question. They recommended a strengthening of the executive branch of the federal government and a subsidiary role for the legislature. Roosevelt concurred and made the report the heart of a reorganization bill he submitted to Congress in January 1937. It called for two new cabinet positions (welfare and public works) and a permanent National Resources Planning Board for central planning, as well as more presidential authority to limit the power of government agencies. Not surprisingly, Congress found the proposal unacceptable. Fear of expanding executive power, especially with the rise of totalitarian regimes in Italy and Germany, rekindled talk of one-man rule rampant during the court-packing brouhaha. As Representative Hamilton Fish said, "This is just a step to concentrate power in the hands of the President and set up a species of fascism or nazi-ism or an American form of dictatorship." Additional opposition came from various governmental units wary of losing influence in any bureaucratic reordering; especially effective, for example, was the Forest Service lobby opposed to moving from the Agriculture Department to the Interior Department. Facing strong opposition, the reorganization bill floundered in both 1937 congressional sessions.[9]

When the bill came before the Senate in March 1938, it had been substantially revised to exempt some agencies from reorganization and to limit the president's ability to create new departments without congressional approval. Nevertheless, opposition surfaced immediately, both inside and outside of Congress. The National Committee to Uphold Constitutional Government chided the president for attempting to usurp more power, as did Father Charles Coughlin. At the radio priest's urging, people from around the country mailed an estimated three hundred thousand telegrams to their senators to voice their opposition. The White House countered with a spirited lobbying effort of its own. With southerners James Byrnes, Pat Harrison, Richard Russell of Georgia, and Cotton Ed Smith of South Carolina remaining loyal, the reorganization bill narrowly passed in the Senate. As the battle shifted to the House, 150 "Paul Reveres" galloped across Washington to warn the people of the threat of dictatorship. As powerful Rules Committee chairman John J. O'Connor spearheaded the opposition, debate on the bill turned malicious. Despite 11th-hour concessions by the president, the House voted to recommit the bill by a vote of 204–196. The rejection of executive reorganization, a measure of special importance to Roosevelt and one for which he labored assiduously, came as the greatest blow yet to his prestige. As one New Dealer recalled, "Congress found out that it could defy Roosevelt without being hit by lightning."[10]

The demise of executive reorganization owed primarily to the fact that, outside of the president and a small number of concerned reformers, few members of the New Deal coalition cared much about the matter. Depression-battered voters and their elected representatives saw no immediate importance in something as esoteric as bureaucratic reshuffling. On the other hand, anti–New Dealers capitalized effectively on Roosevelt's slumping approval ratings and the growing fears of dictatorship fueled by world events. Bent on obtaining some type of legislation, Roosevelt submitted to Congress a watered-down version in 1939 and it passed easily. As historian Richard Polenberg concluded, "Nothing better illustrates the erosion of the New Deal than the contrast between Roosevelt's bold proposals of 1937 and the bland Reorganization bill offered in 1939."[11]

The president suffered another resounding defeat that spring over tax revision. He sought a graduated capital gains tax, a levy on income for government bonds, and, most heinous to the business community, an increase in the undistributed profits tax. In the midst of the recession, the arguments of businessmen like Bernard Baruch that the undistributed profits tax discouraged investment and blocked recovery won many converts. Senate Finance Committee chairman Pat Harrison argued the case for tax cuts to restore investors' confidence and led the fight for revision of the president's bill. Congress subsequently passed a law that eliminated the corporate income tax and virtually did the same to the undistributed profits tax. Recognizing the futility of a veto, Roosevelt took no action and the bill passed without his signature.

Roosevelt did achieve some success with Congress in 1938. When he finally decided to resume spending that spring, the president asked the legislature for a three-billion-dollar appropriation for use by the WPA, FSA, NYA, CCC, and PWA. Conservatives balked at the resumption of pump priming, but both houses of Congress approved a bill authorizing some one hundred million dollars more than Roosevelt requested. Apparently feeling free to oppose the administration on executive reorganization and capital gains taxes—issues that affected very few Americans directly—congressmen bent to the popular will on relief spending. Conservatives had enjoyed some success limiting relief outlays in recent sessions, but the exigencies of the recession radically altered the national mood.

Roosevelt's other success that year came with the passage of the Fair Labor Standards Act (FLSA). Following the bill's resounding defeat in December 1937, the American Federation of Labor's William Green helped draft a new measure providing for a 44-hour maximum workweek and a 25-cents-an-hour minimum wage (to become 40 hours and 40 cents per hour within three years). The new law put no limit on the number of hours a worker could toil but mandated payment at 1½ times the wage rate for overtime. Southerners of both parties opposed the bill, because it threatened the lower wages their region believed it had to pay to be competitive. The threat of a filibuster by southern senators led supporters to compromise; the altered bill allowed Department of Labor advisory boards to rule on regional differentials. In addition, the FLSA exempted large numbers of workers from coverage, including retail and service employees, those engaged in agriculture and fishing, and other seasonal workers. It also ended child labor in most industries. Although the bill survived only after extensive revision, Roosevelt took pride in its passage and rightfully so: it established a standard for wages and hours that could be improved in later years to the benefit of millions of workers. Its adoption marked the New Deal's last reform measure.

Following his overwhelming reelection in 1936, Roosevelt had attempted to consolidate New Deal achievements first by neutralizing the obstructionist Supreme Court and then by controlling the frustrating federal bureaucracy through executive reorganization. Both experiments met with public opprobrium and defeat. As the bright promise of 1936 dimmed in a series of clashes with the rising conservative coalition, the president hoped to regain his mastery over Congress in 1938 by enforcing party discipline. Dissident Democrats, particularly unreconstructed southerners who had repeatedly challenged the president, would have to be eliminated. At the outset of the 1938 primary season New Dealers fared well; incumbents Claude Pepper in Florida and Lister Hill in Alabama won reelection victories over conservative challengers in May and June, respectively. In a June fireside chat Roosevelt informed the nation of his intention to campaign in selected state Democratic primaries for liberals loyal to the New Deal. The president's advisors differed on the wisdom of such involvement in state primaries, Harry Hopkins and Harold Ickes in favor and Jim Farley against, but the president's single-minded determination to purge the party of the disloyal never wavered.

The purge produced some successes. Senate Majority Leader Alben Barkley easily defeated conservative Kentucky governor Albert "Happy" Chandler. In other primaries incumbent senators Robert Bulkley of Ohio, Elmer Thomas of Oklahoma, and Hattie Caraway of Arkansas, and Representative Lyndon Johnson of Texas all won with Roosevelt's backing. In New York the president spoke against John J. O'Connor, a fifteen-year congressman and chairman of the House Rules Committee, and supported challenger James H. Fay. When O'Connor lost the Democratic primary, he entered and won the Republican primary. In the general election Fay won, prompting the *New Republic* to say of the outcome in New York, "This single victory is enough to justify the whole effort." O'Connor lost because of several factors, including the altered demographic composition of the legislative district and the resultant decline of Tammany Hall's influence among voters there. Fay centered his campaign on local concerns and personalities, largely ignoring national issues and Roosevelt's endorsement. In short, it was not at all clear that O'Connor lost because of the purge.[12]

In other contests, the purge came up short. Roosevelt decided not to move against a number of incumbents who, despite their loathsomeness, seemed immune to presidential interference. Senators Augustine Lonergan of Connecticut, Alva Adams of Colorado, Bennett Champ Clark of Missouri, and Pat McCarran of Nevada seemed sure bets for reelection. Roosevelt prepared to oppose incumbent Indiana senator Frederick Van Nuys, but the state Democratic organization could not entice anyone to run against him. In Iowa Roosevelt threw his support behind liberal congressman Otha Wearin, but incumbent senator Guy Gillete won easily. The president intervened most directly in three southern primaries where, based upon the earlier successes of Pepper, Barkley, and Caraway, he believed his endorsement carried the most influence. In the South, traditionally loyal Democrats that Roosevelt referred to as Copperheads had been in the vanguard of the conservative coalition. Some—like Bailey of North Carolina, Byrd and Glass of Virginia, and Harrison of Mississippi—did not stand for reelection in 1938, but Georgia's Walter George, South Carolina's Ed Smith, and Maryland's Millard Tydings did.

Roosevelt intervened directly in those three states, visiting them in person and urging the voters to turn the disloyal Democrats out and elect liberals in their places. He participated directly in the selection of candidates to oppose the incumbents, in Georgia choosing relatively unknown attorney Lawrence Camp, in South Carolina Governor Olin Johnston, and in Maryland liberal congressman David Lewis. In each state the president diverted patronage, lent manpower and campaign funds, and otherwise openly aided his handpicked candidates. Clearly, however, the president's direct involvement backfired. Although George, Smith, and Tydings never attacked Roosevelt directly and claimed to be generally in sympathy with the New Deal, they hammered away incessantly at the president's shameless intervention in local politics. Liberals as well as conservatives disapproved of federal officials insinuating themselves into state affairs, and voters expressed their pique at the polls. The three incumbents all returned to Washington.

The purge failed. Roosevelt again had misjudged the temper of the American people, believing that his personal popularity could be extended to include politicians he supported as well as ideas he favored. The president termed the outcome a meaningless defeat, since he had nothing to lose by trying to oust the conservatives. The worst they could do, Roosevelt argued, was oppose him, and their disloyalty had already been well established. But the ill-conceived campaign against fellow Democrats cost the president dearly thereafter. The senators singled out for expulsion returned to the capital with greater passion fueling their dissension, especially men like Gillette and Tydings, whose apostasy had been limited before. Roosevelt's appeal for party loyalty sounded hollow after the purge, and even those Democrats uninvolved in 1938 campaigns disapproved of the action taken against their colleagues. Most damaging of all, the purge's inglorious result further tarnished the president's ebbing prestige and stiffened his enemies' resolve.

The November elections that year brought more bad news. For the first time in the Roosevelt presidency the Republicans gained ground, adding 12 governors, 8 seats in the Senate, and 81 seats in the House. The Democrats still maintained a two-thirds majority in the Senate and a sizable majority in the House, but with the breakdown in party loyalty and the widening rift between liberals and conservatives, these margins were misleading. In the Senate 23 Republicans and a comparable number of wayward Democrats could combine to derail New Deal legislation. In the House the defection of only 50 Democrats would be sufficient to do the same. As Roosevelt prepared to enter what the American people assumed would be the last two years of his second term—traditionally an unproductive period for lame-duck presidents—he did so with the once estimable New Deal coalition in tatters.

During the last years of the decade Roosevelt became increasingly preoccupied with events in Europe. As he would later remark, Dr. Win-the-War was replacing Dr. New Deal as concerns over the revision of neutrality legislation, selective service, and the destroyers-bases deal took precedence over domestic reform. Fortunately for the president, the conservative coalition invariably broke down over foreign policy issues. Most conservative Democrats, particularly southerners, wholeheartedly backed Roosevelt's decision to bolster the Allies, just as some Progressive New Deal supporters of isolationist sentiment sided with Republicans. For years Roosevelt had accepted neutrality legislation while focusing his energy on domestic reform, and when he turned his attention to events abroad in the years 1939 to 1941, he carried many conservatives along with him.

Even so, Roosevelt's few attempts to rekindle the New Deal coalition in 1939 ran into firm congressional opposition. Besides passing a watered-down executive reorganization bill, the Seventy-sixth Congress gave the president little of what he requested. When Roosevelt asked for $875 million to sustain the WPA, congressional conservatives rallied behind Vice-President John Nance Garner, who insisted instead on sharp reductions in relief spending. Forced to accept a $725 million appropriation, Roosevelt waited only a week after signing the bill to request an additional $150 million. Despite testimony detailing widespread suffering by the unemployed, Congress approved only $100 million more. Since the savings of $50 million or so paled in comparison with the national debt, the defeat of the president's requests seemingly had more to do with an exertion of legislative autonomy than with economy. The conservative coalition was fully in control and defying the president with impunity.

Roosevelt suffered a series of humiliations at the hands of Congress in 1939. Election scandals in 1938, principally in Kentucky, Tennessee, and Pennsylvania, led to charges of illegal WPA interference to aid candidates friendly to the New Deal. Following a well-publicized senatorial investigation, Congress passed the Hatch Act to eliminate the use of relief funds in politics. Although Roosevelt promptly signed the bill and disavowed any Democratic improprieties, the Hatch Act clearly implicated the New Deal. On the same day Congress passed the act, it authorized an investigation of the National Labor Relations Board, a move bitterly opposed by congressional supporters of the CIO. Senator Robert F. Wagner, the great patron of unions and creator of the NLRB, lost that battle along with a vote on a new housing law he had championed. Congress also defeated Roosevelt's program of self-liquidating public works, a modest attempt to revitalize the economy that drew the scorn of liberals hoping for bolder initiatives. By the end of the 1939 legislative session, the conservative coalition seemingly had wrested the initiative totally away from the president and his followers.

Why did the New Deal coalition crumble just when the outcome of the 1936 election had portended even more success in the future? Rising foreign policy concerns late in the decade diverted attention from pressing problems at home, but the New Deal's momentum stalled as early as 1937, before events in Europe began to dominate newspaper front pages. By then the nascent conservative congressional coalition had already dealt the president a series of stunning setbacks, many of which he invited by precipitating crises himself. By introducing the court-packing scheme and attempting to purge disloyal Democrats the following year, Roosevelt allowed his reach to exceed his grasp and his failures strengthened the opposition. His decision to cut spending, resulting in the so-called Roosevelt recession, constituted another severe miscalculation that brought additional public censure. Yet Roosevelt did not create the conservative coalition, as much as he inadvertently nurtured its development. In that sense, Roosevelt was right in continuing to believe in his personal popularity; the people were still with him. They were not, however, for more reform.

Especially resistant to more change, southerners balked at post-1936 New Deal measures. Legislation creating public housing and sustaining high public relief spending levels seemed to favor urban areas, and the South remained the nation's most rural region. The wages-and-hours bill seemed, in the words of one observer, a "sectional bill disguised as a humanitarian reform"; it struck at the heart of the South's low-wage economy. So did the president's refusal to punish the sit-down strikers, since the tactic's success in northern factories boded ill for anti-union southerners. And, of course, antilynching was anathema in Dixie. For years the South had been a Democratic bellwether, assuring presidential candidates 113 electoral votes from 10 states and creating a reliable legislative bloc of 93 votes in the House and 20 in the Senate—all crucial factors in the early success of the New Deal. As the Democratic party's numbers grew in Congress, however, the influence wielded by southerners diminished and they felt increasingly alienated. When such reliables as Pat Harrison and James F. Byrnes broke party ranks to join the Republicans, a viable anti–New Deal coalition became possible.[13]

Disillusionment with New Deal directions surfaced among moderates as well as devoted right-wingers. Many who had backed Roosevelt's policies for years became disenchanted with what they perceived as his insatiable appetite for reform, especially with the success of his earlier measures uncertain. The economic situation also hurt. Believing the emergency over, many former New Dealers grew impatient with persistent calls for pump priming. The WPA made an especially inviting target, since despite enormous expenditures and an egregiously unbalanced budget unemployment remained a problem. Unable to secure recovery, Roosevelt's credibility declined further with the onslaught of recession in 1937. By that time, a great number of people who had supported the president faithfully for years began to have doubts. The New Deal coalition came apart, because the majority in Congress wanted only to maintain the New Deal, perhaps to extend it cautiously in carefully circumscribed ways. The legislators accurately represented the desires of their constituents. Public opinion polls in 1938 and 1939 consistently reported that a substantial majority of Americans favored the consolidation of New Deal achievements rather than additional changes. The rise of the conservative coalition simply reflected the decline in the nation's desire for additional reform.

Their designs on more comprehensive reform thwarted in 1937–39 by the powerful conservative congressional bloc, New Dealers reevaluated their achievements and modified their goals. At least for the immediate future, additional changes would have to come from the institutions created in the earlier legislative bursts of 1933 and 1935, not from the establishment of new reform agencies. Liberals would have to be content with the government's fiscal powers to maintain economic prosperity and ensure its equitable distribution. The cessation of New Deal reform meant that fiscal policy—the ability to tax and spend—assumed increasing importance in the post–World War II years; it provided government with a new means of fine-tuning the political economy. The amount of New Deal reform acceptable to the American people both expanded the power of the state and confined it within new limits.

CHAPTER EIGHT

The Rise of Labor

The dramatic growth of trade unions constituted one of the most remarkable developments of the New Deal era. During Franklin D. Roosevelt's presidency the ranks of organized labor grew more than fourfold, and unions became undeniably vital forces in national life. The American Federation of Labor (AFL) and the fledgling Congress of Industrial Organizations (CIO) became potent political and economic forces, thus securing "big labor's" right to sit at the table with "big business" and "big government." Such New Deal measures as Section 7(a) of the National Industrial Recovery Act, the Wagner Act, and the Fair Labor Standards Act guaranteed the right of workers to organize and bargain collectively; equally important, the implementation of such laws produced a new legal framework for industrial relations. As closed shops replaced company unions and federal bureaucracies sprang up to adjudicate labor-management disputes, the federal government's traditional support of business gave way to a position more congenial to workers and unions. Previously unquestioned management prerogatives fell by the wayside, and organized labor acted with a boldness never before possible. In short, the rules of the industrial relations game altered drastically, and the hegemony enjoyed by management during the halcyon days of the nineteenth century dissolved.

Labor's breakthroughs during the Roosevelt years seemed all the more remarkable considering the sorry state of the unions in the years preceding the New Deal. At the end of the First

World War, the AFL claimed an unprecedented membership of five million workers. AFL president Samuel Gompers's decision to cooperate with the National War Labor Board (specifically, by pledging to forsake strikes and lockouts) resulted in such rewards as eight-hour workdays in many industries and support for workers to organize for collective bargaining. Such inducements led thousands of formerly enervated workers to join the AFL, but the postwar recession of 1920–21 and a disastrous railroad shopmen's strike in 1922 resulted in many members drifting away. Between 1923 and 1929, union membership ebbed gradually, and the Great Depression accelerated the pace of defections. By March 1933, the AFL tallied less than three million members.

Labor's declining fortunes in the 1920s owed to several factors. To counter union blandishments, large corporations provided workers with new pension plans, profit-sharing programs, and a panoply of social and sporting events all designed to foster loyalty to the firm. Such paternalism also surfaced with the proliferation of company unions, which enjoyed huge membership growth during the decade. Public opinion, suffused with paeans to individual rather than collective action, soured on strikes that disrupted everyday life and seemed nonsensical in an age of shared prosperity. Rhetoric extolling the virtues of business naturally undermined the arguments for the need to safeguard workers' interests. The federal government, remaining true to its nineteenth-century proclivities, often intervened to support management, most notably by dispatching troops to break strikes in the steel, mining, and railroad industries. The courts consistently ruled against unions, and judges liberally granted injunctions and upheld yellow-dog contracts. In the landmark case of *Coronado Coal Company* v. *United Mine Workers*, the U.S. Supreme Court ruled in 1922 that strikers could be liable for illegal restraint of trade. Thus, the apparent beneficence of corporations on the one hand and effective government-sanctioned repression on the other in a generally salubrious economic climate undercut much of the support unions could generate.

Even after the onset of the depression, unions continued to flounder. Although Communists and other radical groups organized rent strikes and unemployment demonstrations after the stock market collapse, American workers more often met reduced wages and layoffs with quiet resignation. Union membership slipped inexorably downward and the frequency of strikes lessened in the early 1930s. Struggling unions dispatched fewer organizers, cut officers' salaries, cancelled conventions, ceased publishing newspapers, and retrenched wherever possible to remain solvent. Beset by rumors of infestation by organized crime racketeers, the AFL refused to investigate despite the damage done to its carefully cultivated image of respectability. Labor's only success in the Hoover years came with Congress's passage of the Norris-LaGuardia anti-injunction law in 1932, an achievement tempered by the president's decision to sign the bill but simultaneously issue a letter implying that the courts would surely deem it unconstitutional. (The Supreme Court upheld the law in 1938.) Critics noted that the Norris-LaGuardia Act merely affirmed rights already secured for labor by the Clayton Antitrust Act. Unfortunately, as demoralized workers and union leaders clearly understood, an anti-injunction law yet subject to judicial review did little to alleviate the overwhelmingly negative situation on the eve of the 1932 election.

Franklin Roosevelt's record as governor of New York offered few clues about his views on labor. Several laws passed during his administration aided needy and unemployed workers, but he gave no evidence of desiring to bolster unions as a way of redressing the labor-management imbalance. With the exception of his October 31 address in Boston, Roosevelt's campaign speeches in 1932 touched lightly on the theme of workers' problems. New Dealer Raymond Moley believed that Roosevelt fancied himself a patron of labor but actually gave little thought to the implementation of specific measures. The AFL's executive council affirmed its long-standing policy of nonpartisanship and refused to endorse a presidential candidate. John L. Lewis, bombastic head of the United Mine Workers (UMW), came out for Hoover, as did several other key labor leaders. Although many destitute workers voted for the Democratic candidate, Roosevelt assumed the presidency owing organized labor nothing for his election and committed to no specific labor programs.

Roosevelt's selection of Frances Perkins as secretary of labor incensed labor leaders. The choice of the first woman to serve in a presidential cabinet won Roosevelt plaudits from many quarters, but AFL president William Green asserted that "labor can never become reconciled to the selection." Despite her impressive credentials—following a long career in consumer advocacy she had served as Governor Roosevelt's industrial commissioner—Perkins lacked the one qualification labor leaders deemed essential: unlike all previous labor secretaries, she was neither a union official nor a union member. Sensitive to organized labor's concerns, Perkins tried to decline and urged Roosevelt to choose someone with union ties. Determined to appoint a good friend of unquestioned loyalty and arguing that the labor secretary represented unorganized as well as organized workers, Roosevelt remained adamant and Perkins finally relented. The AFL's concerns grew, for Perkins—much like Roosevelt—voiced concern for workers but expressed no support for legislation concerning labor organizations or collective bargaining.[1]

In the drafting of the National Industrial Recovery Act (NIRA), Secretary Perkins played no role in guaranteeing rights for unions. Intense lobbying by organizing labor, particularly the United Mine Workers, resulted in the inclusion of a collective bargaining provision in Section 7(a). Roosevelt realized that the recovery plan must include benefits for both labor and business but, according to his biographer, Frank Freidel, he did not foresee the sweeping impact of Section 7(a). Moreover, he had not intended to send strong signals of support to unions and probably agreed with New Dealer Francis Biddle's view of Section 7(a) as an "innocuous moral shibboleth."[2]

Obviously, union leaders disagreed. AFL president William Green called 7(a) the "Magna Charta" for labor; the UMW's John L. Lewis likened it to a second emancipation proclamation. Claiming that the government was advocating trade unionism, labor's leadership moved quickly to launch new membership drives. The UMW proved especially skillful in tying its appeals to the NIRA, distributing leaflets that proclaimed, "The President wants you to join a union." The NRA's Hugh Johnson repeatedly denied that a "purpose of the National Recovery Act" was to "unionize labor," but thousands of newly hopeful workers ignored him. Some corporate executives saw the possibility of working with unions to rationalize their industries and welcomed the discipline the interventionist state would provide. For example, the Cotton Textile Institute's inability to curtail night work and the resultant overproduction left its membership amenable to outside intrusion. This was the exception, however, and most industries tried to blunt union recruiting efforts. In the months following the NIRA's passage, company unions grew more rapidly than AFL affiliates. Nevertheless, hundreds of thousands of workers responded to Section 7(a) by returning to dormant unions in the coal and clothing businesses and joining newly chartered locals in the other mass production industries. Whatever the intent of its authors, Section 7(a) had an electrifying effect on American workers.[3]

The revitalization of labor resulted in a plethora of confrontations with management during the spring and summer of 1934. Infused with a new sense of militancy, Minneapolis truckers, Toledo autoworkers, and San Francisco longshoremen clashed with strikebreakers and local authorities. In the lush valleys of California unrest stirred among the perennially impoverished farm workers who had been excluded from the protections of the NIRA. The general textile strike of that year, the largest work stoppage in America to that time, ended when Roosevelt asked the United Textile Workers to go back to work and accept the recommendations of a special mediation board. The strike failed miserably, and the president's role in the affair disturbed union leaders. The increase in labor violence in 1934 reflected, at least in part, the failure of Roosevelt and NRA officials to secure compliance with Section 7(a).

As businesses became more brazen in their disregard for NRA rulings and disgruntled workers left the unions they had so recently joined, the NRA increasingly appeared to be impracticable. An NRA policy statement jointly issued by Hugh Johnson and Donald Richberg in August 1933 ratified proportional representation, denied majority rule in industry, and endorsed company unions. The National Labor Board, formed earlier that year to deal with the wave of strikes sweeping the nation, mediated agreements in many disputes according to the "Reading Formula," whereby striking workers returned to the job and management pledged good-faith bargaining with labor representatives identified through government-supervised elections. The NLB's effectiveness ebbed quickly, however, when corporations challenged the agency's legal underpinnings and ignored its rulings. For Senator Robert F. Wagner, head of the NLB and Congress's foremost champion of labor's rights, the NRA's shortcomings could be rectified only with new legislation correcting the flaws inherent in Section 7(a).

An effective labor bill, Wagner became convinced, should

provide adequate enforcement powers and situate the administrative board apart from the NRA. In conjunction with the AFL, the Department of Labor, and other members of the NLB—but without the participation of NRA officials—Wagner and his legislative secretary, Leon Keyserling, drafted a new bill and submitted it to Congress on March 1, 1934. Unhappy with the bill's provision for majority rule in the shop and conscious of business's staunch opposition, Roosevelt declined to support it. Instead, he opted for a replacement for the NLB, the National Labor Relations Board (NLRB), that would enjoy somewhat greater latitude in resolving disputes. On June 28 the president signed an executive order creating the NLRB, having earlier intervened to prevent Wagner's bill from coming to a vote in the Senate.

Like its predecessor, the NLRB proved ineffective. Under the chairmanship of Lloyd K. Garrison and Francis Biddle, the NLRB grappled with the same knotty problems that confounded the NLB under Robert Wagner—uncooperative employers, endless litigation challenging the board's authority, the impotency of NRA sanctions, and the halfhearted cooperation of the Justice Department. Both the NLB and the NLRB could convene negotiating sessions, offer recommendations, and conduct elections, but neither could mandate union recognition or collective bargaining. The NLRB suffered, as labor historian Irving Bernstein aptly put it, from having "responsibility without authority." His worst fears confirmed, Senator Wagner resolved again to introduce remedial legislation. He hoped to provide on a much grander scale what the 1934 Railway Labor Act guaranteed that industry's workers—the right to organize and an independent agency for grievance settlement. Under Wagner's supervision, Leon Keyserling spent the fall and winter of 1934–35 redrafting a labor disputes bill—this time without the aid of either the AFL or the Department of Labor. President Roosevelt declined to support the final measure, which Wagner submitted to Congress on February 21, 1935.[4]

The National Labor Relations Act established a new National Labor Relations Board with unprecedented power. The remodeled NLRB possessed the authority to identify bargaining units, hold elections, and certify unions as the duly elected representatives of workers—in short, to buttress the principle of collective bargaining with the authority of an autonomous federal agency. The law also proscribed a series of antiunion activities by employers. Whereas the NLB and earlier NLRB had been composed of representatives from labor, industry, and the public, the three members of the new board would all be public appointees. No longer would the agency's principal charge be conciliation to end strikes, a task implicitly grounded in disinterested mediation. Wagner's NLRB clearly existed to enforce labor's rights, as defined in the act.

From March 11 to April 2, 1935, the hearings on the bill before the Senate Labor Committee captured the headlines of the nation's newspapers. Solidly aligned against the measure, big-business organizations like the U.S. Chamber of Commerce and the National Association of Manufacturers testified in opposition and funded a mammoth lobbying campaign. Wagner challenged the contention that his bill would mandate the closed shop, reiterating that it compelled no one to join a union. He further argued for the measure on economic grounds, saying that collective bargaining would elevate wages, equalize the distribution of national income, and thereby promote recovery. Labor leaders William Green and John L. Lewis spoke avidly for the bill, but the AFL officially showed more restraint. The federation offered a series of amendments limiting federal intervention in collective bargaining and only supported the measure grudgingly after their rejection. Though appreciative of the potential gains for workers, the AFL feared a loss of influence when a truly powerful and autonomous NLRB commenced operation. Labor Secretary Perkins wanted the NLRB located in her bailiwick, but when Wagner adamantly refused she offered virtually no comment on the bill. Her laconic assessment of the bill as "very interesting" perfectly represented the administration's noncommittal stance.[5]

After the Senate passed the National Labor Relations Act, Roosevelt eased off the fence and announced his support for the measure. Following the Supreme Court's *Schechter* decision nullifying the NRA, the president promoted the bill to his list of "must" legislation. The House of Representatives passed it without even a roll-call vote, and the president affixed his signature on July 5. How had Wagner's unabashedly prolabor law been passed? Alluding to the spirit of reform that pervaded in 1935, Leon Keyserling argued that it could not have been passed at any other time. The *Schechter* decision undoubtedly played a role, on one hand investing liberals with all the more reason to support labor legislation and on the other hand allowing congressmen confident that the Wagner Act would be found unconstitutional to vote for the bill despite serious misgivings. President Roosevelt's "hands-off" policy, contrasted with his outright opposition to the earlier version, made passage possible. Also influential was the skillful manipulation of the bill through the legislative mine field by one of Congress's consummate tacticians. As Keyserling commented, "There would never have been a Wagner Act or anything like it at any time if the Senator had not spent himself in this cause to a degree which almost defies description."[6]

At first, the NLRB exercised very little influence on labor-management disputes, since antiunion employers openly ignored it pending judicial review. Only after the Supreme Court affirmed the NLRA's constitutionality in the 1937 *Jones and Laughlin Steel* case did the board become more assertive and could labor leaders feel sanguine about its benefit to their organizations. The board's three charter members (Edwin S. Smith, Donald Wakefield Smith, and J. Warren Madden) eagerly anticipated the opportunity to strike a blow for workingmen, and their decisions in the following years quickly established the NLRB's reputation as a liberal haven for union advocates. By December 1939, the NLRB had heard over twenty-five thousand cases involving 5.75 million workers and had held twenty-five hundred elections in which 1.2 million workers cast ballots. And in the four years after the passage of the Wagner Act, union membership rose from 3,753,300 to 6,555,500. Although breakthroughs in the needle trades and mines predated 1935, the newly supportive position of government as articulated in the Wagner Act sparked tremendous growth of unionism in the mass-production industries.

Ironically, just as the NLRB's creation presaged unprecedented success for unions, organized labor fractured in two. Long-simmering problems within the AFL erupted in the mid-1930s as power struggles on the Executive Council, jurisdictional disputes, and philosophical differences bred dissension. The principal division concerned whether or not to unionize low-skilled industrial workers in the mass-production factories. Originally founded as a federation of craft unions representing skilled workers, the AFL evinced for decades an aristocratic disdain for the mass of unskilled workers composed largely of recent immigrants. Further, it insisted that workers be organized on the basis of common skills rather than by industry. In the twentieth century the federation attempted to deal with rapid technological change by initiating organizing campaigns on a small scale among some semiskilled and unskilled workers who replaced skilled laborers. As a result, only about one-fourth of the AFL unions contained skilled workers exclusively by 1915. Despite this new flexibility, however, the AFL made few inroads into the factories with semiskilled and unskilled labor forces in the newer mass-production industries. Moreover, many of the deeply conservative leaders on the AFL Executive Council applauded the continued exclusion of the unskilled immigrant workers.[7]

Section 7(a) seemed to open up the possibility of recruiting millions of unorganized workers, many of them unskilled, who preferred to join industrial unions rather than observe craft jurisdictions. Increasingly, some AFL leaders argued for relaxing traditional distinctions lest a golden opportunity for massive growth be missed. Spearheading the dissidents, the UMW's John L. Lewis campaigned vigorously for a massive organizing drive. Largely indifferent to the arguments regarding the merits of craft or industrial unionism, Lewis argued that practicality demanded the AFL give the millions of restless workers what they wanted—industrial unionism. When AFL president William Green sided with the Executive Council's traditionalists and dismissed Lewis's entreaties, the UMW leader, in conjunction with such like-minded leaders as Sidney Hillman of the Amalgamated Clothing Workers and David Dubinsky of the International Ladies' Garment Workers Union, intensified his agitation and prepared for a struggle for control of the federation.

By 1935 Lewis and his cohorts considered the breach with their antagonists irreparable. That year at the AFL's annual convention in Atlantic City, Lewis demanded a referendum on the question of industrial unionism and lost decisively. Feelings ran high and at one juncture Lewis floored Big Bill Hutcheson of the carpenters union with a punch, and a brief melee ensued. After the convention adjourned Lewis met with several other union presidents to discuss their grievances. On November 9, 1935, the group formed the Committee for Industrial Organization (CIO) to promote industrial organization within the AFL.

The following September the AFL's Executive Council suspended the CIO unions, and at its annual convention in November the AFL formally ejected them. The 10 expelled unions changed their name to the Congress of Industrial Organizations in 1937.

Under John L. Lewis's energetic leadership, the CIO scored several dramatic successes. Lewis, a coal miner of Welsh ancestry known for his florid oratory, fiery personality, and total devotion to the men who labored underground in one of industrialism's most hazardous occupations, had been president of the UMW since 1919. During the 1920s overproduction and resultant wage reductions had cost the UMW over 80 percent of its membership, but Lewis brilliantly exploited early New Deal legislation, particularly Section 7(a), to reenroll within a few months virtually all of the coal miners the union had lost. Elected to the AFL's Executive Council in 1934, he brought the same relentless drive that had saved the UMW to the national labor movement. His brash style and impatience left many of the AFL's stodgier leaders resentful and hostile; few regretted his departure.

No longer constrained by cautious AFL policies, Lewis threw all the resources at the CIO's command into the effort to organize the corporate giants previously considered to be impervious to union campaigns. Recognizing the importance of the New Deal's benign neutrality, Lewis took the CIO into the political arena in a way the AFL had never permitted. In 1936 the CIO contributed over one-half-million dollars to Roosevelt's reelection campaign, laying the foundation for an alliance between organized labor and the Democratic party that would last for decades. Lewis also deviated from traditional AFL practice by accepting the services of highly motivated and exceptionally talented Communist organizers. Serene in his ability to control the influence of Communists in the CIO, Lewis dismissed the notion that they would eventually gain control of the organization. After all, asked Lewis, "Who gets the bird, the hunter or the dog?"[8]

Unafraid to break with past customs and eager to dispute conventional wisdom, the CIO's fate rested with its challenges to the industrial giants in the auto and steel industries. Its first great success came with the campaign against General Motors in 1937. The United Auto Workers (UAW), a CIO affiliate since July 1936, initiated a sit-down strike against General Motors in its sprawling auto plants in Flint, Michigan, on December 30, 1936. The strike lasted six weeks; neither Governor

Frank Murphy nor President Roosevelt succumbed to the rising public pressure to evict the sit-downers. Within a month GM's auto production fell from 15,000 to 150 per week. The prolonged shutdown cost GM an estimated $175 million dollars in sales and forced the corporation finally to the bargaining table. On February 11, 1937, an agreement between the UAW and GM ended the strike. Although the corporation stopped short of granting the union exclusive representation, it did acknowledge the UAW as a party to the collective bargaining process. The UAW became the principal representative of autoworkers in GM factories, its membership growing from fewer than two hundred at the strike's inception to four hundred thousand by mid-1937. Within just a few months the union completed the organization of Chrysler plants as well. The struggle against the violence-prone management at Ford dragged on for years but could not detract from the UAW's sensational breakthrough in the auto industry—an accomplishment that ignited a wave of sit-down strikes in assorted industries involving a half-million men in the years 1936–37.

Shortly after its triumph over GM, the CIO celebrated an equally impressive victory in the heavily fortified U.S. Steel mills. Under the direction of Philip Murray, the CIO's Steel Workers Organizing Committee (SWOC) sought to take control of the many company unions among U.S. Steel's two-hundred-thousand-man work force. The campaign began in the summer of 1936, and by January 1937 U.S. Steel's chairman of the board Myron Taylor had decided to capitulate. He recognized SWOC as the bargaining agent for its members, agreed to the 8-hour day and 40-hour week, and granted a wage increase up to $5 a day. The U.S. Steel agreement, announced on March 3, 1937, made SWOC one of the most powerful unions in organized labor and gave the CIO incalculable prestige. Although other steel companies had urged Taylor not to deal with SWOC, he concluded that collective bargaining could not be avoided indefinitely. Most important, U.S. Steel enjoyed a substantial profit in 1936—its first since the stock market crash—and Taylor resolved to avoid a profit-limiting strike no matter what the cost. Even union recognition became acceptable.

U.S. Steel's submission in 1937 also reflected a sensitivity to negative publicity generated by congressional investigations into the violations of unions' civil liberties. A subcommittee of the

Senate Committee on Education and Labor chaired by Wisconsin's Robert M. LaFollette, Jr., originated to investigate the persecution of the Southern Tenant Farmers Union but quickly expanded its probe to include all antiunion activities. During its existence from 1936 to 1940 the LaFollette Committee focused on four principal management tactics employed against unions for decades—espionage, munitions stockpiling, strikebreaking, and the use of private paramilitary forces. Its exposure of U.S. Steel's infamous espionage network aroused a shocked public, as did its report that General Motors paid over eight hundred thousand dollars to private detective agencies from 1934 to 1936 for information on union activities. John L. Lewis said often that LaFollette Committee disclosures helped the CIO immeasurably, especially by legitimizing union complaints and countering the hostility generated by sit-down strikes. Although the committee's findings may have enhanced public tolerance of union activity, in many instances oppressive labor practices continued and labor still faced formidable opposition.[9]

Despite SWOC's signal victory in February 1937, the struggle in the steel industry intensified. Smaller companies, collectively known as Little Steel, remained adamantly opposed to any rapprochement with labor; they granted wage increases and lowered hours as U.S. Steel had done but denied SWOC recognition. In May the Little Steel strike began and spread to include shutdowns in Illinois, Indiana, Ohio, Michigan, and Pennsylvania. Determined to hold the line, management stockpiled arms and ammunition, while importing private armies to battle the strikers. The LaFollette Committee reported that the arsenal in Republic Steel's South Chicago plant included 552 handguns, 64 rifles, 245 shotguns, 143 gas guns, 2,702 gas grenades, and nightsticks too numerous to count; its private security force numbered 348 in January 1937. With Little Steel companies making such preparations, the ensuing strikes became especially violent.

The 1937 clash between SWOC strikers and local police at the Republic Steel plant in Chicago underscored Little Steel's staunch resistance to union recognition. On Memorial Day an estimated two thousand protesters, including women and children, marched toward the steel factory to protest the Chicago police's refusal to allow picketing. Police met them two blocks from the mill and ordered them to disperse. A fight erupted and as picketers fled, the police opened fire with pistols and clubbed those who fell behind. Union casualties included 10 killed and 30 wounded by gunfire; 60 other picketers suffered injuries from beatings and clubbings. Citing eyewitness interviews and Paramount Newsreel film footage, the LaFollette Committee condemned the Memorial Day Massacre as a police riot. The committee report denounced the police for their willingness to act as strikebreakers as well as for their excessive force. Unfortunately for the SWOC, however, neither the committee's scathing report nor generally negative publicity blunted the effectiveness of Republic Steel's repressive tactics. Little Steel won in Chicago.

Elsewhere, too, the tide began to turn against the unions in the steel industry. By the summer of 1937, strikes against the Bethlehem, Youngstown Sheet and Tube, and Inland companies had all failed; in Pennsylvania and Ohio, Democratic governors deployed National Guard troops to crush the strikes. Frustrated by his inability to resolve the Little Steel dispute, Roosevelt proclaimed "a plague on both your houses," a statement of disinterest that John L. Lewis found difficult to accept in the wake of the substantial financial contributions that the CIO had made to the president's reelection campaign barely a year earlier. "It ill behooves one who has supped at labor's table," Lewis intoned, "to curse . . . with fine impartiality both labor and its adversaries when they become locked in deadly embrace." After an unbroken string of victories, the CIO's setback in Little Steel mirrored the organization's dwindling success in 1937–38. The recession of those years crippled membership drives, as a rash of layoffs and production cutbacks drained union coffers. Particularly damaging to the CIO, which had concentrated its efforts on the mass-production industries, output decreased by more than half in rubber, steel, and automobile factories.[10]

In 1939 additional developments underscored labor's declining fortunes. In *NLRB* v. *Fansteel Metallurgical Corporation,* the Supreme Court outlawed the sit-down strike as outside labor's "normal rights of redress." On January 24, 1939, a member of Congress introduced a resolution to impeach Secretary of Labor Frances Perkins for her failure to deport longshoremen union official Harry Bridges. This action came as the culmination of a movement among conservatives to drive the secretary from office because of her alleged softness on Communistic labor leaders. She voluntarily testified before the Dies Committee in February, and the following month it dismissed the impeachment charges as inadequate. Although Perkins withstood the allegations, the fact that she had to endure such humiliation at all indicates the strength of the rising sentiment against the unions and their friends by the end of the decade. In 1940 the House of Representatives' committee to investigate the NLRB—the Smith Committee—produced a condemnatory report that resulted in the elimination of the board's Economic Research Division. The CIO's magic of 1936–37 was diminishing.

The defense mobilization preceding America's entry into the Second World War ushered in another period of growth for the unions. From June 1940 to December 1941, unemployment fell from 8.5 million to less than 4 million. During the war the CIO concluded the organization of the mass-production industries, toppling the Little Steel corporations and the Ford Motor Company. Such staunch bastions of antiunion sentiment as Goodyear, Armour, and Westinghouse also signed bargaining agreements for the first time. Both the AFL and CIO enjoyed great success organizing the aircraft and shipbuilding enterprises on the West Coast. Throughout the war, workers saw tangible benefits in union membership as newly negotiated agreements steadily—and sometimes spectacularly—raised wage levels. Although the National War Labor Board imposed wage ceilings, the federal government's determination to avoid production-threatening strikes led it to appease workers whenever feasible. The routinization of collective bargaining on such a large scale during the war made it commonplace by 1945. By war's end labor had recruited more than five million new workers, extending its influence far beyond anything approached by unions before and assuring its place of importance in the developing American economy. In short, the war consolidated the unions' gains of the preceding decade.

The New Deal contributed significantly to the rise of organized labor in the twentieth century. According to the National Bureau of Economic Research, union membership rose from 2,805,000 in 1933 to 8,410,000 in 1941 (approximately 23% of the nonagricultural work force). By the mid-1950s, over 15 million workers (one-third of nonagricultural workers) belonged to unions. A movement nearly moribund in the 1920s revived dramatically during the depression and attained a new viability by mid-century. Much of labor's rebirth resulted from the sensational victories of the CIO over the forces of reaction in the sprawling steel, rubber, and auto factories. Although these heavily capitalized mass-production industries employed a relatively small percentage of American workers, their centrality to the United States economy of the 1930s gave them special importance. The New Deal contributed not only through the passage of such laws as the NIRA's Section 7(a) and the Wagner Act, but through the creation of a hospitable environment in which union organizers could proselytize free of persecution. That generally sympathetic climate, in which an epidemic of sit-down strikes seemed to rage, supported the image of Roosevelt as a patron of labor even though he was indifferent to certain crucial legislative measures.

The growth in union membership in the 1930s and early 1940s, despite the high visibility of the CIO's recruiting efforts, occurred primarily in the AFL. The defection of several unions to the CIO during 1936–37 cost the AFL over 1 million members, but it initiated another 760,000 new recruits during that same time. Between 1937 and 1945 the CIO recruited nearly 2 million new members, but the AFL claimed nearly 4 million. The AFL enjoyed great success in nonmanufacturing industries like transportation, communication, construction, restaurants, and public service. Such AFL affiliates as the Teamsters, Hotel and Restaurant Employees, and Retail Clerks in particular enjoyed remarkable growth. Although the CIO's aggressiveness undoubtedly pushed AFL organizers to greater efforts, in relatively few instances did either organization grow at the expense of the other; between 1938 and 1946 only 13 percent of the representation elections conducted by the NLRB involved workers choosing between the two organizations. Overall, the AFL and CIO appealed to separate groups, and New Deal reforms allowed workers to improve their conditions by joining unions in a wide variety of jobs and industries.[11]

Improvements for workers went beyond higher wages and shorter hours. Unions established the seniority principle, a vital concern during the depression because of the need for layoffs and rehiring. In better times, seniority figured in promotions, transfers, and other personnel matters. Organized labor also instituted formal grievance procedures on the shop floor; no longer could employers arbitrarily punish or discharge workers without showing just cause. As a result of the union presence, shop stewards championed the interests of the often inarticulate laborer against the previously omnipotent foremen and management representatives. For the first time workers knew what to expect as rationality and predictability replaced the discretionary system of rewards and punishments long operative in the factories. Labor gained a new dignity and respect, creating a new relationship between worker and employer.

Union successes came more grudgingly in the South, where the drive to attract new industry centered on cheap labor. As a heavily rural region having minimal experience with large-scale unionism, the South offered several intractable problems to organizers. Deeply held rural values and the popularity of religious denominations emphasizing suffering in this world for salvation in the hereafter undermined worker militance. Much southern-based industry existed in small shops and mills widely scattered in sparsely populated rural areas. As a result, although the textile industry had relocated largely from New England to the southern piedmont, the International Ladies Garment Workers Union counted fewer than one thousand members in the South by 1940. Between 1936 and 1939, 19 union organizers were killed in southern mill towns. Failure in the textile mills, the touchstone of southern industry, denied the CIO the kind of dramatic victories it had achieved in the northern auto and steel plants. The CIO's necessary acceptance of black workers in the drive for mass unionization of the unskilled also generated hostility in a region long committed to racial inequality. Such unions as the United Mine Workers, which reserved the offices of vice-president and secretary in all of their locals for blacks, posed a real threat to the southern caste system. In the larger cities like Memphis, Atlanta, and Birmingham, campaigns of terror and intimidation limited the effectiveness of unions' organizing efforts. To be sure, dedicated unionists persevered in the 1930s and laid the foundation for more extensive gains thereafter. Even so, in 1940 only 10.7 percent of the South's labor force belonged to unions, roughly half of the national percentage of 21.5. The CIO's massive Operation Dixie, launched with great expectations in 1946, quietly ended in 1953 after disappointing results. Long after the New Deal, union membership rates in Dixie remained far below those in other regions.

The New Deal's impact on workers also profoundly altered

American politics, undermining organized labor's traditional neutrality and tying unions to the emerging Democratic coalition forged by the Roosevelt revolution. Certainly Roosevelt fell short of labor leaders' expectations on occasion—most notably in the Little Steel strike—and by the end of the decade he and CIO president John L. Lewis feuded openly. On the whole, however, labor supported Roosevelt strongly; when Lewis supported Republican presidential candidate Wendell Willkie in 1940, the CIO remained loyal to the Democrats. Although it may be true, as labor historian David Brody says, that "one carries away a distinct impression of *inadvertency* in the role the New Deal played in the expansion of the labor movement," workers correctly perceived a sympathy toward labor never previously exhibited by the national government. Labor's electoral support for the Democratic party made sense, because Roosevelt's administration paved the way for substantial union advances.[12]

Significantly, the increased political activism among workers in the 1930s found an outlet within one of the two major existing political parties. Talk of an independent workingman's party increased in the depression years as some union leaders thought of extending their influence from the union hall to city hall. To mobilize support for Roosevelt's reelection in 1936, CIO leaders formed Labor's Non-Partisan League, which provided considerable economic and logistical support for the campaign. Considering independence from the Democratic party, CIO leaders supported candidates for elections in 1937 in New York, Pittsburgh, Detroit, Akron, and other industrial communities. Hopes soared especially in Akron, a city widely thought to have the most union members per capita of any U.S. community, where Labor's Non-Partisan League sponsored a slate of candidates for local contests, including the mayoralty. The overwhelming defeat of labor candidates in Akron where the possibilities for success seemed greatest, and in other cities across the nation, destroyed the notion of the CIO acting as an autonomous presence in American politics. The CIO (later, the AFL–CIO) maintained its political activism but exclusively as an agent of the Democratic party.

Organized labor's marriage to a mainstream political party vitiated whatever influence radical parties wielded previously. The provision for workers of an institutional voice forestalled the popularity of fringe groups questioning capitalism's responsiveness to workers' concerns. The New Deal's record of reform in the workplace blunted the Marxist message that the capitalist state would never challenge the ruling class on behalf of the people. The Socialist party, which historically had commanded a loyal if small following among workers, lost its remaining influence during the 1930s. Its leader, Norman Thomas, explained the loss succinctly: "It was Roosevelt in a word." The Communist party enjoyed some success in a handful of CIO unions, particularly the International Brotherhood of Electrical Workers, but never captured the political allegiances of more than a small minority of American workers. American laborers expressed little interest in revolution, concerning themselves instead with the more pragmatic goals of higher wages, protective legislation, and job security. Seeking such objectives, they found the Democratic party's advocacy of collective bargaining altogether more attractive than the fundamental transformation promised by the left.[13]

Overall, collective bargaining became the New Deal's greatest bequest to labor. It was, however, a curse as well as a gift. Federal intervention protected the unions and assured their growth, but at the cost of regulation. The NLRA safeguarded labor's right to organize and bargain collectively, but by giving the NLRB the power to determine appropriate bargaining units, it left unions hostage to public policy. Indeed, whereas unions and management had negotiated traditionally for their own interests, the Wagner Act turned this essentially private activity into a public one. It also formalized the process, creating new institutions with clearly articulated roles within a structure regulated by the state. Organized labor placed its trust in the state's benign influence and although the NLRB arguably rewarded that trust in the vast majority of cases, a loss of union autonomy resulted. The courts and the NLRB constructed a new framework for labor relations, one that guaranteed stability and minimized conflict. For better or worse, the New Deal granted the unions the stamp of legitimacy and a secure place in the American capitalist system.[14]

CHAPTER NINE

A New Deal for Blacks?

Thinking back to conditions he and other African Americans encountered in the 1930s, boxing champion Archie Moore said: "The white people were jumping out of windows. I don't remember any black people jumping. We were used to depression." Indeed, the affluence supposedly characteristic of the 1920s bypassed most blacks, who continued to occupy the lowest rung on the socioeconomic ladder. Traditionally "last hired and first fired," blacks held the lowest-paying jobs and enjoyed the least employment security. Economics aside, blacks also endured a second-class citizenship based upon a rigid Jim Crow system of segregation in the South and an equally confining—if less formalized—caste structure in the North. Political disfranchisement guaranteed black powerlessness, while residential segregation and minuscule budgets damaged black education. Lynchings occurred with alarming frequency, and the Ku Klux Klan enjoyed a resurgence in the first half of the post–World War I decade. From their disadvantaged position on the fringes of "Coolidge prosperity," blacks expressed scant concern with the stock market crash and the ensuing economic downturn—and with good reason, since they had been experiencing hard times for as long as they could remember. Unfortunately, the worsening depression took its heaviest toll on society's most vulnerable citizens; blacks found themselves sinking into even greater poverty.[1]

In 1930 over half the nation's blacks, including about 97 percent of black farmers, lived in the rural South, yet less than 20 percent owned their own land. The vast majority—sharecroppers, tenant farmers, and wage hands—suffered severely as cotton prices plummeted from 18 cents per pound in 1929 to 6 cents per pound four years later. An estimated two-thirds of blacks engaged in cotton farming earned no profits in the early 1930s. The absence of rural relief left roughly two million black farmers in the South without sustenance. Some remained on the land, scavenging, begging, or relying on the charity of their white employers. Many left for the cities, more commonly for the nearest urban center but occasionally for the metropolises of the North. In the 1920s roughly eight hundred thousand blacks migrated northward, followed by another four hundred thousand in the 1930s.

In the cities blacks found little succor. Spreading unemployment eliminated "Negro Work" as downwardly mobile whites took over menial jobs traditionally monopolized by blacks, such as elevator operator, cook, waiter, hotel bellboy, filling-station mechanic, maid, chauffeur, drugstore delivery boy, steward, and hospital attendant. In Georgia the Black Shirts aroused jobless whites by blaming their unemployment on competition from black workers. In Mississippi white vigilantes working for the Illinois Central Railroad killed black firemen in a dispute over unskilled labor opportunities. Everywhere urban unemployment rates for blacks dwarfed the rates for whites. In 1931 in New Orleans and Birmingham the jobless rate for black males was twice that of white males. By 1932 Atlanta and Philadelphia blacks composed one-half of the city's unemployed, in Houston and Memphis approximately one-third. Half of Harlem's families received unemployment relief by 1933. In Gary, Indiana, half the black population collected full relief; another 30 percent qualified for partial assistance. A Howard University sociologist ruefully concluded that nationwide "fully a third of the race is unemployed and another third under-employed."[2]

Indigent blacks suffered in all cities but especially in the South. In part, this resulted from that region's parsimony in awarding the nation's lowest relief benefits, a decision based upon the South's purportedly low cost of living. Additionally, however, southern communities established more rigorous relief qualification standards for blacks and subsequently paid larger monthly sums to whites than to black recipients. Many privately funded philanthropic organizations systematically excluded blacks. Consequently, formerly secure blacks often fell into grinding poverty in a remarkably short time. A concerned Memphian described a scene repeated frequently in other southern cities: "I happened to pass one of the city's garbage dumps. I was astounded to see 25 or 30 colored men and women with rakes, hoes, and other digging tools, with buckets and baskets, digging around in the garbage and refuse for food and any other articles which they might be able to use."[3]

Like other Americans, disconsolate blacks increasingly chided President Herbert Hoover for failing to ease their suffering. Heeding Frederick Douglass's famous dictum that "the Republican party is the ship, all else the sea," blacks supported Hoover's candidacy in 1928, albeit with little enthusiasm. Leading black Republican Robert R. Church, Jr., plaintively concluded that "the Republican party offers us little. The Democratic party offers us nothing." Once ensconced in the White House, Hoover seemed to go out of his way to rebuff blacks. Determined to purge the integrated "black-and-tan" party factions in some southern states, he supported the "lily-white" organizations and terminated the Republican National Committee's Negro Division. Hoover nominated to the Supreme Court John J. Parker, an outspoken southern opponent of black enfranchisement, and drastically reduced the number of black appointees to federal office. And despite heated black protest, he insisted on the total segregation of mothers and widows of U.S. soldiers sailing for Europe to visit grave sites. His insensitive treatment of these black "Gold Star Mothers" led many black voters by 1932 to question their historic commitment to the party of Lincoln.[4]

For all of Hoover's shortcomings, however, blacks' ties to the Republican party remained strong and, perhaps more important, so did their long-standing aversion to the Democratic party. The Democrats' traditional southern orientation—affirmed as recently as Woodrow Wilson's presidency—left many blacks concerned, as did presidential candidate Franklin D. Roosevelt's choice of Texan John Nance Garner as his running mate in 1932. Blacks bridled at Roosevelt's boast that as assistant secretary of the navy in 1915 he had written Haiti's constitution, a repressive document that bound that nation closely to an imperialistic United States. As New York's governor, Roosevelt had shown no interest in black affairs, making few appointments and supporting virtually no legislation to achieve racial parity. In 1932 Pittsburgh *Courier* editor Robert L. Vann claimed, "I see millions of Negroes turning the pictures of Abraham Lincoln to the wall," but that year's election returns belied his assessment. Even with all of Hoover's liabilities, more than two-thirds of black voters cast their ballots for him rather than for the Democrat. As political scientist Samuel Lubell noted, "Negroes defected in smaller numbers in the 1932 election than did any other group of Republican voters."[5]

Having supported Hoover, blacks had no claim on Roosevelt's loyalties and the early days of the New Deal appeared to confirm their pessimism. Presidential aide Thomas G. Corcoran later commented that "when Roosevelt came in in 1933, there were many more things to worry about than what happened to civil rights," and Roosevelt seemed to ignore blacks with a vengeance. He appointed whites as ministers to Haiti and Liberia and as register of the treasury, posts traditionally reserved for blacks. His apparent indifference to blacks' sensibilities no doubt reflected the race's relative weakness as a political pressure group. In the 1930s the vast majority of blacks still lived in the South, where Jim Crow statutes limited their voting. Moreover, the paucity of blacks living above the Mason-Dixon Line indicated that race was a southern problem, not a national concern. As a northern politician heading a predominantly southern party, the newly elected president seemed unlikely to support a group whose voters would have denied him national office.[6]

On the other hand, the strength of southern Democrats in Congress dictated the president's reluctance to challenge the South's racial customs. A list of prominent southerners in Washington in 1933 included the vice-president, the majority leaders of the Senate and the House, and most of the chairmen of major congressional committees. Hailing from a one-party region where Jim Crow restrictions kept blacks from voting, these Dixie politicians parlayed their seniority into powerful positions. Committee chairmen could report New Deal measures for consideration by the entire legislative body or keep them off the floor; majority leaders could enforce party discipline or ignore an administration measure. Roosevelt urgently needed the support—and votes—of southerners in Congress to pass New Deal relief and recovery legislation; racial matters assumed far less significance.

New Deal programs crafted during the Hundred Days offered blacks little and, despite the inclusion of legislative language to the contrary, they frequently practiced racial discrimination. Blacks found the National Recovery Administration (NRA) particularly unpalatable. NRA codes ignored the three-fourths of blacks employed as domestics and farm workers. The National Industrial Recovery Act (NIRA) said nothing about lower wages and more hours for black workers. To be sure, the NRA repeatedly denied the appeals of southern entrepreneurs for race-based pay differentials, but NRA code draftsmen cleverly invented ways of assuring lower pay for blacks without use of explicit language. They exempted low-paying occupations in which blacks predominated from NRA-sanctioned minimum-wage standards. More than one hundred codes outlined geographical variations that allowed southern industries to pay their workers, many of whom were black, lower wages. Drawing on the example of grandfather clauses used to curtail voting, southern businesses wrote codes that tied wage rates for certain labor groups to standards prevalent at a specific time in the past. Informed of such practices, Roosevelt responded, "It is not the purpose of this Administration to impair Southern industry by refusing to recognize traditional differentials."[7]

Not only did government punish the vast majority of black workers when approving NRA codes, but the enforcement of code standards also favored whites. When the NRA required management to pay equal wages regardless of race, many employers fired blacks and replaced them either with white workers or machines. Benefiting not at all as laborers, blacks suffered as consumers when the NRA forced prices higher. Blacks viewed the NRA blue eagle as a "predatory bird," and the black press suggested that the acronym NRA stood for "Negro Removal Act," "Negroes Ruined Again," "Negro Rarely Allowed," and "Negro Run Around."[8]

Black farmers found the Agricultural Adjustment Administration (AAA) equally disappointing. Secretary of Agriculture Henry A. Wallace refused to appoint a special black advisor in his department, arguing that to do so would be "patronizing" and "discriminatory." By 1939, out of fifty-two thousand employees in the Department of Agriculture, only about eleven hundred were blacks, nearly three-fourths of whom were custodians. The exclusion of blacks permeated all levels of the AAA's structure, as nowhere in the South did blacks serve on the county committees that tailored general agency policies to local conditions. According to Swedish sociologist Gunnar Myrdal, the AAA uprooted over two hundred thousand black farmers. Frequently black owners lost their land and became tenants; black tenants often descended to sharecropping. Arguably the depopulation of the southern farms would have come in any event, but the original AAA expended no effort to protect blacks from the rapaciousness of white landlords. The first AAA refused to intervene to ensure that blacks shared proportionately in the benefit payments awarded for crop reductions. In short, the AAA's influence made certain that whatever recovery accrued in the agricultural South would aid only whites.[9]

The Civilian Conservation Corps (CCC) also proved hostile to blacks. CCC director Robert Fechner, a southerner fully committed to racial segregation, contended that communities throughout the nation objected to the location of CCC camps for blacks in their vicinity. He insisted that camps in the South remain strictly segregated, even though a modicum of race mixing occurred in camps elsewhere. Because blacks could not be employed in white camps throughout much of the nation, a surplus of nonwhites awaiting placement always existed. By the end of 1933 blacks composed only about 5 percent of CCC enrollments despite legal guarantees that "no discrimination shall be made on account of race, color, and creed." During its nine-year existence, the CCC enrolled approximately 2.5 million men, of whom nearly 200,000 (8%) were black. Given the high percentage of blacks among the nation's poor, however, they never achieved adequate representation in the program. In Georgia, Florida, Alabama, and Arkansas, state CCC offices agreed to enroll blacks only after being threatened with the withholding of all funds. In 1935 Fechner announced that black applicants would be selected thereafter only when vacancies opened up in existing black camps. Roosevelt approved but asked that his name not be associated with the new policy.[10]

Racial segregation and discrimination also became hallmarks of the Tennessee Valley Authority (TVA). David Lilienthal, director of the TVA for much of the 1930s, heralded the "grass-roots democracy" made possible by the agency's insistence on local control, but blacks recognized that such decentralization merely allowed southern officials to enforce prevailing racial mores. As a result, reported a National Association for the Advancement of Colored People (NAACP) investigating team, local TVA officials resisted employing black workers and consigned them to the lowest-paying menial jobs. The new model town of Norris, Tennessee, barred blacks from purchasing homes, while other TVA communities maintained segregated housing and workplaces. In all, fewer than 1 percent of the workers on the TVA payroll were black.

New Deal housing programs closely adhered to the principle of racial separation both in the North and South. The few subsistence homesteads constructed during the decade barred blacks, but more significantly, the Home Owners Loan Corporation (HOLC) and the Federal Housing Administration (FHA) established policies of segregation that affected millions of home owners. The HOLC refinanced mortgages based upon a new, uniform system of housing appraisal designed to predict neighborhood development. HOLC appraisers categorized neighborhoods in all cities according to housing stock and the occupation, income level, and ethnicity of the population. Large residential security maps divided each city into four types of neighborhoods by color—green, blue, yellow, and red—in descending order of preferability. By always designating black neighborhoods as least desirable, the HOLC created the practice of redlining. The HOLC maintained that its classification system did not promote segregation and, indeed, the agency awarded some mortgages to residents in red neighborhoods. By making their maps available to private lending institutions, however, HOLC officials provided the means for segregationists to defend existing racial exclusionary policies. More significant in the long run, the FHA adopted HOLC appraisal techniques without emulating its egalitarian values.

Prior to guaranteeing a loan to a prospective home buyer, the FHA required an "unbiased professional estimate" that included an evaluation of the neighborhood as well as the property itself and the prospective borrower. Expressing a concern with "inharmonious racial or nationality groups," the FHA refused to recommend loans to redlined neighborhoods and urged property owners to adopt restrictive racial covenants. (Subsequent to a Supreme Court decision banning such covenants, the FHA disavowed them in 1950 but continued to redline predominantly black living areas.) Obviously, neither the HOLC nor the FHA pioneered in reducing the value of real estate on the basis of racial occupancy; private interests had been making such judgments for decades. But as urban historian Kenneth T. Jackson has noted: "For perhaps the first time, the federal government embraced the discriminatory attitudes of the marketplace. Previously, prejudices were personalized and individualized; FHA exhorted segregation and enshrined it as public policy."[11]

Acceptance of local customs in direct opposition to federal policies also characterized the provision of both direct and work relief to blacks. The Federal Emergency Relief Administration (FERA) expressly forbade racial discrimination, yet state and local officials frequently made awards and determined amounts in accord with prevailing customs of racial inequality. These administrators hired all available whites before considering blacks, who only received jobs requiring unskilled labor, and paid whites considerably higher wages. In 1935, for example, Atlanta's average monthly relief award to whites was $32.66 and to blacks $19.29; in Norfolk, Virginia, FERA's emergency education program paid blacks $25–$75 per month and whites $90–$125. Southern politicians asserted that blacks required less compensation and regional mores demanded such racial discrepancies.

The Works Progress Administration (WPA) retained FERA's policies on race despite Roosevelt's executive order to the contrary and explicit administrative guidelines banning discrimination. Although the WPA proved a godsend for thousands of poverty-stricken blacks, they never received the benefits their percentage of the unemployed warranted. Blacks also continued to receive smaller stipends than did whites and seldom obtained skilled or white-collar appointments. Fewer than one hundred blacks out of four thousand WPA recipients in St. Louis worked on professional and service projects. Blacks also complained about the handling of unskilled labor; the Birmingham NAACP charged that black women had to perform physically taxing work on city streets (such as rolling wheelbarrows and swinging picks and shovels) normally done by men. In Jackson, Mississippi, black female construction workers toiled under the supervision of armed guards. T. Arnold Hill, acting executive secretary of the National Urban League (NUL), concluded that "the Negro remains that most forgotten man in a program planned to deal new cards to the millions of workers neglected and exploited in the shuffle between capital and labor." Or as Howard University political scientist Ralph J. Bunche put it, the New Deal for blacks meant "the same thing, but more of it."[12]

In addition to deploring the inadequacy of New Deal programs, blacks criticized Roosevelt for his failure to support actively an antilynching bill. After the number of lynchings dropped significantly in the 1920s, the onset of the depression brought a resurgence of racial tension resulting from economic competition. From a low of 7 lynchings in 1929, the number of incidents rose to 21 in 1930, 1931, and 1932, and 28 in 1933. No other single issue symbolized so well the helplessness and inferior status of blacks in American society, and in the 1930s the NAACP shifted its focus from litigation to an antilynching campaign. Walter White, executive secretary of the NAACP, recruited Senators Robert F. Wagner of New York and Edward P. Costigan of Colorado to introduce an antilynching bill into Congress in early 1934. The measure penalized state and local officials who failed to protect prisoners or prosecute lynchers and prescribed harsher sanctions for law-enforcement officers who joined lynch mobs. The bill also stipulated that counties where lynchings occurred would be fined ten thousand dollars. When the Senate Judicial Committee favorably reported the bill in March 1934, White called on the president to endorse the measure. On two separate occasions that spring, Roosevelt told White and others that he fully supported an end to the heinous practice but for political reasons could not say so publicly:

> I did not choose the tools with which I must work. Had I been permitted to choose them I would have selected quite different ones. But I've got to get legislation passed by Congress to save America. The Southerners by reason of the seniority rule in Congress are chairmen or occupy strategic places on most of the Senate and House committees. If I come out for the anti-lynching bill now, they will block every bill I ask Congress to pass to keep America from collapsing. I just can't take that risk.[13]

Without the president's backing, the bill never came up for a vote in that session. The following year the Senate considered the measure at greater length, resulting in a six-day filibuster by southerners who managed to keep the bill from being voted on. Unwilling to risk the loss of support for his Second New Deal measures, Roosevelt acquiesced. Each year from 1937 to 1940 Congress considered an antilynching bill, and in 1938 southern senators responded with a filibuster that lasted more than six weeks. After a cloture vote failed, Roosevelt asked for the bill's withdrawal so that an urgently needed emergency relief appropriation could be considered. In 1939 Eleanor Roosevelt publicly endorsed the bill, but again her husband demurred. By the end of the decade, the necessity to retain southern votes for the burgeoning defense program relegated antilynching legislation to certain defeat. Although appreciating the political exigencies Roosevelt faced, black leaders never fully accepted his refusal to endorse their cause. In a letter to the president, Walter White affirmed his "belief that the utterly shameless filibuster could not have withstood the pressure of public opinion had you spoken out against it."[14]

Yet, despite the president's timorous approach to racial issues and the failure of many New Deal agencies to provide relief in color-blind fashion, much in the Democratic administration appealed to African Americans. If nothing else, numerous New Dealers expressed their concern about racial inequality. Although Roosevelt seemed genuinely uninterested in civil rights issues, an unprecedented number of people in Washington felt no compunction about speaking out boldly in behalf of blacks—so much so, in fact, that white southerners became increasingly displeased with the rhetoric concerning racial equality emanating from the capital. And simultaneously with their public declarations Harold Ickes, Aubrey Williams, Will Alexander, Clark Foreman, Eleanor Roosevelt, and others close to the president took every opportunity to lobby him for more daring civil rights initiatives.

During the 1930s no one spoke out more often or more eloquently for civil rights than did Eleanor Roosevelt. Like her husband, the First Lady knew very little about such matters—and, in fact, knew very few blacks—when she came to Washington in 1933. Initially she saw racial matters only within the context of economics, impervious to the necessity for remediation apart from New Deal relief and recovery measures. But as she became friends with Walter White of the NAACP and Mary McLeod Bethune, president of the National Council of Negro Women, the First Lady changed her views and urged special consideration of racial inequality, Jim Crowism, lynching, and political disfranchisement. As an ally of civil rights organizations, she publicly began to advocate stronger action to redress such grievances. Her increasingly outspoken support of civil rights antagonized many Americans of more traditional racial views—particularly southern Democrats. In 1938 she caused an uproar by sitting in the "colored" section of the auditorium at the Southern Conference of Human Welfare in Birmingham, Alabama. Local police forced her to move, so she placed her chair in the aisle between the white and colored sides. When the Daughters of the American Revolution (DAR) prohibited black contralto Marian Anderson from singing in Constitution Hall, Mrs. Roosevelt resigned her membership in the organization and helped locate an alternative concert site.

Perhaps Eleanor Roosevelt contributed most to the civil rights cause by acting as the voice of blacks in the White House. She became an unofficial ombudsman, articulating blacks' complaints and requests to New Deal administrators otherwise impervious to such sentiments. Walter White quickly learned that Eleanor Roosevelt provided the surest access to the otherwise inaccessible chief executive, and on countless occasions she pestered the president to meet black leaders or consider their ideas. Regardless of the actual results of her efforts, African Americans knew that for the first time they had a voice in the highest councils of government. Constantly preoccupied with the political ramifications of his actions, Roosevelt received from his wife the view from the high road. She was, said presidential advisor Robert Sherwood, "the keeper of and constant spokesman for her husband's conscience."[15]

Second only to Eleanor Roosevelt as a proselytizer for civil rights causes, Secretary of the Interior Harold L. Ickes brought to the New Deal a lifelong commitment to improved race relations. A former president of the Chicago NAACP chapter, Ickes wasted no time in effecting change in Washington racial customs. He promptly desegregated Department of Interior cafeterias and restrooms and proclaimed an end to all segregation within his bailiwick. As head of the Public Works Administration (PWA), he instituted a quota system based on the 1930 census that reserved a certain percentage of both skilled and unskilled relief jobs for black workers. In addition, Ickes hired an unprecedented number of blacks in white-collar positions, integrated housing projects in the North, and commenced the gradual desegregation of southern national parks. Although his efforts frequently fell short, Ickes's dogged persistence and unswerving commitment won him the gratitude of thankful black suppliants.

Ickes campaigned for the establishment of a government position specifically designated to protect black interests in New Deal recovery efforts and offered to make a home for this person in the Department of Interior. When the Julius Rosenwald Fund volunteered to pay the salary, Roosevelt agreed to the plan. Ickes selected Clark Foreman, a Columbia University Ph.D. in political science, former member of the Commission on Interracial Cooperation, and Rosenwald Fund staff member. Foreman, a white native of Atlanta, Georgia, initially hesitated to accept the appointment, arguing that a black person should fill the position, but eventually relented under the condition that he would serve only until a black man could be found to succeed him. Black leaders strongly protested the selection of a white man to represent their concerns, accusing Ickes of paternalism. Stung by the criticism, Ickes agreed to appoint a black man along with Foreman, and the Rosenwald Fund provided the additional money. Foreman chose Robert Weaver, a Harvard Ph.D. in economics and member of the Joint Committee on National Recovery. Foreman and Weaver found their task foreboding since they could easily spot instances of racial discrimination in government agencies but found correction of such inequities exceedingly difficult. The two investigators could only report their findings to Ickes, who urged the delinquent agencies to reform. Some cabinet departments and New Deal agencies named race relations advisors, and a special interdepartmental committee on Negro affairs met briefly before disbanding. These and other initiatives by Ickes, Foreman, and Weaver frequently foundered, but blacks applauded the attempts. Certainly no previous administration had made such efforts.

Other prominent white liberals assumed highly visible positions in the New Deal and in some instances implemented quite successfully more enlightened racial policies in New Deal agencies. Will W. Alexander, a Methodist clergyman and student of the cotton tenancy conundrum in the South, resigned his pastorate and founded the Commission on Interracial Cooperation in 1919. As the commission's director and principal spokesman since its inception, Alexander emerged by the 1930s as one of the leaders of southern white liberalism. Succeeding Rexford G. Tugwell as director of the Farm Security Administration (FSA) in 1937, Alexander constantly battled a hostile Congress and made do with an inadequate budget but nevertheless scored some notable victories. The FSA employed a greater percentage of blacks in supervisory positions than any other agency. Furthermore, Alexander insisted that blacks receive FSA loans in numbers proportionate to their percentage of the population and in the same amounts as white recipients. By 1940 black families composed one-fourth of the FSA homestead tenants and over half the residents of FSA rental cooperatives. Remarkably, Alexander even managed to integrate a few FSA projects in the South.

Aubrey Willis Williams, another esteemed white liberal southerner, likewise left his mark on New Deal agencies. A social worker by training, Williams served as Harry Hopkins's assistant in the WPA from 1935 to 1938 and as director of the National Youth Administration (NYA) thereafter. In the WPA Williams reinforced Hopkins's own liberal racial proclivities but made so many powerful enemies in the process that he could not be confirmed as WPA head when Hopkins became secretary of commerce. Under his direction the NYA became a paragon of racial equality, mandating equal pay for blacks and whites in the South and elsewhere. Almost all of the nation's black colleges received NYA student aid, and Williams insisted that black youths participating in the out-of-school work programs be included in all the skilled labor training and preprofessional programs. Altogether, over three hundred thousand black youngsters received some form of NYA assistance.

Because of the efforts of administrators like Ickes, Alexander, and Williams, some New Deal agencies developed sterling records on race in direct contrast to the more conservative NRA, AAA, and CCC. In addition to the FSA and NYA, which clearly stood out for their enlightened racial practices, the United States Housing Authority (USHA) won acclaim for its demand that black workers be hired on public housing construction sites equal to their proportion of the local population. The USHA also hired Robert Weaver as a special advisor on race. And although blacks castigated the FERA for its record of racial discrimination, they generally applauded the operation of the WPA after 1935. The WPA employed 350,000 blacks annually, and its education program taught an estimated 250,000 to read and write. Decentralization exacted a cost, especially in the South, but Harry Hopkins made a concerted effort to include blacks in the WPA's special projects and to equalize wage scales. In some communities the percentage of blacks employed by the agency equaled five times their proportion of the local population. The WPA never fulfilled the hopes of African Americans, but honest efforts by Harry Hopkins and Aubrey Williams deflected much of the criticism away from Washington.

The Roosevelt administration also compiled an enviable record of making appointments of and dispensing patronage to blacks. During the 1930s the number of blacks working for the federal government more than tripled; significantly, the ranks of the newly hired included lawyers, engineers, architects, and other professionals—not just token appointments of custodians, night watchmen, and domestics. With great fanfare Roosevelt appointed William Hastie the first black federal judge, Robert L. Vann and William Houston assistant attorneys general, Mary McLeod Bethune director of Negro affairs for the NYA, and Ira DeA. Reid to the Social Security Board. Other well-known blacks such as Forrester Washington, Lawrence W. Oxley, Eugene K. Jones, and Ambrose Caliver served for varying amounts of time as racial advisors within executive departments. Never before had blacks been so visible in the federal government.

By 1935 New Deal agencies and cabinet departments employed about 45 blacks, who designated themselves the Federal Council on Negro Affairs; the press referred to them as the Black Brain Trust or, more commonly, the Black Cabinet. An informal network of blacks sharing only a common desire to advance the interests of their race in federal government bureaucracies, the Black Cabinet met sporadically and informally. Much older than most of her male colleagues, Mary McLeod Bethune assumed the unofficial role of discussion leader and hosted most Black Cabinet meetings at her home. This group, with its fluctuating membership, exerted little direct influence on policy matters but served several useful functions—sharing ideas, plotting strategy, providing inside information to civil rights groups, and focusing public attention on civil rights issues. Like so many other New Deal innovations, the significance of the Black Cabinet was always primarily symbolic.

In a less obvious way, the New Deal aided the cause of civil rights through the president's Supreme Court appointments. Legal breakthroughs came grudgingly in the 1930s, the principal courtroom victory coming in the 1938 case, *Missouri ex rel Gaines* v. *Canada,* in which the Court instructed the University of Missouri Law School to admit a black applicant since the state provided racial minorities no other opportunities for legal education. Missouri's willingness to erect a separate law school for blacks rather than integrate the existing institution tarnished the victory somewhat, but elated blacks cheered the decision as the beginning of the end of Jim Crow education. Blacks also applauded when the Supreme Court overturned Alabama courts' dubious convictions of black defendants accused of raping white women in the celebrated *Scottsboro* case. At the same time, however, the Court approved white-only primaries as a right of political parties. In the long run, Roosevelt's eight Supreme Court appointees provided the greatest hope for legal victories since, with the lone exception of James F. Byrnes, they all supported civil rights for blacks. Among them, Frank Murphy, Felix Frankfurter, Hugo Black, and William O. Douglas forthrightly worked to ensure constitutional protection for minorities and played a leading role in subsequent landmark civil rights decisions. As historian Harvard Sitkoff observed, "What would culminate in the Warren Court clearly began in the Roosevelt Court."[16]

Promising developments within the federal government reflected the quickened pace of activity among black civil rights groups during the 1930s. In part, the activism of such organizations as the NAACP and the National Urban League pushed the New Deal toward a greater attention to racial matters; at the same time, good news from Washington about bold departures by the Roosevelt administration (if not by the president himself) spurred blacks on to greater efforts. Blacks picketed, marched, lobbied, litigated, and protested with an unprecedented fervor and more frequently than ever before. They launched Don't Buy Where You Can't Work campaigns, boycotted exploitative merchants, and conducted rent strikes against avaricious landlords. New organizations representing the radical left and organized labor also emerged to invoke the cry for racial justice and equality.

In 1933 black leader John P. Davis organized the Joint Committee on National Recovery as a lobby for black interests in the

New Deal. Although it represented some 20 organizations, the committee limped along with just a two-person staff and an annual budget under five thousand dollars. In 1935 a frustrated Davis, along with Ralph Bunche and union leader A. Philip Randolph, created the National Negro Congress (NNC) in hopes of forging a broader-based national organization with more influence. Local NNC councils sprang up around the nation, especially in such large black population centers as Chicago, New York, and Washington, D.C. By the end of the decade, however, Davis's goal of a massive national organization uniting all black factions seemed unattainable, in part because of the hostility of the NAACP and the NUL. Davis's call for black political independence went unheeded in 1936 when grateful blacks voted for Roosevelt and the New Deal in huge numbers. Failing to attain black unity, Davis and the NNC began to emphasize the interracial harmony of economic interests. By the end of the decade, the NNC lost much of its support among blacks as it came to be dominated by the American Communist party and, to a lesser extent, the CIO. In 1940 Randolph resigned as NNC president, and Davis later followed suit.

The Communist party's conquest of the NNC was part of its major effort during the 1930s to recruit blacks. Communists repeatedly led the way in civil rights protests, condemning racial injustice at every turn, defending blacks in the celebrated *Scottsboro* and *Angelo Herndon* cases, challenging the federal government to make relief programs nondiscriminatory, and taking dangerous positions in defense of blacks in the violence-racked South. The Communist party readily accepted black members and practiced total integration; its nomination of a black man, James Ford, as its vice-presidential candidate won praise even from the historically skeptical black press. The Communists' tireless activities in the 1930s helped publicize racial inequality, and they garnered some recruits for their efforts, particularly among black intellectuals. Most African Americans, however, found the party an unappealing alternative. Because most blacks coveted inclusion in the American capitalist system—not its destruction—the radical doctrine of Marxism ultimately proved unsatisfactory. Ironically, the Communist party's well-publicized activities on behalf of racial change added to the ferment that induced the New Deal to move slightly more leftward.

Similar pressures on the federal government came from the

CIO, whose chances for successful organization of labor's unskilled and semiskilled workers depended largely upon black support. This backing, in turn, resulted from the CIO's embrace of racial equality. While AFL president William Green gradually recognized the need to accept black workers in the unions of a changing work force, the CIO's John L. Lewis took the plunge without hesitation. The CIO unions made way for blacks in their administrative hierarchies, issued public proclamations supporting racial equality, and donated substantial sums of money to black organizations. To be sure, discrimination still existed in locals of the CIO as well as the AFL, but the CIO's national leadership firmly staked out a position endorsing interracialism. As black sociologist Charles S. Johnson remarked in 1939, "Negro workers are now recognizing in the CIO the most strategic weapon for their advance as a class."[17]

Like the CIO, African Americans in the 1930s came to believe that their political fortunes rested with Franklin D. Roosevelt and the New Deal. Election returns in 1934 indicated that the ambivalence black voters felt in 1932 was changing to a clear preference for the Democratic party. For the first time in history blacks voted Democratic that year, a reaction not only to the changes instituted in their behalf in Washington but also to striking advances made in local politics in several locations. In Chicago the Kelly-Nash Democratic machine enthusiastically courted black voters and lured top black politicians like William Dawson and Arthur Mitchell away from the Republicans. Mayor Ed Kelly provided the critical support for Mitchell, who bested black Republican congressman Oscar De Priest and became the first black Democrat to serve in the U.S. Congress. In New York City the Tammany Hall Democratic machine chose its first black district leader that year. Some old-line black Republican leaders like Robert R. Church, Jr., of Memphis, Percy Howard of Mississippi, and Henry Lincoln Johnson of Georgia remained loyal to the party of emancipation, but many younger blacks gravitated toward the Democratic party where a dearth of black members opened up leadership opportunities. The New Deal created a whole new generation of black politicians who owed their status and even their livelihood to the Democratic party.

In 1936, much to the dismay of white southern Democrats, their party made unprecedented overtures to black voters. At its national nominating convention the Democratic party for the first time seated black delegates (10 regular and 22 alternates) and desegregated the press box. A black clergyman delivered an invocation, prompting South Carolina senator Ellison "Cotton Ed" Smith to walk out of the convention hall. "By God, he's as black as melted midnight!" loudly exclaimed Smith as he departed. Later he added, "I am not opposed to any Negro praying for me, but I don't want any blue-gummed, slew-footed Senegambian praying for me politically!" Smith ceremoniously exited again when Congressman Arthur Mitchell became the first black to address a Democratic convention by seconding Roosevelt's nomination. Blacks applauded the abrogation of the two-thirds rule, by which southerners had long exercised a veto over presidential candidate selection, in favor of simple majority rule. After the convention the Democrats persisted in their pursuit of black votes, especially emphasizing the vital economic relief provided by New Deal agencies. The Democratic party produced a 16-minute film, *We Work Again,* which extolled the WPA's role in aiding unemployed blacks. The film played to appreciative audiences in theaters, Urban League meetings, and Elks Club gatherings nationwide. Members of the New Deal's Black Cabinet, the president's wife, and even the Roosevelts' maid campaigned among black voters that autumn.[18]

No longer wavering as they had four years earlier, African Americans fully joined the ranks of the incipient Roosevelt coalition in 1936. Although a few black newspapers refrained from endorsing the president, the majority—including the New York *Amsterdam News,* Pittsburgh *Courier,* Atlanta *World,* Chicago *Metropolitan News,* and St. Louis *Argus*—did so. According to Gallup polls an estimated 76 percent of blacks in the North voted for Roosevelt, including 81 percent of black voters in Harlem, 75 percent in Pittsburgh and Indianapolis, and over 67 percent in Cincinnati, Cleveland, St. Louis, and Kansas City. In Chicago the Democratic vote in black wards increased from 23 percent in 1932 to 49 percent four years later. In the South poll taxes, intimidation, and a host of discriminatory registration requirements disfranchised all but a few black voters (fewer than 5% of eligible black voters cast ballots in the 1930s). Nevertheless, election returns in the handful of Tennessee, Texas, and North Carolina cities where blacks could vote showed their disenchantment with the Republicans as well.

In 1940 Robert L. Vann urged blacks to practice "loose-leaf

politics," that is, to remain independent and vote for whichever party offered the best deal. To underscore his commitment to pragmatic opportunism, he endorsed Republican presidential candidate Wendell Willkie. The NAACP withheld an endorsement of Roosevelt subsequent to his announced opposition to segregation in the 1940 defense act. Willkie promised desegregation in the armed forces and antilynching legislation while lambasting Roosevelt for failure to achieve either. Faced with absolute intransigence from the military—Navy Secretary Frank Knox threatened to resign if Roosevelt attempted desegregation, and Secretary of War Henry L. Stimson refused to consider any alterations in army racial policies—Roosevelt could only promote Benjamin O. Davis, Jr., as the first black man to achieve the rank of general in the U.S. Army. But despite the criticisms of black leadership, the voters still backed the incumbent and, especially, the New Deal. Votes for Roosevelt came in greatest numbers in the poorest black neighborhoods, areas where New Deal relief programs meant the most. Whereas Roosevelt's percentage of the popular vote declined from 60.8 percent in 1936 to 54.7 percent in 1940, his support in black districts remained stronger (the percentage of the black vote decreased from 71% in 1936 to 67% in 1940). For all of the wear and tear of incumbency, blacks remained the most loyal members of the Roosevelt coalition.[19]

By the end of the 1930s the Democratic party had captured the black vote, but the value of the prize was not at all clear. Disfranchised in the South and composing a small portion of the population in northern states with large electoral vote totals, blacks did not register or vote in great numbers anywhere. Roosevelt owed neither his 1936 nor 1940 reelections to black voters. And yet blacks continued to move northward at a rapid rate, some four hundred thousand during the 1930s alone. Some northern states—Illinois, Michigan, Missouri, New York, Pennsylvania, and Ohio—experienced a one-third growth in their black populations during that decade. The overwhelming number of these migrants settled in cities, reinforcing a development ongoing for generations. Urbanized blacks in the North became less docile, more politically active, increasingly demanding. Historian Harvard Sitkoff noted that "because of such numbers, and because those blacks who had migrated in earlier decades gradually emancipated themselves from their former Southern patterns of behavior and thought, the Negro now had political power in the North." As this demographic change accelerated in subsequent years, emerging black political power increased. The black vote, not decisive in 1930s elections, became a cornerstone of the Democratic party in later years. On the other hand, the cost of the prize—the defection of the southern white electorate—would damage the presidential candidacies of Democrats like Walter Mondale and Michael Dukakis, neither of whom earned 30 percent of the white vote in the South.[20]

The revolution in black politics occurred primarily because the New Deal provided relief in the Great Depression. To be sure, it was never enough. As a downcast Aubrey Williams wrote Harry Hopkins in 1934: "The Negroes don't get a fair deal. I don't know how to secure one for them." The Social Security program excluded agricultural and domestic workers, occupational categories accounting for two-thirds of black employment, and assigned administration of retirement pensions to the states at a time when local control inevitably resulted in greater racial discrimination. But as W. E. B. DuBois explained: "Any time people are out of work, in poverty, have lost their savings, any kind of a 'deal' that helps them is going to be favored. Large numbers of colored people in the United States would have starved to death if it had not been for the Roosevelt policies." At one time as many as one million black families relied on the WPA as their sole means of support. One bitter Georgia politician noted that blacks began voting Democratic "since Roosevelt became Santa Claus." Patronage, recognition, and assorted symbolic gestures no doubt elevated the Democratic party in the estimation of blacks, but economic aid remained most important. "It was not civil rights," remarked Franklin Williams, president of the Phelps-Stokes Fund, "it was jobs" that coaxed black voters away from the Republican party.[21]

Blacks changed political parties for the same reason that they lionized Franklin D. Roosevelt—because he did more for their race than any other president in memory. Never deeply committed to civil rights, the president could have done much more but shied away from controversy. The NAACP's Roy Wilkins demanded "that now, while the Government is pouring millions of dollars into the South, is the time for it to insist upon the correction of some of the evils of the plantation system as a condition of government aid." But this called for Roosevelt to take extraordinary action at a time when no consensus existed among the American people on racial matters—and a time when a powerful, highly motivated portion of the white population strongly resisted reform. As the NAACP's official organ, *Crisis,* editorialized after Roosevelt's death: "It is true that the millennium in race relations did not arrive under Roosevelt. But cynics and scoffers to the contrary, the great body of Negro citizens made progress." In the context of the times and given what had come before, the achievements of the New Deal seemed substantial.[22]

Moreover, the changes initiated by the New Deal, modest though they may have been, laid the foundation for the much more sweeping alterations of the Second Reconstruction a generation later. The pioneering efforts of black activists in the 1930s constituted, in historian Bernard Sternsher's phrase, a "prelude to revolution." The federal government, a key player in the civil rights drama of the 1950s and 1960s, recognized blacks and their concerns during the depression years on a scale never approached before. The New Deal fell far short of alleviating the wretched conditions and attacking the second-class citizenship under which African Americans lived, but its modest inroads made possible significant changes later on. As the example of the FHA demonstrated, increased federal involvement did not always advance the cause of racial justice. Relatedly, the public housing program initiated by the PWA and USHA accepted residential segregation as a prerequisite to improved housing for racial minorities. The result, intended or not, was the continued ghettoization of African Americans. And the New Deal's expansion of federally funded relief, charged the National Urban League at the time and other critics later, created a permanently dependent welfare class among urban blacks. Regardless of outcome, however, the New Deal established race as a legitimate area of government interest and thereby made the civil rights movement possible. The extension of black legal and political rights at least became more feasible, an achievement most Americans would celebrate. If the 1930s produced disappointingly few breakthroughs, New Deal partisans could claim as part of its legacy the metamorphosis of government into an active agent for social change. To blacks and other oppressed groups the future looked brighter as a result.[23]

CHAPTER TEN

Women and the New Deal

During her peregrinations on behalf of Harry Hopkins, Lorena Hickok discovered in 1933–34 a nation ravaged by the Great Depression. Hickok's letters to the FERA administrator told feelingly of the suffering experienced by all types of people, but her reports often bespoke a special sensitivity to the plight of women whose vulnerability frequently led to heart-rending stories. For example, she wrote Hopkins about a man walking the streets of Houston who was frequently propositioned by doleful young women turned to prostitution. The man finally said to one woman: "I can't. I haven't any money." The woman replied: "Oh, that's alright. It only costs a dime." On another occasion Hickok relayed the story of a meeting of prominent Baltimore businessmen, one of whom suggested that women who refused jobs as live-in housemaids at three dollars per week forfeit their relief benefits. When someone pointed out that women with children to care for at night could not accept such an arrangement, the businessman urged that the children be taken from the mother and placed in an institution. "I think we owe it to the taxpayers," Hickok quoted him as saying. Such stories about women, married and unmarried, young and old, challenged the belief that widespread unemployment affected only men and that housewives remained at home impervious to the worst effects of the Great Depression.[1]

Clearly, women as well as men suffered from the economy's collapse. Housewives grimly tried to keep beleaguered households together with dwindling resources, adopting the adage, "Use it up, wear it out, make it do, or do without." Many families sustained their living standards only because women worked harder at home in compensation for goods and services they could no longer afford. Housewives baked bread and canned food instead of purchasing them at the grocers', and sewed and patched clothing rather than buying factory-made garments. Often they wore their own clothes until threadbare, then stayed at home to hide their shabby appearance. These women also had to cope with bitter, unemployed husbands who saw their inability to support their families as a personal failure. Often the men dawdled around the house, spreading gloom and a deepening sense of frustration.[2]

Of course, not all women enjoyed the protection of the home during the depression. In 1930 over 10.5 million women worked in the labor force, 29 percent of whom were married. Contrary to the widely held belief that women worked outside the home simply to earn "pin money," U.S. Women's Bureau investigators showed that economic necessity had always been the reason. Economic exigencies in the 1930s forced many women who had previously been supported by their husbands or parents to enter the work force, resulting in a 50 percent increase in the number of married women wage earners during the decade. The specter of needy women seeking jobs at a time of scarce employment opportunities aroused hostility in some quarters. As magazine editor Norman Cousins prescribed: "Simply fire the women, who shouldn't be working anyway, and hire the men. Presto! No unemployment. No relief rolls. No depression." Along with the prevalence of such opinions in a male-dominated work force, severe belt-tightening and the frantic search for precious jobs in a collapsed labor market made the depression an especially perilous time for women.[3]

Women, like men, looked expectantly to the New Deal and experienced both stirring successes and disappointing setbacks. The Roosevelt administration enjoyed a well-deserved reputation for elevating women to highly visible positions in the federal government and for appointing women to second- and third-tier posts as well. More so than in any previous administration, women held positions of real authority. In addition to selecting Frances Perkins as secretary of labor, Roosevelt could claim a number of other firsts among his female appointments, namely Ruth Bryan Owen as U.S. minister to Denmark, Florence Allen as judge in the Sixth U.S. Circuit Court of Appeals, Nellie Tayloe Ross as director of the mint, and Marion Glass Banister as assistant treasurer of the United States. High-level administrators within New Deal relief agencies included Hallie Flanagan as head of the Federal Theatre Project; Hilda Worthington Smith, director of the WPA Workers Education Project; and Ellen Sullivan Woodward, head of WPA's Women's and Professional projects. True enough, Roosevelt stopped short of elevating women to the highest administrative levels—he declined to support Florence Allen for a Supreme Court justiceship, for instance—and included only men among his closest advisors. Nevertheless, the Roosevelt record on prestigious appointments for women had no equal to that time.

At the secondary and tertiary levels in New Deal agencies, women also fared well. Within the Labor Department, Clara Beyer held an important position at the Labor Standards Division, as did Grace Abbott and Katherine Lenroot in the Children's Bureau and Mary Anderson in the Women's Bureau. The National Recovery Administration employed Rose Schneiderman, Mary Harriman Rumsey, and Emily Newell Blair, among others. Jane Hoey acted as director of public assistance for several years. Ellen Sullivan Woodward served on the three-member Social Security Board from 1938 to 1946, Molly Dewson for a few months in 1937–38. From 1929 to 1939 the percentage of women employed by the federal government increased from 14.3 to 18.8, bringing to 175,000 the number of women holding civil service jobs. Having dominated the social work profession for years, women possessed the skills and knowledge needed for hastily formed relief programs, and New Deal administrators like Harry Hopkins appointed them in great numbers. In a related development, many women rose to prominence in the Democratic party. In addition to director of the Women's Division Molly Dewson, Caroline Wolfe, Gladys Tillett, and Dorothy McAllister rose in the hierarchy of this previously all-male enclave.

Much of the New Deal's notoriety was owed to the efforts of approximately 25 women who developed a network of cooperation in Washington. These female reformers shared common goals based upon their past experiences in the women's suffrage crusade and in various Progressive social movements. At the center of this network stood Eleanor Roosevelt, whose seemingly endless activities on behalf of women, as well as several other constituencies, proved of incalculable benefit. A firm believer in women's capabilities and devoted to numerous causes affecting women, she publicized certain issues through press conferences and the daily newspaper columns she wrote for years. As First Lady, Eleanor Roosevelt's greatest contribution may have been the direct access to the president she provided for women activists. As Molly Dewson recalled, "When I wanted help on some definite point, Mrs. Roosevelt gave me the opportunity to sit by the President at dinner and the matter was settled before we finished our soup."[4]

Despite her privileged and isolated upbringing in a prominent New York family, Eleanor Roosevelt developed a social conscience and bonafide credentials as a reformer. Through her work with the Women's City Club of New York and several settlement houses, Eleanor observed firsthand urban poverty and unfit working conditions. From the National Consumers League and the League of Women Voters she learned about practical politics. No dilettante, she became friends and colleagues with the premier women reformers in the nation, including Lillian Wald of the Henry Street Settlement, Greenwich House's Mary Simkhovitch, National Consumers League president Florence Kelley, and Rose Schneiderman of the Women's Trade Union League. By the time of her husband's election to the presidency, Eleanor Roosevelt had become an eminent advocate of social reform, and she unhesitatingly used her newly acquired influence to bring other such women into the New Deal.

Almost as highly visible as the First Lady, Secretary of Labor Frances Perkins brought comparable reform credentials to her Washington post. An ardent suffragist and settlement house worker, she served on the New York commission to examine factory conditions after the tragic Triangle shirtwaist factory fire that killed 146 female garment workers in 1911. As a consequence of that experience, she initiated a lifelong crusade to improve working conditions that eventually led to her cabinet appointment. Always quick to deny that she was a feminist, Perkins opposed the Equal Rights Amendment because of her fear that it would endanger such special programs for women as maternity aid and mothers' pensions. Instead, she backed legislation to improve working conditions for men and women equally. Behind the scenes, however, she unobtrusively aided women's causes. Most important, she brought several talented women into Labor Department jobs and worked for social reform in conjunction with other women New Dealers.

Less well known than either the First Lady or the secretary of labor, Mary "Molly" Dewson was the driving force behind the women's network. A veteran of the women's suffrage movement and member of the National Consumers League, Dewson worked diligently to attain additional opportunities for women in public life. Through her work for the Democratic party in the 1920s, she became a close friend of both Franklin and Eleanor Roosevelt. The president especially valued her candor and willingness to vie with the party's crustier politicians. It was Dewson, and not Eleanor Roosevelt as many people supposed, who managed the nationwide campaign for the appointment of a female cabinet member. Dewson championed Frances Perkins's candidacy to the president, just as she would do for many other women appointment-seekers during the 1930s.

Franklin Roosevelt chose Dewson to revitalize the Women's Division of the Democratic National Committee, a task she performed with consummate skill. Under Dewson's leadership, the Women's Division dispatched some eighty thousand volunteers to proclaim the New Deal's achievements. She introduced the Reporter Plan, whereby county Democratic organizations assigned women to serve as reporters for each New Deal agency and chronicle their accomplishments to the local electorate. The Women's Division supplied 90 percent of the Democratic National Committee's campaign literature in the 1936 election at an estimated savings of one million dollars over the 1932 expenditure. It also published *Democratic Digest,* a monthly periodical that boasted a peak circulation of 26,500 in 1938. Dewson set as one of her principal goals increased participation of women in Democratic party affairs, and although her efforts were only partially successful, she could claim more women serving on party committees and more female representation at national meetings. By the late 1930s, she noted proudly, 17 state Democratic organizations had equal numbers of men and women on all party committees.

Dewson viewed politics as an exercise in education, and her emphasis left an indelible stamp on the Democrats' Women's Division. Leaving the job of mobilizing the big-city bosses and party faithful to Jim Farley and Louis Howe, Dewson sought to inform independent voters about the Roosevelt administration's accomplishments. In the process, she hoped to recruit women by convincing them of the New Deal's relevance to their lives; issues like social justice, safety in the workplace, and economic opportunity, she argued, should have a special appeal to women voters. As Dewson's biographer, Susan Ware, has noted, "The issue-oriented approach to politics, which Dewson mastered, has characterized women's political participation ever since."[5]

Ellen Sullivan Woodward, the fourth key member of the women's network, served as the Federal Emergency Relief Administration's director of women's work from 1933 to 1935, then directed all of the Works Progress Administration's nonconstruction programs. In that capacity she supervised all the WPA's arts and professional projects and those undertakings designated specifically for women. Uniquely well prepared by her earlier career in public affairs, Woodward had been elected to the state legislature in her native Mississippi and came to Washington with considerable political savvy. She bore the responsibility for administering programs aiding approximately 460,000 women, nearly one-fifth of all relief recipients, and used her influence to urge that the sexes receive equal pay for equal work. Like the other network members, Woodward never achieved parity for women in her purview but won better treatment for them in relief and work relief agencies.[6]

The activities of this network in the capital and the elevation of a few notable women to high-level government positions made women appear to be active participants in the New Deal. Certainly, women of talent and ambition enjoyed greater opportunity than ever before for public service in Washington, D.C., and elsewhere. The New Deal's impact on the majority of women at the grass-roots level remains much more difficult to assess, however. The successes of individuals like Frances Perkins, Ellen Sullivan Woodward, and others—uplifting though they may have been for women long starved for role models—had relatively few consequences for the many women seeking melioration from depression conditions. The New Deal compiled a mixed record on the provision of relief to unemployed women, just as its social programs produced an ambiguous legacy. As a result, the Roosevelt administration's impact on the American work force and on gender roles left women ambivalent.

The only New Deal agency specifically excluding women was the Civilian Conservation Corps (CCC), which employed 2.5 million men to perform conservation tasks in the countryside. In response to criticism about the preclusion of women, the Federal Emergency Relief Administration (FERA) created a modest program for females (dubbed the "she-she-she") in 1934 that initially included 28 camps. At its peak in 1935 the program operated 45 camps for eighty-five hundred women. With the dissolution of the FERA, it moved briefly to the National Youth Administration (NYA); in 1937 Congress discontinued funding altogether. During the brief life of the experiment, which had in common with the CCC only its rural venues, women performed no physical labor and received no wages. The CCC's military trappings and rugged outdoor imagery never seemed appropriate for the societal role most Americans ascribed to women.

As the cornerstone of the New Deal's recovery plan, the National Industrial Recovery Act (NIRA) affected American women on a much grander scale. The agency's Women's Section attempted little more than urging housewives to buy only at stores displaying the blue eagle, but National Recovery Administration (NRA) codes regulated the activities of four million women workers (about half the total in the labor force). Because NRA codes overlooked a number of female-dominated occupations, many women found themselves excluded from the improved wages-and-hours provisions. And since women had long earned less than men, they stood to gain more when government imposed even a 25-cents-an-hour minimum. Moreover, about one-fourth of the codes paid women less than men for the same work—a practice the NRA justified with reference to "long established customs." Women complained heatedly about such pay differentials, which ranged from 5 cents to 25 cents per hour, but the practice continued. The Fair Labor Standards Act of 1938 allowed the Department of Labor, which administered the law, to establish different wage minimums and hour maximums for the sexes. The Social Security Act produced some notable gains specifically for women, such as aid to mothers with dependent children and maternal aid, but excluded great numbers of farm workers from coverage. More alarming, it exempted the great majority of women who worked in the home but could not claim to be a part of the labor force. The NRA, Social Security Act, and FLSA all omitted the millions of domestic workers from coverage. Women protested the deficiencies in these laws but also recognized the significant improvements in many workers' lives they made possible.

Unemployment remained the greatest concern for both women and men, and again New Deal programs yielded mixed results. Women received only about 12 percent of the jobs created by the FERA and only 7 percent by the Civil Works Administration (CWA). Both agencies paid men approximately one dollar per hour for construction work, an opportunity that women lacked. Instead, they found themselves assigned "women's work" at 30 to 40 cents per hour. In addition to work-relief projects, the FERA operated worker education camps for young women. Camp residents learned such housekeeping skills as cooking and cleaning, which, according to project director Hilda Worthington Smith, would prepare them for their later marital duties. The more generously endowed WPA affected many more women. An average of 300,000 women worked for the agency at various times, as many as 405,000 in 1938. At a time when women constituted 24 percent of the work force, the inclusion of women on WPA payrolls peaked at 19 percent. Additional problems existed. Because the WPA limited employment to one person per family and assumed the male to be the principal breadwinner, a woman could not be certified unless she could prove herself the economic head of a household. During winter months when husbands could not work outside, wives could not obtain positions with indoor projects because their spouses were still considered household heads. If WPA officials termed a woman's husband undeserving, that is, physically able to work but refusing to do so, she could not be employed either. And like its predecessors, the FERA and CWA, the WPA paid women lower wages.

Women often prospered in the WPA special projects under the direction of Ellen Sullivan Woodward. Only about one-seventh of the musicians hired by the Federal Music Project were women, but this proved the exception for these projects rather than the rule. Women constituted 41 percent of the enrollees in the Federal Arts Project, which hired such talented young artists as Lee Krassner, Alice Neel, and Louise Nevelson. During Hallie Flanagan's administration, the Federal Theatre Project employed hundreds of actresses and behind-the-scenes workers. Under the auspices of the Federal Writers Project, Katherine Kellock supervised the writing, editing, and publication of the WPA state guidebooks. Women also worked in great numbers in the Historical Records Survey and in local endeavors to rationalize city record keeping.

The WPA assigned the vast majority of its female employees to menial household work, however, a source of real concern to women who decried the lack of preparation they received for more remunerative work after the depression. In 1936 the WPA employed nearly three hundred thousand women in nine thousand sewing rooms, not only providing "suitable" work for women but also apparel that could be given free to indigents. By October 1937, WPA workers had distributed 122 million free articles of clothing to the needy. A WPA official noted that "for unskilled men we have the shovel. For unskilled women we have only the needle." In addition, many women worked in canning projects, school lunchrooms, mattress factories, bookbinderies, libraries, and public health services. The WPA often set up temporary schools to instruct black women to be maids, cooks, dishwashers, and laundresses, then worked with the U.S. Employment Service to find them jobs. Eventually fifteen thousand women between the ages of 18 and 25 enrolled in the Household Workers' Training Program in 17 states and the District of Columbia, 93 percent of whom were black. WPA offices in Louisiana and Mississippi assigned no white women to the housekeeping aide project. In Memphis maid trainees, working beneath a banner proclaiming that "dishwashing is an ancient art but few are proficient at it," received instruction, according to a local newspaper, "that goes to make a well-rounded servant." Responding to the charge that sewing rooms might reduce the number of women available for domestic service, Woodward ordered many sewing projects to devote the last hour of every workday to domestic training. Thus, when the demand for household servants returned, an adequate supply of maids would be ready. WPA training programs and employment opportunities reinforced traditional ideas about women's work.[7]

Married women workers often found themselves the brunt of severe criticism for two reasons—taking work away from males responsible for supporting their families and failing to satisfy a woman's traditional role in the home as mother and housekeeper. Prior to its repeal in 1937, Section 213 of the 1932 National Economy Act prohibited employment of both spouses by the federal government. Since men invariably earned higher wages, women usually resigned if their husbands obtained work. During the five years Section 213 existed, the federal government discharged sixteen hundred married female employees. Twenty-six states also adopted comparable statutes affecting millions of married women.

In private enterprise the same policy prevailed. Such companies as the Northern Pacific Railroad and the New England Telephone and Telegraph Company dismissed married women, beginning as early as January 1931. A National Education Association survey of fifteen hundred cities revealed that 77 percent of school districts refused to hire married women applying for teaching positions and 63 percent dismissed women instructors if they married. At decade's end, according to a National Industrial Conference Board study, 84 percent of insurance companies, 65 percent of banks, and 63 percent of public utilities observed certain restrictions on the employment of married women.

Societal pressures reinforcing traditional women's roles, often reflected in husbands' disapproval, also operated to keep women in the home. While the dearth of attractive jobs often discouraged women from entering the labor market, for many the unceasing demands of family life were overwhelming. Guilt over providing inadequate housecleaning and child care proved daunting hurdles for many potential working women. And, as historian Winifred Wandersee has hypothesized, "the emergence of the companionship marriage as the middle-class ideal may have caused many women to have a positive perception of their marital status. Most married women looked to the family for their psychological satisfaction and simply did not see work as a means of improving their personal status." Some partners opted for "depression divorce," whereby husband and wife ended their marriage so they both could be employed, and the incidence of desertion, the "poor man's divorce," rose during the 1930s. But for most women the strength of family ties remained paramount.[8]

Despite the powerful forces operating to keep women at home, the number of women in the labor force increased by two million (from 24.3% to 25.4%) during the 1930s and the number of married women by a remarkable 50 percent. This apparent anomaly resulted from the rigid segmentation of private employment into men's and women's work, so that the decline of the former did not necessarily occur also with the latter. The contraction of such industries as coal mining, construction, and manufacturing sent men into the streets looking for work but had little impact on women. Less affected by the economic downturn, clerical work, domestic and personal service, and nursing, among other jobs traditionally held by women, provided greater security. Even though industrial production ebbed, paperwork proliferated during the depression. As a result, clerical work was the fastest-growing sector of the labor force, resulting in a 25 percent increase in the number of female workers from 1930 to 1940. Moreover, the stigma attached to such pink-collar occupations kept men from taking them away from women. Ironically, the stereotyping of women's work gave females a substantial amount of protection, but only if they agreed to accept low-status jobs paying meager wages. Regardless of cost, the feminization of the American labor force, a trend ongoing throughout the twentieth century, continued unabated in the dismal 1930s.

Black women experienced decidedly different changes during the depression years. Their dire socioeconomic situations had long forced many black women to work outside the home; in 1930 approximately two-fifths of black married women, as compared to less than 10 percent of their white counterparts, did so. Depression exigencies led many white women to accept household employment, an area of work previously held almost exclusively by black women. This displacement visited new hardships on black families, for at a time when two incomes became necessary for survival, the percentage of married black women in the labor force decreased from 43.3 in 1930 to 37.8 in 1940. For the decade black female employment declined 12.7 percent. Moreover, black women continued to receive the least desirable jobs. Barred from working in sewing rooms and canneries, they often found landscaping and construction jobs entailing strenuous physical labor the only positions available to them.

Although the New Deal contributed to the growth of organized labor during the 1930s, the unions' growing influence in American life aided women less than men. The NIRA's Section

7(a), the Wagner Act, and the FLSA bettered the lot of all workers to some degree, as wages rose and government mandated more and better programs for employees. From 1929 to 1939 female membership in unions tripled to an estimated eight hundred thousand, but great numbers remained unorganized. With few exceptions, union hierarchies continued to be all-male bastions, and women seldom achieved much recognition. Even the International Ladies Garment Workers Union and the Amalgamated Clothing Workers Union, both of which had predominantly female memberships, maintained male leadership with only token representation for women on governing boards. The unions persisted in accepting contracts with favorable provisions for male members, often to the detriment of the generally tiny female membership. Overall, women found the American Federation of Labor (AFL) leadership more culpable in that regard, whereas the Congress of Industrial Organizations (CIO) seemed more committed to the recruitment of women workers, especially after 1937 when the CIO strongly endorsed a minimum wage tied to job rather than gender.

Feminists in the 1930s criticized labor's campaigns for legislation protecting women in the workplace, accusing it of "wearing a mask of altruism." Demanding that women work only in pristine environments, these critics charged, allowed union leaders to pilfer their jobs under the guise of chivalry. Protective legislation, they concluded, both demeaned women and limited their employment opportunities. Moreover, ardent feminists inveighed against the social reforms championed by members of the New Deal women's network for essentially the same reasons. The National Woman's Party (NWP), the decade's foremost feminist organization, criticized Labor Secretary Frances Perkins for her support of gender-specific reform legislation and lamented the fact that Franklin Roosevelt was a "peninsula, almost completely surrounded by women who believe in protective labor legislation for women only." Members of the NWP expressed contradictory feelings about Eleanor Roosevelt, decrying her active participation in the women's network but applauding her independent life-style and outspoken defense of a woman's right to a career. Journalist and NWP member Ruby Black concluded that the First Lady "talks like a social worker and acts like a Feminist."[9]

Like so many of their peers, Eleanor Roosevelt and Frances

Perkins avidly opposed the Equal Rights Amendment. The NWP first introduced the ERA in Congress in 1923 and repeatedly thereafter for the next two decades. To the NWP membership support for the amendment was the true test of feminism, because it remained the only means of ensuring total equality for the sexes in the marketplace. In addition to influential women New Dealers, organizations like the League of Women Voters and the U.S. Women's Bureau opposed the ERA in fear that its passage would threaten many of the specific benefits already won for women and possibly even result in female conscription. The ERA's continued defeat throughout the 1930s symbolized for radical feminists the deficiencies in the entirely too timid Roosevelt administration. *Equal Rights,* the NWP's official journal, sadly editorialized that "the early New Deal work relief programs had done nothing for the 'forgotten woman,' except further to sacrifice her to the forgotten man."[10]

To the majority of women in the 1930s, however, the feminist critique of Roosevelt's initiatives seemed harsh. Interested more in relief than in constitutional assurances of equality, most women praised the WPA for the benefits it provided their families. If they rued the fact that one-fourth of NRA codes provided lower wages for women than men, they also applauded the fact that three-fourths did not. Further, they gloried in the enhanced status afforded women in government and Democratic party circles. No one could gainsay the solid increases in the number of women employed in civil service posts as well as in more glamorous upper-level appointments. On the debit side of the ledger, the differential in wage rates for the sexes altered little because of New Deal influence. The Social Security Administration reported in 1937 that men's annual income remained almost twice as much as women's, $1,027 to $525. New Deal programs frequently discriminated in favor of males and discouraged women from working in occupations where they might compete with men.

The Great Depression contributed to the continuing growth of the female labor force and reinforced the trend toward older, married women workers; New Deal work relief programs, though frequently biased in favor of men in hiring and wage policies, failed to arrest this development. The women who served in the New Deal, the veterans of many social reform battles, born in the late nineteenth century and closing their public careers with service in Washington in the 1930s, pressed for expanded opportunities for women within the larger context of societal improvement. They acquiesced in the operation of New Deal agencies that shunted women into low-status occupations and ratified traditional views of female labor. Saving the choicest white collar jobs for men, New Deal administrators assumed that the restoration of economic prosperity would allow women to return to their natural state of domesticity. As in so many other areas of American life, the New Deal intended to break no new paths as much as it sought the return of normal conditions.

New Deal social programs, which frequently reflected sexist societal norms, aided women not as a special group but as a large contingent of Americans suffering in the depression. Just as much as men, women benefited from home-owner loans, rural electrification, agricultural resettlement programs, federally funded relief, and wages-and-hours standards. They profited from New Deal largess as individuals and as housewives concerned with the well-being of both husbands and children. Historian Martha Swain observed: "It may be true that the economic progress of women in the 1930s was not translated into permanent gains, but the community services of the Women's and Professional Projects were institutionalized. Federal, state, and local governments continued hot school lunches, nursery schools for low income groups, library extension, historic preservation, and delivery systems for social services." Historian Susan Ware concluded that "the most long-lasting legacy of the New Deal for women may be the founding of the modern welfare state, which has improved women's lives along with men's." As women's participation in the labor force continued to increase in the twentieth century, this safety net woven by the New Deal assumed greater significance for more and more women. Roosevelt's administration failed by feminist standards, and men continued to enjoy privileged status in a society where women's "place" remained the home. The best that could be said for women was that their lives improved insofar as New Deal reforms improved the quality of life for all people.[11]

CHAPTER ELEVEN

The New Deal and Urban America

Observers of American cities in the 1930s were understandably dismayed by the starkly visible signs of depression at every turn. Visitors arriving by train disembarked alongside hoboes, who warmed themselves by fires and sought shelter in makeshift quarters in or near the switchyards. In other vacant lots throughout the cities, ramshackle Hoovervilles blighted the landscape. Hundreds queued up in breadlines, in front of soup kitchens, and before unemployment offices. The hungry combed through garbage dumps and congregated outside restaurants and hospitals, hoping for scraps and only partially spoiled food. Panhandlers and beggars, once few in number and confined to certain low-rent neighborhoods, descended on central business districts where greater opportunities for handouts existed. Boston authorities reported that men with self-inflicted wounds sought refuge from the cold in hospitals and jails. Even those people fortunate enough to retain jobs, homes, and financial security saw around themselves the unmistakable reminders of the city's worsening condition. As one Chicagoan wrote movingly of the city's plight, "You can ride across the lovely Michigan Avenue bridge at midnight" with "the lights all about making a dream city of incomparable beauty, while twenty feet below you, on the lower level of the same bridge, are 2,000 homeless, decrepit, shivering and starving men, wrapping themselves in old newspapers to keep from freezing, and lying down in the manure dust to sleep."[1]

Rising unemployment rates and a quickening pace of business failures led inevitably to tragic consequences. Jobless men and women missing too many mortgage payments lost their homes to financially threatened banks and lending agencies forced to collect debts. In 1932 alone, 273,000 people lost their homes; the following year foreclosures occurred at the rate of one thousand names daily. Penniless apartment renters often learned of their evictions by finding their furniture and other possessions piled high on the sidewalks. Municipal payrolls dwindled by necessity as city coffers emptied. Initially, many cities trimmed the salaries of municipal workers (by an average of 25% in Cleveland, for example) and required charity contributions from employees, but all too often they had to lay off policemen, firemen, schoolteachers, and other civil servants. Because state constitutions and city charters mandated balanced budgets, municipal government found no recourse but to reduce dramatically the level of services it could provide the citizenry.

With fewer and fewer people receiving paychecks, the taxes paid city governments decreased accordingly. Declining property values posed part of the problem—the assessed valuation of real property in the nation's largest cities fell nearly 18 percent from 1929 to 1933—but tax delinquency accounted for a greater portion of the shortfall. In 1930 the 145 largest American cities reported 11 percent of local taxes unpaid; three years later the same cities failed to collect over 25 percent of their levies. In Chicago embattled home owners conducted a highly organized and very effective tax strike, and when Mayor Edward J. Kelly assumed office there in 1933 the tax delinquency lists filled 260 newspaper pages. Unfortunately, this decline in revenue exacerbated an already hazardous situation, because many cities entered the depression in financial crisis. Earlier in the century, especially during the buoyantly optimistic 1920s, the possibilities of urban expansion seemed boundless and cities invested well beyond their means. On the outer edges of cities and in adjacent suburbs, empty lots and unused sidewalks sprouting weeds provided testament to unrealistic expectations. Bond issues floated earlier came due in the 1930s and, unable to pay principal or interest, cities defaulted. Crushing financial burdens incurred in the past left cities doubly susceptible to capital shortages.

Already overextended, many cities met their financial obligations through a series of emergency schemes that were usually effective only for the short term and often of questionable legality. Some cities sold tax anticipation warrants to banks, predicated upon the future collection of unpaid levies. Others depleted their sinking funds (usually modest sums reserved for dire emergencies) and, as a result, municipal bond ratings plummeted. Many cities issued scrip to their employees, although the courts frequently disallowed this practice. By 1934 debt charges accounted for 78 percent of the Los Angeles budget, an indication of why that city and others found banks wary of lending them money. Powerless mayors avoided bankruptcy by going hat in hand to bankers asking for loans, an experience the chief executives found degrading. In Houston powerful bankers not only required budget cuts as prerequisites for loans but even stipulated which positions be eliminated and whose salaries be pared.

The lack of money became a cancer that ate away at the cityscape itself. Building virtually ceased, and slums spread into previously respectable areas. The construction of residential property declined by 95 percent from 1928 to 1933, while the amount spent annually on housing repairs fell from $55 million to $500,000. During the building boom of the 1920s in Chicago, over 40,000 dwelling units rose annually; in 1933 Windy City builders erected a total of 137 residential units. The lifeless construction industry presented an acute problem in the 1930s, because economists considered a building revival central to economic recovery. Unfortunately for cities, the inaccessibility of housing to so many people eliminated any chance that renewed construction would stimulate the economy.

While city officials overwhelmingly agreed about the problems confronting urban America, they differed widely in the solutions they favored. Daniel W. Hoan, Socialist mayor of Milwaukee, urged a "pay as you go" fiscal policy to safeguard the solvency of local governments. He recommended the approval of only those relief projects that could be financed without emptying the city treasury. Birmingham, Alabama, chief commissioner Jimmy Jones concurred, saying, "I am as much in favor of relief for the unemployables as anyone, but I am unwilling to continue this relief at the expense of bankrupting the City of Birmingham." Believing in the supreme importance of prudent spending, many local and state officials rejected greater relief expenditures no matter how harsh the conditions. As New

Jersey state budget commissioner John Reddan intoned: "I think we are being welfared to death. People brought up on the land of Daniel Boone and Buffalo Bill should not need coddling." Harold S. Buttenheim, the highly influential editor of *American City,* feared that too much activity by the federal government would turn "Uncle Sam" into "Boss Sam."[2]

On the other hand, many experts on municipal affairs strongly urged increased expenditures for relief and invited more federal government involvement. Dismissing his misgivings about excessive governmental authority, Buttenheim warned against "a blind retrenchment of public spending" when "we must collectively put into use enough currency and credit to restore" prosperity. Believing that local governments could preserve cities' autonomy, urban chief executives like Mayor Fiorello LaGuardia of New York City and City Manager C. A. Dykstra of Cincinnati ardently sought as much federal largess as they could attract. As depression conditions plumbed new depths by 1933, increasing numbers of embattled mayors across the nation clamored for aid from Washington. Concerned that wretched conditions might lead to violence, Chicago mayor Anton Cermak advised the U.S. House of Representatives Banking and Commerce Committee that "it would be cheaper for Congress to provide a loan . . . to the City of Chicago, than to pay for the services of Federal troops at a future date."[3]

Mayor Frank Murphy of Detroit took the lead in pleading the cities' case to the federal government. Murphy's efforts to help his constituents won him national acclaim, as did his eloquent and impassioned pleas for charity. He argued that balancing of the municipal ledger was "only an objective. It isn't a god, a sacred thing that is to be accomplished at all costs. It is not right to shatter living conditions and bring human beings to want and misery to achieve such an objective. . . . To sacrifice everything to balance the budget is fanaticism." At Murphy's invitation 26 big-city mayors met in 1932 and decided to ask the federal government to fund a five-billion-dollar public works program. Although unsuccessful in this venture, these petitioners helped form the United States Conference of Mayors (USCM) as a permanent urban lobby in the nation's capital. For the first time, a vehicle existed for the administrators of big cities (membership was limited to mayors of cities with populations of fifty thousand or more) to present their shared concerns to the president and Congress. In the 1930s, the USCM fought many losing battles but achieved some successes as well; in 1937–38, for example, the mayors' lobbying effort turned the tide in Congress against Senator James F. Byrnes's proposal that local government contribute at least 40 percent of WPA costs. As former city manager and New Dealer Louis Brownlow observed in the wake of such USCM activity, "It has been said that the Federal Government has discovered the cities; it is equally true that the cities have discovered the Federal Government."[4]

The mayors found only a marginally sympathetic ear in the White House. Franklin D. Roosevelt recognized the necessity of concentrating federal money in densely populated metropolitan areas, but he neither liked cities nor envisioned a New Deal–generated urban renaissance. Rexford Tugwell characterized the president as a "child of the country" who saw cities as nothing "other than a perhaps necessary nuisance." During the Hundred Days Roosevelt refused the USCM's request that the Reconstruction Finance Corporation (RFC) purchase tax delinquency and tax anticipation warrants to expand short-term credit. He explained that "the less the Federal Government has to do with running a municipality in this country the better off we are going to be in the days to come." Sounding an additional warning, Roosevelt argued, "If the Federal Government started to finance cities, it would give us some kind of obligation to see that they were run right."[5]

Guided by an abiding attachment to rural life, an interest in natural resource conservation, and an expertise in agriculture, Roosevelt favored "back-to-the-land" schemes for the treatment of urban industrial ills. He took special interest in the Civilian Conservation Corps and various programs to resettle the city's unemployed in nearby bucolic settings, heeding Henry Ford's famous remark, "We shall solve the problem of cities by leaving the city." To implement his designs Roosevelt chose Rexford Tugwell, who carefully outlined his approach: "My idea is to go just outside centers of population, pick up cheap land, build a whole community and entice people into it. Then back to the city and tear down whole slums and make parks of them."[6]

Tugwell foresaw a need for three thousand such planned greenbelt towns, but money existed for the construction of only three—Greenbelt, Maryland, outside Washington, D.C.; Greenhills, Ohio, outside Cincinnati; and Greendale, Wisconsin, outside Milwaukee. The National Industrial Recovery Act (NIRA) provided for the creation of one hundred subsistence homesteads near major cities, but they contributed little to the decentralization effort. Sprawling cities absorbed many of the homesteads, and in others inhabitants returned to the city when economic recovery ensued. Depopulation of the cities never occurred on a large scale, in part because of hardening congressional opposition in the late 1930s to Tugwell's "Communist towns." Moreover, as historian Paul Conkin notes, "the time and expense required in developing successful communities proved to be much above earlier expectations. In a period when quick results were demanded, the community idea soon appeared to be very impractical."[7]

While resettlement proved unwieldy, the New Deal aided cities through myriad programs infusing federal money for relief and public works. Federal funds made possible significant improvements in the infrastructures of hundreds of towns and cities, both through the construction of new facilities and the refurbishment of existing edifices. Public works programs not only provided emergency employment for the cities' unemployed, but also left countless brick-and-mortar achievements that served the cities for years thereafter. The Works Progress Administration (WPA) built 500,000 miles of streets, 500,000 sewerage connections, and 110,000 public buildings in American cities. In its most expensive project, the WPA built New York City's LaGuardia International Airport, spending over forty million dollars and employing at one time twenty-three thousand workers. In Chicago the WPA completed the 17-mile Outer Drive along Lake Michigan, including the Outer Drive Bridge over the Chicago River, and landscaped adjacent Lincoln Park. The WPA provided Cleveland a lakefront highway, Boston the Huntington Avenue Subway, and Kansas City the better part of its skyline.

The Public Works Administration (PWA) employed fewer workers, operated with a smaller budget, and, largely due to the caution of Harold L. Ickes, spent much less money than the WPA, but also left its mark on urban America. The list of its contributions includes New York City's Lincoln Tunnel and Triborough Bridge, Chicago's State Street Subway, Philadelphia's Thirtieth Street Railroad Station, a remodeled state capitol and new Tennessee Supreme Court Building in Nashville, and Oklahoma City's new civic center. Moreover, the PWA built hospitals, municipal buildings, port facilities, sewage systems, public housing, and 70 percent of the new schools erected between 1933 and 1939. The federal government allowed Baltimore to combine WPA and PWA grants (the only city so favored), which made possible a massive overhaul of the city's streets, bridges, sewers, and harbor. Despite recurring complaints about the inefficiency of the agency's "semicolon" boys, the PWA gave many downtowns a major face-lift.

Public works proved especially beneficial in southern cities, where urban development traditionally lagged behind. Historian David R. Goldfield noted of the New Deal era that "the federal government paid for the capital facilities in southern cities that northern cities had paid for themselves in earlier decades and on which they were still paying off the debt. The almost-free modernization received by southern cities would prove to be an important economic advantage in subsequent decades." Because of New Deal generosity, New Orleans restored the historic *Vieux Carre* around Jackson Square, built three new bridges over Orleans Canal, and constructed Charity Hospital (the nation's second-largest health care facility). In Memphis the WPA built the municipal zoo, and, in conjunction with the U.S. Army Corps of Engineers, the PWA completed Riverside Drive alongside the Mississippi River. Atlanta built Chandler Airport, Grady Memorial Hospital, and an extensive sewer system that became the largest WPA project in the South. Houston received funds for a new city hall and city-county hospital, Dallas its Museum of Natural History, and Birmingham a dam and industrial water supply system critical for iron and steel plants. The federally financed renovation of Key West, Florida, along with the construction of an overseas highway across the keys, converted that community from a bankrupt backwater to a thriving resort. Further, New Deal–sponsored malaria control projects, in which workers poured concrete into ditches and other low-lying mosquito-infested areas, virtually eradicated what had previously been a serious health hazard in the subtropical southern climate.[8]

The New Deal also affected urban development through its housing policies. The Home Owners Loan Corporation (HOLC), which refinanced loans at low interest with long-term notes, assumed one-sixth of urban mortgages and halved the number of foreclosures from 1933 to 1937. The Federal Housing Administration (FHA) insured loans made by private institutions, and by the adoption of the self-amortizing mortgage extended the length of the loans from 8–10 years to 20–30 years. It also reduced both the amount of down payments from approximately 50 percent to 10–20 percent and the subsequent amount of monthly payments. The Federal Savings and Loan Insurance Corporation, created along with the FHA in 1934, insured savings up to five thousand dollars in savings-and-loan and building-and-loan associations. Having generally eliminated the need for second mortgages and made first mortgages more accessible for potential home buyers, the FHA extended the possibility of ownership to many more people. (From 1934 to 1972, owing to the availability of FHA and Veterans Administration funds, the percentage of home owners in the American populace increased from 44 to 63.) Franklin Roosevelt saw home ownership as a cherished American goal, and these New Deal innovations aided the private construction industry by subsidizing low-density, single-family housing units. With the FHA unwilling to underwrite virtually any other types of dwelling units and limiting stipends for repair of existing structures, the agency encouraged new construction on the periphery and suburbanization. For Roosevelt, as well as the FHA, high-density multifamily dwellings offered few attractions.

For the one-third of the American people "ill-housed, ill-clad, ill-nourished," whose circumstances kept them from taking advantage of HOLC and FHA programs, the New Deal provided a limited number of low-rent units. In 1932 famed housing reformer Lawrence Veiller claimed that U.S. cities "have the worst slums in the civilized world." Nevertheless, spirited resistance to public housing came from the National Association of Real Estate Boards, the U.S. Chamber of Commerce, and banks and other lending institutions concerned about any competition for the private building industry. Public housing advocates cited studies in Cleveland and Boston that showed city services to be costlier in slum areas and argued that improved housing for the disadvantaged would enable them to rise out of poverty. Section 202(d) of the National Industrial Recovery Act provided for a Housing Division in the PWA and stimulated the creation of local housing authorities to apply for grants.[9]

"Housers" initially cheered PWA administrator Harold L. Ickes, long reputed to be an enthusiastic supporter of low-cost housing, but soon became critical of his maddening attention to detail and insistence upon meeting unrealistic standards. Of 533 applications to the PWA Housing Division for loans to finance limited-dividend corporations, Ickes approved only 18 and later rescinded 10. Other developments also militated against substantial building. In December 1934, Roosevelt diverted $110 million of the $150 million allocated for low-cost housing to relief, and in 1935 a U.S. district court ruled in *U.S.* v. *Certain Lands in the City of Louisville* that the federal government could not condemn private property to construct public housing. A later court decision overruled the *Louisville Lands* precedent and restored to Washington the power of eminent domain, but the litigation took additional time. By 1937 the PWA had launched construction of just 21,800 dwellings in 51 public housing projects, far short of expectations.

Disappointed housing reformers worked closely with New York Senator Robert F. Wagner and his aide, Leon F. Keyserling, to draft a new housing bill. In 1935 and 1936 their efforts failed in Congress, largely due to the lack of support from the White House. Admitting his lack of interest in public housing, Roosevelt flippantly told a visiting delegation from the International Housing Study Commission his solution for clearing slums from New York City's Lower East Side: "You don't need money and laws; just burn it down." According to housing expert Ernest Bohn, "the President could not get interested in tearing down a few slums in a few cities. If FDR wanted to lend his support to public housing a bill could have passed in 1935." In 1937 Roosevelt finally provided a tepid endorsement, and the Wagner-Steagall Act creating the United States Housing Authority (USHA) became law. Congress empowered the USHA to extend 60-year loans at 3 percent interest to local housing authorities for up to 90 percent of a project's cost and to underwrite the cost of construction and maintenance. Such generous conditions quickened the tempo of activity; within a year 221 communities established housing authorities and by 1941 the USHA had sponsored 130,000 new units in over three hundred projects nationwide. Yet the Wagner-Steagall Act represented at best a limited commitment to public housing. The law authorized $500 million in loans and $60 million in subsidies at a time when experts estimated a cost of $2.5 billion just to demolish tenements in

New York City alone. Reformers saw the 1937 law as a modest beginning.[10]

For head of the fledgling USHA, Senator Wagner and the bulk of the housing experts supported the relatively unknown Nathan Straus. Born and raised in New York City, the heir to the Macy's department store fortune, son of a world-renowned Zionist-philanthropist, Straus had served three terms in the New York State Senate in the 1920s, where he and Wagner worked unsuccessfully for minimum-wage and maximum-hours legislation. At the outset of his 1928 gubernatorial campaign, Franklin Roosevelt chose Straus for lieutenant governor but later switched to Herbert Lehman at Al Smith's suggestion. Straus remained close to Roosevelt, however, providing generous campaign contributions and later accepting the president's offer to become NRA director for New York State. Straus had developed an interest in housing and with RFC loans built Hillside Homes in the Bronx, one of the few successful limited-dividend endeavors of the Hoover years. Hoping to control the new agency, Ickes suggested one of his PWA subordinates to administer the USHA. Roosevelt honored Wagner's request that Straus administer the USHA, however, and agreed that he report directly to the White House and not to Ickes. Straus and the USHA enjoyed virtual autonomy.

True to his convictions, Straus battled real estate interests, congressional critics, and others interested in housing who held conflicting views throughout his stormy five-year tenure. Like such housing experts as Catherine Bauer, Henry Wright, and Lewis Mumford, Straus urged that the construction of public housing take precedence over slum clearance, so that the interests of the poor supersede those of profit-minded builders and developers. Opposing the pressure for downtown slum clearance exclusively, Straus advocated the construction of low-rent housing on vacant land scattered throughout the metropolitan area and slum clearance only after uprooted families had been provided substitute lodging. As a result, he often ignored a clause in the Wagner-Steagall Act stipulating that every project must result in the demolition, condemnation, or repair of a number of dwellings roughly equal to the number constructed; by 1941 the USHA had erected approximately one hundred thousand new dwellings but destroyed fewer than seventy thousand.

Straus admitted that the USHA constructed roughly one-third of its projects on land not located in central city slum sites. Indeed, the USHA's penchant for choosing building sites in relatively cheap vacant lots far from downtown sparked vigorous protest from private enterprise.

The increasingly controversial Straus also failed to establish good relations with Congress, a vital necessity since the USHA depended upon funding approval from Capitol Hill at regular intervals. In 1938 Congress raised its contribution level to the USHA but refused to vote any additional appropriations during the remainder of Straus's tenure. In 1940 Congress passed the Lanham Defense Housing Act, an omnibus measure calling for the construction of nearly seven hundred thousand units from 1941 to 1944 but specifying that these units be disposed of after the wartime emergency passed. Further, it failed to mention the USHA and specifically forbade subsidized housing for persons of low income. Faced with what he considered to be the irrevocable demise of the USHA, Straus bitterly criticized public housing's opponents in Congress and the federal bureaucracy. On January 5, 1942, he resigned.

For the duration of the Second World War "demountable" housing, rather than any permanent form, predominated so that real estate interests would face no competition from government after the conflict. Straus and his reformist constituency, who saw decent low-cost housing as part of a comprehensive reform program, learned that the New Deal was a much more cautious and modest assault on existing institutions than they hoped. Straus proved to be an ineffective administrator whose recalcitrance poisoned relations with an already unsympathetic Congress, yet it seems doubtful that anyone else could have done better against the powerful real estate interests and deeply ingrained preference of Americans for individual home ownership. USHA efforts resulted in the demolition of dilapidated housing and replacement with superior dwellings on a relatively small scale. Because applicants for public housing needed to be employed and earning monthly incomes six times the amount of the monthly rent they would pay, the lower middle class qualified and the poor did not. A Charleston, South Carolina, newspaper editor remarked dryly that only "negro economic royalists" could afford public housing rents. The New Deal demonstrated that a local-federal partnership could provide low-rent housing, but continually fell far short of generating an adequate amount.[11]

Even if Washington had made available many more dollars for low-cost housing, the impetus for additional construction rested with local housing authorities. As with other New Deal experiments, local control tempered the expanded federal presence. To be sure, the federal-city relationship became much closer, often at the expense of state governments. The cities began to look to Washington for information, inspiration, additional services, and, most important, new funding sources. Nevertheless, the cities jealously guarded their prerogatives and refused to surrender autonomy in exchange for federal perquisites. Local politicians and elected leaders, who frequently clashed with hostile governors and rural-dominated state legislatures, welcomed federal assistance but insisted on exercising power in their own bailiwicks. By and large, they succeeded.

At first many local politicians, Democrats as well as Republicans, feared that New Deal programs would undermine their control of city hall. In Pittsburgh, for example, Mayor William McNair refused a $24 million PWA project and only belatedly dropped his opposition to any WPA projects in his city. When McNair resigned in 1936, his successor, Cornelius Scully, opened the city's treasury to all available federal funds. Fearing that acceptance of WPA funds would require federal supervision and thereby decrease the chances of politically connected contractors receiving bids, the Davidson County (Nashville, Tennessee) highway commission refused a $236,000 grant. Only after being assured that federal dollars came with few—if any—strings attached did some local leaders fully welcome the New Deal.

Even those mayors unsympathetic to increased relief appropriations and expanded federal involvement went along because of the political capital to be gained with their constituents. In countless cities municipal leaders pledged their fealty to Roosevelt and the New Deal for practical, and sometimes partisan, but not always ideological reasons. Alliances between big-city Democratic machines and the Roosevelt administration could serve both parties. Mindful of the precariousness of a national party allying labor, blacks, the big cities' polyglot masses, and a conservative South, the president carefully cultivated the support of urban bosses while overlooking their deviations from official policies. Liberal backers of Roosevelt and the New Deal had difficulty reconciling support for the president from such unsavory bosses as Kansas City's Tom Pendergast, Jersey City's Frank Hague, and Boston's James Michael Curley. But Roosevelt, always a cold-blooded realist, saw in these powerful Democrats a source of votes that he could not spurn for reasons of ideological purity. As long as they delivered their precincts and kept their criminal activities to an acceptable limit, such disreputable politicos remained in the president's good graces.

Roosevelt's willingness to do business with big-city bosses obviated many of the tenets of the Last Hurrah thesis, which attempted to explain the demise of big-city political machines. Based upon Edwin O'Connor's best-selling novel, *The Last Hurrah,* this thesis suggested that the New Deal destroyed urban political machines by terminating the dependence of the poor upon city hall and substituting federal suzerainty. The new network of services created by the New Deal supposedly rendered obsolete the unofficial social welfare functions performed by the political machines. The collapse of many such machines in the 1930s—some directly as a result of hostile action initiated by the Roosevelt administration—seemed to lend credence to the Last Hurrah thesis. But, as historian Lyle W. Dorsett has shown, Roosevelt undercut Tom Pendergast and James Michael Curley simply because their machines' corruption reached unacceptable proportions, and the president cast his lot with their politically ascendant rivals. The welfare state spared—indeed aided—bosses who remained locally viable. Dorsett notes that "under the New Deal many welfare programs were financed in Washington, but they were *directed* at the local level." When in good favor with Roosevelt, Pendergast controlled 200,000 federal jobs, Curley 100,000 jobs, and Chicago mayor Edward J. Kelly 40,000 WPA jobs alone. Tammany Hall, the New York City Democratic machine with which Roosevelt feuded in his early political career, survived into the 1960s, and the Chicago Democratic machine, which formed during the depression decade, remained viable into the 1980s. In short, any generalization positing the New Deal's lethal effects on urban bosses and machines collapses upon closer scrutiny.[12]

The political situation in Chicago provided a perfect example of Roosevelt's tolerance of bossism. Mayor Edward J. Kelly endlessly praised the New Deal, often campaigning under the slogan,

Roosevelt Is My Religion. Kelly cultivated a good relationship with Harry Hopkins, Jim Farley, and other key bureaucrats in addition to the president, and clearly reaped rewards for his efforts. The primary contribution of the New Deal to the nascent Democratic organization lay in the financial windfall it provided during the threadbare depression years. The city saved its own slender resources and spent great sums of federal money for the support of the indigent and unemployed. With this capital, neither patronage nor city services needed to be reduced. At a time when the gravest threat to the Democratic machine came from financial disaster rather than from a robust Republican opposition, New Deal largess assured Chicago's solvency. In 1936 Roosevelt carried Chicago by over five hundred thousand votes, and both parties to the alliance remained totally satisfied.

In Pittsburgh the New Deal catalyzed the formation of a Democratic machine that supplanted a Republican organization. "For Pittsburgh's Republicans the advent of the New Deal signified 'the Last Hurrah,'" wrote historian Bruce Stave, "for the city's Democrats it sounded 'the First Hallelujah.'" David Lawrence, boss of the city's Democrats from the 1930s to the 1960s, worked to unseat Mayor William McNair and replace him with a more reliable organization Democrat. In subsequent years Mayor Lawrence and other New Deal veterans cemented ties between the Democratic machine and the city's business elite, resulting in the downtown renewal and smoke abatement projects constituting the "Pittsburgh Renaissance." New Deal labor reforms, so critical in iron-and-steel-dominated Pittsburgh, also served to bolster the emerging Democracy.[13]

In Memphis, Tennessee, one of the few southern cities in which political machines operated, a tenuous alliance existed between Boss Edward H. Crump and the president. Crump averred that "Roosevelt . . . has done more for the South than any president—aid to the farmers, public works, TVA." The boss clashed with Roosevelt on occasion, particularly when he thought that New Deal measures threatened southern racial norms, but remained loyal because of the resources afforded his machine and the autonomy he enjoyed in presiding over their distribution. Shelby County, with roughly one-ninth of the state's population, received one-seventh of the WPA jobs. Over the years the combined enrollment of the FERA, CWA, WPA, and PWA brought thousands of jobs to Memphis—jobs that, though created and funded by the federal government, passed into the hands of needy Memphians through the good offices of the Crump organization. A 1938 congressional investigation unearthed clear evidence of electoral illegalities but, remarkably, the Senate committee took no action. Because of detailed newspaper coverage, Memphis's already sullied reputation, besmirched by reports of widespread gambling, prostitution, and violence, descended even further in the public esteem. Nevertheless, Roosevelt's New Deal still had room for the politically potent Crump machine.[14]

Likewise in New Orleans, Roosevelt demonstrated his willingness to associate with an infamous political machine—in fact, whichever machine appeared to hold the upper hand. Mayor T. Semmes Walmsley, standard-bearer for the Old Regular (Choctaw) Democratic machine, clashed with Governor Huey Long, whose drive for hegemony in Louisiana depended upon control of New Orleans. When the Long-dominated legislature cut state aid to its leading city, the federal government reduced its contributions to New Orleans and other cities in the Pelican State. Mayor Walmsley issued several plaintive appeals to the president, affirming his loyalty to the New Deal and arguing that he and his city were being unfairly punished for Long's indiscretions. Although Roosevelt had no affinity for the Kingfish, he refused to intervene on Walmsley's behalf. Many of the Choctaws defected to Long, and the remaining Old Regulars ostracized the mayor for his inability to govern effectively. Walmsley resigned in 1936, and the legatees of Long's organization chose Robert Maestri for mayor. In many ways more loathsome than Ed Crump, Maestri became embroiled in numerous scandals involving income tax delinquency, organized crime, and "hot oil" profiteering. He did, however, move with dispatch to mend fences with Roosevelt, and the resumption of federal dollars flowing to New Orleans indicated his success. In a struggle for control of New Orleans's Democratic leadership, Roosevelt resumed relations with the eventual winner, despite its connections with Huey Long and its sordid reputation.

Just as the president showed considerable forbearance in his associations with a variety of allies in state and national politics, so too did he usually suffer in silence his relations with big-city bosses. The New Deal worked through local city halls but, barring any potential political damage, exerted little influence over those who made policy in them. It seemed unlikely that Roosevelt would obtrude in the affairs of the cities that were becoming Democratic strongholds and, indeed, no heavy-handed federal intrusions altered the existing federalist system of local autonomy. As historian Richard Wade observed, "The New Deal might have produced a revolutionary rearrangement in formal governmental institutions and agencies, but it left most of the country's urban fabric intact." Or as Charles H. Trout noted about the impact of the New Deal in one city, "During the entire New Deal policies from Washington altered Boston, but just as surely Boston modified federal programs." If the New Deal altered American federalism by introducing new links between city halls and the federal government, it stopped well short of demanding the surrender of home rule.[15]

Roosevelt possessed no blueprint for federal involvement in the cities after the depression and, in fact, operated without an urban program in the 1930s. He reacted to vacillating unemployment figures and the blandishments of the suddenly aggressive big-city mayors. Historian Mark I. Gelfand has concluded that "his program was urban only in the sense that it assisted people who lived in cities: guarantees of collective bargaining for the organized; work relief for the jobless; public housing for the slum resident; judgeships for the immigrant blocs." Nevertheless, intended or not, New Deal policies produced significant consequences in later years for American cities. Principally, they contributed to the deconcentration of population in metropolitan areas that had been ongoing for decades. Rather than arrest centrifugal forces, the New Deal enhanced suburbanization in several ways.[16]

First, the New Deal altered the American housing market by making detached single-family homes more accessible to great numbers of middle- and working-class families. The HOLC introduced the long-term, self-amortizing mortgage, and the FHA insured such mortgage loans to make them available to even more people. Moreover, the Internal Revenue Service allowed home owners to deduct mortgage interest and property taxes from their federal income tax returns. Simply stated, the federal government made it cheaper to buy than rent. Because of the paucity of FHA loans for repairs to existing structures and the agency's clear preference for single-family units rather than multi-family dwellings, loans invariably went to residential neighborhoods far removed from the urban core.

Second, the New Deal enhanced the nation's automobility. In seven years during the 1930s, the number of motor registrations increased; from 1929 to 1940 the number of registered autos shot up by 4.5 million. Many emergency work projects entailed highway construction, thereby improving the flow of traffic in and out of cities' central business districts. As a result of federal dollars, civil engineers and local officials introduced several new innovations in automobile transit, including limited-access highways, divided expressways, and cloverleaf exchanges. Bridges designed to connect central cities with a sprawling hinterland, like the eight-mile San Francisco Oakland Bay Bridge, became economically practical with the addition of federal funds to state and local dollars. Mass transit may have experienced a brief increase in ridership during the depression because of relatively cheap fares, but the New Deal's subsidization of expressway construction paved the way for the automobiles' growing importance thereafter.

New Deal labor legislation, which reduced the workweek by as much as one-third in some industries and raised the laborer's disposable income, gave blue- and white-collar workers more time and money to spend on housing. With more leisure time for family activities and home improvements, many workers found commuting an increasingly attractive alternative. And as more and more people migrated outward, factories, retail outlets, department stores, and theaters followed.

While so many policies encouraged suburbanization, the New Deal also pioneered in attempting to serve citizens too poor to pay market rates for housing. Ironically, however, the 1937 Wagner-Steagall Act, ostensibly designed to improve inner city housing stock, underscored decentralization. Because local housing authorities decided where—and indeed whether—to build public housing, inner cities built racially segregated projects and suburbs usually built none at all. As a result, public housing projects invariably appeared in the bleakest sections of central cities. Public housing policies initiated in the 1930s and continued in subsequent decades concentrated the indigent in inner cities and contributed to suburbia's developing status as a haven for the wealthier classes.

In 1939 FHA official Seward H. Mott told an American Institute of Planners Convention that "decentralization is taking place. It is not a policy, it is a reality—and it is as impossible for us to change this trend as it is to change the desire of birds to migrate to a more suitable location." Indeed, the New Deal's policies toward large cities constituted not so much a radical departure as the reaffirmation of a clearly identifiable trend. The federal government's inadvertent support of suburbanization, ongoing for decades, dovetailed nicely with the attitudes and desires of most Americans. By promoting better automobile transportation, buttressing the house construction industry, providing a limited amount of low-cost dwellings within inner cities, and attempting unsuccessfully to resettle part of the urban population in greenbelt communities, the New Deal underscored the growth around central cities so dominant since the nineteenth century. By keeping hands off local housing authorities and city halls, it allowed cities and suburbs to continue to develop as they always had—as a result of the minimal interaction between private real estate interests and restrained local governments. Unlike European cities where community action and planned growth had played a much larger role, American cities represented the triumph of a privatist ethic whereby cities grew haphazardly as a result of thousands of independent economic decisions made by entrepreneurs. The New Deal imposed no order on urban growth, allowing Americans to continue their exodus toward the greener pastures of suburbia.[17]

Conclusion

At the close of the Hundred Days, Franklin D. Roosevelt said, "All of the proposals and all of the legislation since the fourth day of March have not been just a collection of haphazard schemes, but rather the orderly component parts of a connected and logical whole." Yet the president later described his approach quite differently. "Take a method and try it. If it fails admit it frankly and try another. But above all, try something." The impetus for New Deal legislation came from a variety of sources, and Roosevelt relied heavily at various times on an ideologically diverse group of aides and allies. His initiatives reflected the contributions of, among others, Robert Wagner, Rexford Tugwell, Raymond Moley, George Norris, Robert LaFollette, Henry Morgenthau, Marriner Eccles, Felix Frankfurter, Henry Wallace, Harry Hopkins, and Eleanor Roosevelt. An initial emphasis on recovery for agriculture and industry gave way within two years to a broader-based program for social reform; entente with the business community yielded to populist rhetoric and a more ambiguous economic program. Roosevelt suffered the opprobrium of both the conservatives, who vilified "that man" in the White House who was leading the country down the sordid road to socialism, and the radicals, who saw the Hyde Park aristocrat as a confidence man peddling piecemeal reform to forestall capitalism's demise. Out of so many contradictory and confusing circumstances, how does one make sense of the five years of legislative reform known as the New

Deal? And what has been its impact on a half century of American life?[1]

A better understanding begins with the recognition that little of the New Deal was new, including the use of federal power to effect change. Nor, for all of Roosevelt's famed willingness to experiment, did New Deal programs usually originate from vernal ideas. Governmental aid to increase farmers' income, propounded in the late nineteenth century by the Populists, surfaced in Woodrow Wilson's farm credit acts. The prolonged debates over McNary-Haugenism in the 1920s kept the issue alive, and Herbert Hoover's Agricultural Marketing Act set the stage for further federal involvement. Centralized economic planning, as embodied in the National Industrial Recovery Act, flowed directly from the experiences of Wilson's War Industries Board; not surprisingly, Roosevelt chose Hugh Johnson, a veteran of the board, to head the National Recovery Administration. Well established in England and Germany before the First World War, social insurance appeared in a handful of states—notably Wisconsin—before the federal government became involved. Similarly, New Deal labor reform took its cues from the path-breaking work of state legislatures. Virtually alone in its originality, compensatory fiscal policy seemed revolutionary in the 1930s. Significantly, however, Roosevelt embraced deficit spending quite late after other disappointing economic policies and never to the extent Keynesian economists advised. Congress and the public supported the New Deal, in part, because of its origins in successful initiatives attempted earlier under different conditions.

Innovative or not, the New Deal clearly failed to restore economic prosperity. As late as 1938 unemployment stood at 19.1 percent and two years later at 14.6 percent. Only the Second World War, which generated massive industrial production, put the majority of the American people back to work. To be sure, partial economic recovery occurred. From a high of 13 million unemployed in 1933, the number under Roosevelt's administration fell to 11.4 million in 1934, 10.6 million in 1935, and 9 million in 1936. Farm income and manufacturing wages also rose, and as limited as these achievements may seem in retrospect, they provided sustenance for millions of people and hope for many more. Yet Roosevelt's resistance to Keynesian formulas for pump priming placed immutable barriers in the way of recovery that only war could demolish. At a time calling for drastic inflationary methods, Roosevelt introduced programs effecting the opposite result. The NRA restricted production, elevated prices, and reduced purchasing power, all of which were deflationary in effect. The Social Security Act's payroll taxes took money from consumers and out of circulation. The federal government's $4.43 billion deficit in fiscal year 1936, impressive as it seemed, was not so much greater than Hoover's $2.6 billion shortfall during his last year in office. As economist Robert Lekachman noted, "The 'great spender' was in his heart a true descendant of thrifty Dutch Calvinist forebears." It is not certain that the application of Keynesian formulas would have sufficed by the mid-1930s to restore prosperity, but the president's cautious deflationary policies clearly retarded recovery.[2]

Although New Deal economic policies came up short in the 1930s, they implanted several "stabilizers" that have been more successful in averting another such depression. The Securities and Exchange Act of 1934 established government supervision of the stock market, and the Wheeler-Rayburn Act allowed the Securities and Exchange Commission to do the same with public utilities. Severely embroiled in controversy when adopted, these measures have become mainstays of the American financial system. The Glass-Steagall Banking Act forced the separation of commercial and investment banking and broadened the powers of the Federal Reserve Board to change interest rates and limit loans for speculation. The creation of the Federal Deposit Insurance Corporation (FDIC) increased government supervision of state banks and significantly lowered the number of bank failures. Such safeguards restored confidence in the discredited banking system and established a firm economic foundation that performed well for decades thereafter.

The New Deal was also responsible for numerous other notable changes in American life. Section 7(a) of the NIRA, the Wagner Act, and the Fair Labor Standards Act transformed the relationship between workers and business and breathed life into a troubled labor movement on the verge of total extinction. In the space of a decade government laws eliminated sweatshops, severely curtailed child labor, and established enforceable standards for hours, wages, and working conditions. Further, federal action eliminated the vast majority of company towns in such industries as coal mining. Although Robert Wagner and Frances Perkins dragged Roosevelt into labor's corner, the New

Deal made the unions a dynamic force in American society. Moreover, as Nelson Lichtenstein has noted, "by giving so much of the working class an institutional voice, the union movement provided one of the main political bulwarks of the Roosevelt Democratic party and became part of the social bedrock in which the New Deal welfare state was anchored."[3]

Roosevelt's avowed goal of "cradle-to-grave" security for the American people proved elusive, but his administration achieved unprecedented advances in the field of social welfare. In 1938 the president told Congress: "Government has a final responsibility for the well-being of its citizenship. If private co-operative endeavor fails to provide work for willing hands and relief for the unfortunate, those suffering hardship from no fault of their own have a right to call upon the Government for aid; and a government worthy of its name must make fitting response." The New Deal's safety net included low-cost housing; old-age pensions; unemployment insurance; and aid for dependent mothers and children, the disabled, the blind, and public health services. Sometimes disappointing because of limiting eligibility requirements and low benefit levels, these social welfare programs nevertheless firmly established the principle that the government had an obligation to assist the needy. As one scholar wrote of the New Deal, "More progress was made in public welfare and relief than in the three hundred years after this country was first settled."[4]

More and more government programs, inevitably resulting in an enlarged administrative apparatus and requiring additional revenue, added up to a much greater role for the national government in American life. Coming at a time when the only Washington bureaucracy most of the people encountered with any frequency was the U.S. Postal Service, the change seemed all the more remarkable. Although many New Deal programs were temporary emergency measures, others lingered long after the return of prosperity. Suddenly, the national government was supporting farmers, monitoring the economy, operating a welfare system, subsidizing housing, adjudicating labor disputes, managing natural resources, and providing electricity to a growing number of consumers. "What Roosevelt did in a period of a little over 12 years was to change the form of government," argued journalist Richard L. Strout. "Washington had been largely run by big business, by Wall Street. He brought the government to Washington." Not surprisingly, popular attitudes toward government also changed. No longer willing to accept economic deprivation and social dislocation as the vagaries of an uncertain existence, Americans tolerated—indeed, came to expect—the national government's involvement in the problems of everyday life. No longer did "government" mean just "city hall."[5]

The operation of the national government changed as well. For one thing, Roosevelt's strong leadership expanded presidential power, contributing to what historian Arthur Schlesinger, Jr., called the "imperial presidency." Whereas Americans had in previous years instinctively looked first to Capitol Hill, after Roosevelt the White House took center stage in Washington. At the same time, Congress and the president looked at the nation differently. Traditionally attentive only to one group (big business), policymakers in Washington began responding to other constituencies such as labor, farmers, the unemployed, the aged, and to a lesser extent, women, blacks, and other disadvantaged groups. This new "broker state" became more accessible and acted on a growing number of problems, but equity did not always result. The ablest, richest, and most experienced groups fared best during the New Deal. NRA codes favored big business, and AAA benefits aided large landholders; blacks received relief and government jobs but not to the extent their circumstances merited. The long-term result, according to historian John Braeman, has been "a balkanized political system in which private interests scramble, largely successfully, to harness governmental authority and/or draw upon the public treasury to advance their private agendas."[6]

Another legacy of the New Deal has been the Roosevelt revolution in politics. Urbanization and immigration changed the American electorate, and a new generation of voters who resided in the cities during the Great Depression opted for Franklin D. Roosevelt and his party. Before the 1930s the Democrats of the northern big-city machines and the solid South uneasily coexisted and surrendered primacy to the unified Republican party. The New Deal coalition that elected Roosevelt united behind common economic interests. Both urban northerners and rural southerners, as well as blacks, women, and ethnic immigrants, found common cause in government action to shield them from an economic system gone haywire. By the end of the decade the increasing importance of the urban North in the Democratic party had already become apparent. After the economy recovered from the disastrous depression, members of the Roosevelt coalition shared fewer compelling interests. Beginning in the 1960s, tensions mounted within the party as such issues as race, patriotism, and abortion loomed larger. Even so, the Roosevelt coalition retained enough commitment to New Deal principles to keep the Democrats the nation's majority party into the 1980s.[7]

Yet for all the alterations in politics, government, and the economy, the New Deal fell far short of a revolution. The two-party system survived intact, and neither fascism, which attracted so many followers in European states suffering from the same international depression, nor communism attracted much of a following in the United States. Vital government institutions functioned without interruption and if the balance of powers shifted, the national branches of government maintained an essential equilibrium. The economy remained capitalistic; free enterprise and private ownership, not socialism, emerged from the 1930s. A limited welfare state changed the meld of the public and private but left them separate. Roosevelt could be likened to the British conservative Edmund Burke, who advocated measured change to offset drastic alterations—"reform to preserve." The New Deal's great achievement was the application of just enough change to preserve the American political economy.

Indications of Roosevelt's restraint emerged from the very beginning of the New Deal. Rather than assume extraordinary executive powers as Abraham Lincoln had done in the 1861 crisis, the president called Congress into special session. Whatever changes ensued would come through normal governmental activity. Roosevelt declined to assume direct control of the economy, leaving the nation's resources in the hands of private enterprise. Resisting the blandishments of radicals calling for the nationalization of the banks, he provided the means for their rehabilitation and ignored the call for national health insurance and federal contributions to Social Security retirement benefits. The creation of such regulatory agencies as the SEC confirmed his intention to revitalize rather than remake economic institutions. Repeatedly during his presidency, Roosevelt responded to congressional pressure to enact bolder reforms, as in the case of the National Labor Relations Act, the Wagner-Steagall Housing Act, and the FDIC. The administration forwarded the NIRA only after Senator Hugo Black's recovery bill mandating 30-hour workweeks seemed on the verge of passage.

As impressive as New Deal relief and social welfare programs were, they never went as far as conditions demanded or many liberals recommended. Fluctuating congressional appropriations, oscillating economic conditions, and Roosevelt's own hesitancy to do too much violence to the federal budget left Harry Hopkins, Harold Ickes, and others only partially equipped to meet the staggering need. The president justified the creation of the costly WPA in 1935 by "ending this business of relief." Unskilled workers, who constituted the greatest number of WPA employees, obtained but 60 to 80 percent of the minimal family income as determined by the government. Roosevelt and Hopkins continued to emphasize work at less than existing wage scales so that the WPA or PWA never competed with free labor, and they allowed local authorities to modify pay rates. They also continued to make the critical distinction between the "deserving" and "undeserving" poor, making sure that government aided only the former. The New Deal never challenged the values underlying this distinction, instead seeking to provide for the growing number of "deserving" poor created by the Great Depression. Government assumed an expanded role in caring for the disadvantaged, but not at variance with existing societal norms regarding social welfare.

The New Deal effected no substantial redistribution of income. The Wealth Tax Act of 1935 (the famous soak-the-rich tax) produced scant revenue and affected very few taxpayers. Tax alterations in 1936 and 1937 imposed no additional burdens on the rich; the 1938 and 1939 tax laws actually removed a few. By the end of the 1930s less than 5 percent of Americans paid income taxes, and the share of taxes taken from personal and corporate income levies fell below the amount raised in the 1920s. The great change in American taxation policy came during World War II, when the number of income tax payers grew to 74 percent of the population. In 1942 Treasury Secretary Henry Morgenthau noted that "for the first time in our history, the income tax is becoming a people's tax." This the New Deal declined to do.[8]

Finally, the increased importance of the national government exerted remarkably little influence on local institutions. The New

Deal seldom dictated and almost always deferred to state and local governments—encouraging, cajoling, bargaining, and wheedling to bring parochial interests in line with national objectives. As Harry Hopkins discovered, governors and mayors angled to obtain as many federal dollars as possible for their constituents but with no strings attached. Community control and local autonomy, conditions thought to be central to American democracy, remained strong, and Roosevelt understood the need for firm ties with politicians at all levels. In his study of the New Deal's impact on federalism, James T. Patterson concludes: "For all the supposed power of the New Deal, it was unable to impose all its guidelines on the autonomous forty-eight states. . . . What could the Roosevelt administration have done to ensure a more profound and lasting impression on state policy and politics? Very little."[9]

Liberal New Dealers longed for more sweeping change and lamented their inability to goad the president into additional action. They envisioned a wholesale purge of the Democratic party and the creation of a new organization embodying fully the principles of liberalism. They could not abide Roosevelt's toleration of the political conservatives and unethical bosses who composed part of the New Deal coalition. They sought racial equality, constraints upon the southern landholding class, and federal intrusion to curb the power of urban real estate interests on behalf of the inveterate poor. Yet to do these things would be to attempt changes well beyond the desires of most Americans. People pursuing remunerative jobs and the economic security of the middle class approved of government aiding the victims of an unfortunate economic crisis but had no interest in an economic system that would limit opportunity. The fear that the New Deal would lead to such thoroughgoing change explains the seemingly irrational hatred of Roosevelt by the economic elite. But, as historian Barry Karl has noted, "it was characteristic of Roosevelt's presidency that he never went as far as his detractors feared or his followers hoped."[10]

The New Deal achieved much that was good and left much undone. Roosevelt's programs were defined by the confluence of forces that circumscribed his admittedly limited reform agenda—a hostile judiciary; powerful congressional opponents, some of whom entered into alliances of convenience with New Dealers and some of whom awaited the opportunity to build on their opposition; the political impotence of much of the populace; the pugnacious independence of local and state authorities; the strength of people's attachment to traditional values and institutions; and the basic conservatism of American culture. Obeisance to local custom and the decision to avoid tampering with the fabric of American society allowed much injustice to survive while shortchanging blacks, women, small farmers, and the "unworthy" poor. Those who criticized Franklin Roosevelt for an unwillingness to challenge racial, economic, and gender inequality misunderstood either the nature of his electoral mandate or the difference between reform and revolution—or both.

If the New Deal preserved more than it changed, that is understandable in a society whose people have consistently chosen freedom over equality. Americans traditionally have eschewed expanded government, no matter how efficiently managed or honestly administered, that imposed restraints on personal success—even though such limitations redressed legitimate grievances or righted imbalances. Parity, most Americans believed, should not be purchased with the loss of liberty. But although the American dream has always entailed individual success with a minimum of state interference, the profound shock of capitalism's near demise in the 1930s undermined numerous previously unquestioned beliefs. The inability of capitalism's "invisible hand" to stabilize the market and the failure of the private sector to restore prosperity enhanced the consideration of stronger executive leadership and centralized planning. Yet with the collapse of democratic governments and their replacement by totalitarian regimes, Americans were keenly sensitive to any threats to liberty. New Deal programs, frequently path breaking in their delivery of federal resources outside normal channels, also retained a strong commitment to local government and community control while promising only temporary disruptions prior to the return of economic stability. Reconciling the necessary authority at the federal level to meet nationwide crises with the local autonomy desirable to safeguard freedom has always been one of the salient challenges to American democracy. Even after New Deal refinements, the search for the proper balance continues.

Notes

INTRODUCTION

1. Robert S. McElvaine, ed., *Down and Out in the Great Depression: Letters from the Forgotten Man* (Chapel Hill: University of North Carolina Press, 1983), pp. 14, 15, 220.

2. Ibid., pp. 13, 203.

3. Carl Degler, *Out of Our Past: The Forces That Shaped Modern America* (New York: Harper, 1959); William E. Leuchtenburg, "The Achievement of the New Deal," in Harvard Sitkoff, ed., *Fifty Years Later: The New Deal Evaluated* (New York: Alfred A. Knopf, 1985), p. 213.

4. Barton J. Bernstein, "The New Deal: The Conservative Achievements of Liberal Reform," in Barton J. Bernstein, ed., *Towards a New Past: Dissenting Essays in American History* (New York: Pantheon, 1968), p. 246; Paul Conkin, *The New Deal* (New York: Thomas Y. Crowell, 1967), p. 73.

5. Leuchtenburg, "The Achievement of the New Deal," p. 213; Jerold S. Auerbach, "New Deal, Old Deal, or Raw Deal: Some Thoughts on New Left Historiography," *Journal of Southern History* 35 (February 1969), p. 21.

CHAPTER 1: HERBERT HOOVER AND THE GREAT DEPRESSION

1. Herbert Hoover, *The Memoirs of Herbert Hoover* (New York: Macmillan, 1952) 3:30 (Mellon quotation); Thomas Kessner, *Fiorello H.*

LaGuardia and the Making of Modern New York (New York: McGraw-Hill, 1989), pp. 170–71 (Coolidge quotations).

2. Broadus Mitchell, *Depression Decade: From New Era through New Deal, 1929–1941* (New York: Rinehart, 1947), p. 15 (Coolidge quotation).

3. Kessner, *Fiorello H. LaGuardia and the Making of Modern New York,* p. 167 (Harvard quotation); Robert S. McElvaine, *The Great Depression: America, 1929–1941* (New York: Times Books, 1984), p. 77 (Ford quotation).

4. John A. Garraty, *The Great Depression* (Garden City, N.Y.: Doubleday, 1987), p. 162 (Keynes quotation).

5. Kessner, *Fiorello H. LaGuardia and the Making of Modern New York,* p. 167 (Baruch quotation); Arthur M. Schlesinger, Jr., *The Age of Roosevelt: The Crisis of the Old Order* (Boston: Houghton Mifflin, 1957), p. 188 (Keynes quotation).

6. Anthony J. Badger, *The New Deal: The Depression Years, 1933–1940* (New York: Farrar, Straus, and Giroux, 1989), p. 41 (Hoover quotation).

7. McElvaine, *The Great Depression,* p. 65 (Hoover quotation).

8. Jordan A. Schwarz, *The Interregnum of Despair: Hoover, Congress, and the Depression* (Urbana: University of Illinois Press, 1970), pp. 33 (LaGuardia quotation), 35 (Hoover quotations).

9. Udo Sautter, "Government and Unemployment: The Use of Public Works Before the New Deal," *Journal of American History* 73 (June 1986), p. 82 (Hoover quotation and first Gifford quotation); Albert U. Romasco, *The Poverty of Abundance: Hoover, the Nation, the Depression* (New York: Oxford University Press, 1965), p. 166 (second Gifford quotation).

10. James Stuart Olson, *Herbert Hoover and the Reconstruction Finance Corporation, 1931–1933* (Ames: Iowa State University Press, 1977), pp. 35 (LaGuardia quotation), 43 (Norris quotation); Susan Estabrook Kennedy, *The Banking Crisis of 1933* (Lexington: University Press of Kentucky, 1973), p. 42 (Hoover quotation).

11. For a reappraisal of Hoover's presidency, see David Burner, *Herbert Hoover: A Public Life* (New York: Alfred A. Knopf, 1979); Joan Hoff Wilson, *Herbert Hoover, Forgotten Progressive* (Boston: Little, Brown, 1975); and Martin L. Fausold and George T. Mazuzan, eds., *The Hoover Presidency: A Reappraisal* (Albany: State University of New York Press, 1974).

12. Romasco, *The Poverty of Abundance,* p. 233.

13. Kessner, *Fiorello H. LaGuardia and the Making of Modern New York,* p. 170 (first Hoover quotation); Schlesinger, *The Crisis of the Old Order,* p. 242 (second Hoover quotation).

14. Schlesinger, *The Crisis of the Old Order,* p. 291 (Lippmann

quotation); James MacGregor Burns, *Roosevelt: The Lion and the Fox* (New York: Harcourt, Brace, and World, 1956), p. 157 (Holmes quotation).

15. Burns, *Roosevelt,* p. 144 (Hoover quotation); McElvaine, *The Great Depression,* p. 133 (Roosevelt quotation).

16. Arthur M. Schlesinger, Jr., *The Cycles of American History* (Boston: Houghton Mifflin, 1986), p. 239 (Hoover quotation); Samuel I. Rosenman, ed., *The Public Papers and Addresses of Franklin D. Roosevelt* (New York: Random House, 1938) 1:788 (Roosevelt quotation).

17. Fausold and Mazuzan, *The Hoover Presidency,* p. 71 (Hoover quotation).

18. On the Brains Trust, see Elliot A. Rosen, *Hoover, Roosevelt, and the Brains Trust: From Depression to New Deal* (New York: Columbia University Press, 1977).

19. Frank Freidel, "The Interregnum Struggle between Hoover and Roosevelt," in Fausold and Mazuzan, *The Hoover Presidency,* p. 145 (Hoover quotation); John T. Flynn, *The Roosevelt Myth* (New York: Devin-Adair, 1948), p. 31 (Roosevelt quotation).

20. Schlesinger, *The Crisis of the Old Order,* pp. 477 (first Hoover quotation), 481 (second Hoover quotation).

CHAPTER 2: THE HUNDRED DAYS

1. Frank Freidel, *Franklin D. Roosevelt: Launching the New Deal* (Boston: Little, Brown, 1973), pp. 201–3.

2. Ibid., p. 205 (Roosevelt quotations); Arthur M. Schlesinger, Jr., *The Age of Roosevelt: The Coming of the New Deal* (Boston: Houghton Mifflin, 1959), p. 1 (Eleanor Roosevelt quotation).

3. See Kennedy, *The Banking Crisis of 1933.*

4. Ibid., p. 168 (Thomas quotation); Schlesinger, *The Coming of the New Deal,* p. 5 (Cutting quotation); William E. Leuchtenburg, *Franklin D. Roosevelt and the New Deal* (New York: Harper and Row, 1963), p. 44 (last quotation).

5. Freidel, *Launching the New Deal,* p. 265.

6. James E. Sargent, *Roosevelt and the Hundred Days: Struggle for the Early New Deal* (New York: Garland, 1981), p. 122 (*New Republic* quotation).

7. Ronald A. Mulder, *The Insurgent Progressives in the U.S. Senate and the New Deal, 1933–1939* (New York: Garland, 1979), p. 78 (Wheeler quotation); Schlesinger, *The Coming of the New Deal,* p. 40 (Martin quotation).

8. Burns, *Roosevelt: The Lion and the Fox,* p. 170.

9. Schlesinger, *The Coming of the New Deal,* p. 464 (Rayburn quotation).

10. Herbert Hoover, *Memoirs: The Cabinet and the Presidency, 1920–1933* (New York: Macmillan, 1952), p. 304 (Hoover quotation).

11. Katie Louchheim, ed., *The Making of the New Deal: The Insiders Speak* (Cambridge: Harvard University Press, 1983), p. xviii (first quotation); Schlesinger, *The Coming of the New Deal,* p. 16 (second quotation).

12. Sargent, *Roosevelt and the Hundred Days,* p. 177 (Douglas quotation).

13. Freidel, *Launching the New Deal,* p. 409 (Roosevelt quotation).

14. Ibid., p. 434 (first two quotations); Schlesinger, *The Coming of the New Deal,* p. 102 (last quotation).

15. Kennedy, *The Banking Crisis of 1933,* p. 222.

16. Ronald L. Feinman, *Twilight of Progressivism: The Western Republican Senators and the New Deal* (Baltimore: Johns Hopkins University Press, 1981), p. 66 (Norbeck quotation).

17. Schlesinger, *The Coming of the New Deal,* p. 22 (Lippmann quotation); Rosenman, *The Public Papers and Addresses of Franklin D. Roosevelt* 1:165 (Roosevelt quotation).

18. Ronald L. Heinemann, *Depression and New Deal in Virginia: The Enduring Dominion* (Charlottesville: University Press of Virginia, 1983), p. 47 (Glass quotation).

19. Graham J. White, *Franklin D. Roosevelt and the Press* (Chicago: University of Chicago Press, 1979), p. 10 (Brown quotation).

20. Frank Freidel, *Franklin D. Roosevelt: A Rendezvous with Destiny* (Boston: Little, Brown, 1990), p. 73.

21. Arthur M. Schlesinger, Jr., "Getting FDR's Ear," *New York Review of Books* 36 (February 16, 1989), p. 20 (Roosevelt quotation); Frances Perkins, *The Roosevelt I Knew* (New York: Viking, 1946), p. 239 (Perkins quotation).

CHAPTER 3: AGRICULTURAL ADJUSTMENT

1. Van L. Perkins, *Crisis in Agriculture: The Agricultural Adjustment Administration and the New Deal, 1933* (Berkeley: University of California Press, 1969), pp. 49 (Roosevelt quotation), 59 (Wallace quotation).

2. Richard S. Kirkendall, "The New Deal in Agriculture," in Alonzo L. Hamby, ed., *The New Deal: Analysis and Interpretation* (New York: Longman, 1969), p. 63 (Peek quotation).

3. Gilbert C. Fite, *George N. Peek and the Fight for Farm Parity* (Norman: University of Oklahoma Press, 1954), p. 258 (Wallace quotation); David E. Conrad, *The Forgotten Farmers: The Story of the Sharecrop-*

pers in the New Deal (Urbana: University of Illinois Press, 1965), p. 39 (Peek quotation).

4. Conrad, *The Forgotten Farmers,* p. 106 (Pressman quotation).

5. Ibid., p. 52.

6. Gilbert C. Fite, *Cotton Fields No More: Southern Agriculture, 1865–1980* (Lexington: University Press of Kentucky, 1984), p. 143 (Wallace quotation).

7. Ibid., p. 153.

8. Theodore Saloutos, "New Deal Agricultural Policy: An Evaluation," *Journal of American History* 61 (September 1974), p. 416.

CHAPTER 4: THE BLUE EAGLE

1. Ellis W. Hawley, *The New Deal and the Problem of Monopoly* (Princeton: Princeton University Press, 1966), p. 19 (Harriman quote).

2. John Kennedy Ohl, *Hugh S. Johnson and the New Deal* (DeKalb: Northern Illinois University Press, 1985), p. 104 (first Johnson quotation); Bernard Bellush, *The Failure of the NRA* (New York: W. W. Norton, 1975), p. 60 (second Johnson quotation).

3. Ohl, *Hugh S. Johnson and the New Deal,* p. 123.

4. Ibid., p. 180 (Johnson quotation).

5. Ibid., p. 181 (first Johnson quotation); Bellush, *The Failure of the NRA,* p. 95 (second Johnson quotation).

6. Bellush, *The Failure of the NRA,* pp. 70 (Johnson quotation).

7. Ohl, *Hugh S. Johnson and the New Deal,* pp. 189 (Johnson quotation), 190 (editor quotation).

8. See Gavin Wright, *Old South, New South: Revolutions in the Southern Economy Since the Civil War* (New York: Basic Books, 1986).

9. Bellush, *The Failure of the NRA,* p. 140 (Lippmann quotation).

10. Ohl, *Hugh S. Johnson and the New Deal,* p. 171 (Johnson quotation).

11. Leverett S. Lyon et al., *The National Recovery Administration: An Analysis and Appraisal* (Washington, D.C.: Brookings Institution, 1935), p. 291.

12. Heinemann, *Depression and New Deal in Virginia: The Enduring Dominion,* p. 59 (quotation).

CHAPTER 5: RELIEF AND SOCIAL WELFARE

1. Robert H. Bremner, "The New Deal and Social Welfare," in Harvard Sitkoff, ed., *Fifty Years Later: The New Deal Evaluated* (New York:

Alfred A. Knopf, 1985), p. 69 (first quotation); Leuchtenburg, "The Achievement of the New Deal," ibid., p. 230 (second quotation).

2. Janet Poppendieck, *Breadlines Knee-Deep in Wheat: Food Assistance in the Great Depression* (New Brunswick, N.J.: Rutgers University Press, 1986), p. 105 (Hopkins quotation).

3. George McJimsey, *Harry Hopkins: Ally of the Poor and Defender of Democracy* (Cambridge: Harvard University Press, 1987), p. 54 (Hopkins quotation).

4. Jane Walker Herndon, "Ed Rivers and Georgia's 'Little New Deal,'" *Atlanta Historical Journal* 30 (Spring 1986), pp. 98–99.

5. Betty M. Field, "The Politics of the New Deal in Louisiana" (Ph.D. diss., Tulane University, 1973), pp. 157–61.

6. Michael P. Malone, *C. Ben Ross and the New Deal in Idaho* (Seattle: University of Washington Press, 1970), p. 52 (first quotation); Heinemann, *Depression and New Deal in Virginia: The Enduring Dominion*, p. 84 (second quotation).

7. James T. Patterson, *America's Struggle against Poverty, 1900–1980* (Cambridge: Harvard University Press, 1981), p. 59 (first quotation); Donald T. Critchlow and Ellis W. Hawley, eds., *Poverty and Public Policy in Modern America* (Chicago: Dorsey Press, 1989), p. 128 (second quotation); Bremner, "The New Deal and Social Welfare," pp. 73 (third quotation), 75 (fourth quotation).

8. John M. Allswang, *The New Deal and American Politics* (New York: Wiley, 1978), p. 26 (quotation).

9. McJimsey, *Harry Hopkins*, pp. 89 (first quotation), 91 (second quotation).

10. Robert E. Burton, "The New Deal in Oregon," in John Braeman, Robert H. Bremner, and David Brody, eds., *The New Deal: The State and Local Levels* (Columbus: Ohio State University Press, 1975), p. 364 (Martin quotation); David E. Rison, "Arkansas During the Great Depression" (Ph.D. diss., University of California, Los Angeles, 1974), p. 113 (Hopkins quotation).

11. Robert Sherwood, *Roosevelt and Hopkins: An Intimate History* (New York: Harper and Brothers, 1948), p. 57 (Hopkins quotation); Jane DeHart Matthews, *The Federal Theatre, 1935–1939: Plays, Relief, and Politics* (Princeton: Princeton University Press, 1967), p. 311 (second quotation).

12. W. Andrew Achenbaum, *Social Security: Visions and Revisions* (Cambridge: Cambridge University Press, 1986), pp. 22–23 (Roosevelt quotation).

13. Bremner, "The New Deal and Social Welfare," p. 79.

14. George B. Tindall, *The Emergence of the New South, 1913–1945* (Baton Rouge: Louisiana State University Press, 1967), p. 478 (quotation).

15. Bremner, "The New Deal and Social Welfare," p. 75 (Hopkins quotation).

16. Ibid., p. 86.

CHAPTER 6: THE POLITICS OF PREEMPTION, 1934–1936

1. John F. Bauman and Thomas H. Coode, *In the Eye of the Great Depression: New Deal Reporters and the Agony of the American People* (DeKalb: Northern Illinois University Press, 1988), p. 108.

2. Richard Lowitt and Maurine Beasley, eds., *One Third of a Nation: Lorena Hickok Reports on the Great Depression* (Urbana: University of Illinois Press, 1981), p. 218.

3. Schlesinger, *The Coming of the New Deal,* p. 507 (quotation).

4. *New York Times,* November 6, 1934.

5. McElvaine, *The Great Depression,* p. 231.

6. Ibid., p. 232.

7. T. Harry Williams, *Huey Long* (New York: Alfred A. Knopf, 1969), p. 640 (quotation).

8. McElvaine, *The Great Depression,* p. 252 (quotation).

9. McJimsey, *Harry Hopkins,* p. 77.

10. The cost and benefits of work relief are carefully weighed in William R. Brock, *Welfare, Democracy, and the New Deal* (Cambridge: Cambridge University Press, 1988).

11. Perkins, *The Roosevelt I Knew,* p. 239.

12. Mark Leff, *The Limits of Symbolic Reform: The New Deal and Taxation, 1933–1939* (Cambridge: Cambridge University Press, 1984), p. 137 (quotation).

13. Ibid., p. 139 (quotation).

14. Burns, *Roosevelt: The Lion and the Fox,* p. 226 (Roosevelt quotation).

15. Rosenman, *The Public Papers and Addresses of Franklin D. Roosevelt* 5:232–33.

16. William E. Leuchtenburg, "Election of 1936," in Arthur M. Schlesinger, Jr., ed., *History of American Presidential Elections, 1789–1968* 3:2818 (quotation).

17. Ibid., p. 2827 (quotation).

18. Alan Brinkley, *Voices of Protest: Huey Long, Father Coughlin, and the Great Depression* (New York: Alfred A. Knopf, 1982), p. 261 (Coughlin quotation).

19. Schlesinger, *The Coming of the New Deal,* p. 642 (Farley quotation).

20. Burns, *Roosevelt,* p. 380.

CHAPTER 7: THE NEW DEAL IN ECLIPSE, 1937–1939

1. Rosenman, *The Public Papers and Addresses of Franklin D. Roosevelt* 6:5.

2. Tony Freyer, *Hugo L. Black and the Dilemma of American Liberalism* (Glenview: Scott, Foresman, Little, Brown, 1990), p. 66 (quotation).

3. James T. Patterson, *Congressional Conservatism and the New Deal* (Lexington: University Press of Kentucky, 1967), p. 86 (Roosevelt quotation).

4. Burns, *Roosevelt: The Lion and the Fox*, p. 294 (quotation).

5. Patterson, *Congressional Conservatism and the New Deal*, p. 116 (first quotation); Martha H. Swain, *Pat Harrison: The New Deal Years* (Jackson: University Press of Mississippi, 1978), p. 147 (second quotation).

6. Patterson, *Congressional Conservatism and the New Deal*, p. 127.

7. Freyer, *Hugo L. Black and the Dilemma of American Liberalism*, p. 69 (quotation).

8. *New York Times*, December 16, 1937.

9. Richard Polenberg, *Reorganizing Roosevelt's Government: The Controversy over Executive Reorganization, 1936–1939* (Cambridge: Harvard University Press, 1966), p. 50 (quotation).

10. Ibid., p. 180 (quotation).

11. Ibid., p. 185.

12. Richard Polenberg, "Franklin Roosevelt and the Purge of John O'Connor: The Impact of Urban Change on Political Parties," *New York History* 49 (July 1968), p. 325 (quotation).

13. Patterson, *Congressional Conservatism and the New Deal*, p. 243 (quotation).

CHAPTER 8: THE RISE OF LABOR

1. George Martin, *Madam Secretary: Frances Perkins* (Boston: Houghton Mifflin, 1976), p. 3 (quotation).

2. James A. Hodges, *New Deal Labor Policy and the Southern Cotton Textile Industry, 1933–1941* (Knoxville: University of Tennessee Press, 1986), p. 46.

3. Irving Bernstein, *Turbulent Years: A History of the American Worker, 1933–1941* (Boston: Houghton Mifflin, 1971), p. 41 (first quotation); Hodges, *New Deal Labor Policy and the Southern Cotton Textile Industry, 1933–1941*, p. 46 (second quotation).

4. I. Bernstein, *Turbulent Years*, p. 322.

5. Irving Bernstein, *The New Deal Collective Bargaining Policy* (Ber-

keley: University of California Press, 1950), p. 99 (Perkins quotation).

6. J. Joseph Huthmacher, *Senator Robert F. Wagner and the Rise of Urban Liberalism* (New York: Atheneum, 1968), p. 197 (quotation).

7. On the AFL–CIO split, see Christopher L. Tomlins, "AFL Unions in the 1930s: Their Performance in Historical Perspective," *Journal of American History* 65 (March 1979), pp. 1021–42.

8. I. Bernstein, *Turbulent Years*, p. 783 (quotation).

9. Jerold S. Auerbach, *Labor and Liberty: The LaFollette Committee and the New Deal* (Indianapolis: Bobbs-Merrill, 1966), p. 121 (Lewis quotation).

10. I. Bernstein, *Turbulent Years*, p. 496 (first quotation); Leuchtenburg, *Franklin D. Roosevelt and the New Deal*, p. 243 (second quotation).

11. Tomlins, "AFL Unions in the 1930s," pp. 1022–23, 1040.

12. David Brody, *Workers in Industrial America: Essays on the Twentieth Century Struggle* (New York: Oxford University Press, 1980), p. 145.

13. Schlesinger, *The Coming of the New Deal*, p. 180 (quotation).

14. See Christopher L. Tomlins, *The State and the Unions: Labor Relations, Law, and the Organized Labor Movement in America, 1880–1960* (Cambridge: Cambridge University Press, 1985).

CHAPTER 9: A NEW DEAL FOR BLACKS?

1. Frank Deford, "The Ageless Warrior," *Sports Illustrated* 70 (May 8, 1989), p. 112 (quotation).

2. Harvard Sitkoff, *A New Deal for Blacks: The Emergence of Civil Rights as a National Issue, the Depression Decade* (New York: Oxford University Press, 1978), p. 37 (quotation).

3. George W. Lee, *Beale Street Where the Blues Began* (New York: Robert O. Ballou, 1934), p. 210 (quotation).

4. Nancy J. Weiss, *Farewell to the Party of Lincoln: Black Politics in the Age of FDR* (Princeton: Princeton University Press, 1983), p. 12 (Church quotation).

5. Ibid., pp. 28 (first quotation), 29 (second quotation).

6. Ibid., p. 35 (quotation).

7. Raymond Wolters, *Negroes and the Great Depression: The Problem of Economic Recovery* (Westport, Conn.: Greenwood, 1970), p. 145 (quotation).

8. Weiss, *Farewell to the Party of Lincoln*, p. 56 (quotation).

9. Wolters, *Negroes and the Great Depression*, pp. 42–43 (first quotation); Allen F. Kifer, "The Negro under the New Deal, 1933–1941" (Ph.D. diss., University of Wisconsin, 1961), p. 152 (second quotation).

10. John A. Salmond, *The Civilian Conservation Corps, 1933–1942:*

A New Deal Case Study (Durham: Duke University Press, 1967), p. 88 (quotation).

11. Kenneth T. Jackson, *Crabgrass Frontier: The Suburbanization of the United States* (New York: Oxford University Press, 1985), p. 213 (quotation).

12. Weiss, *Farewell to the Party of Lincoln*, p. 177.

13. Ibid., pp. 169–70 (quotation).

14. Ibid., pp. 113–14 (quotation).

15. Sitkoff, *A New Deal for Blacks*, p. 61 (quotation).

16. Harvard Sitkoff, "The New Deal and Race Relations," in Harvard Sitkoff, ed., *Fifty Years Later: The New Deal Evaluated* (New York: Alfred A. Knopf, 1985), pp. 104–5.

17. John B. Kirby, *Black Americans in the Roosevelt Era: Liberalism and Race* (Knoxville: University of Tennessee Press, 1980), p. 199 (quotation).

18. Allan A. Michie and Frank Ryhlick, *Dixie Demagogues* (New York: Vanguard, 1939), pp. 266, 281 (Smith quotations).

19. James H. Brewer, "Robert Lee Vann, Democrat or Republican: An Exponent of Loose-Leaf Politics," in Bernard Sternsher, ed., *The Negro in Depression and War: Prelude to Revolution, 1930–1945* (Chicago: Quadrangle, 1969).

20. Sitkoff, *A New Deal for Blacks*, p. 91.

21. Weiss, *Farewell to the Party of Lincoln*, pp. 179 (first quotation), 286 (DuBois quotation), 233 (politician quotation), 216 (fourth quotation).

22. Wolters, *Negroes and the Great Depression*, p. 45 (first quotation); Weiss, *Farewell to the Party of Lincoln*, p. 298 (second quotation).

23. Bernard Sternsher, ed., *The Negro in Depression and War: Prelude to Revolution, 1930–1945* (Chicago: Quadrangle, 1969).

CHAPTER 10: WOMEN AND THE NEW DEAL

1. Lowitt and Beasley, *One Third of a Nation: Lorena Hickok Reports on the Great Depression*, pp. 223, 350.

2. Susan Ware, *Holding Their Own: American Women in the 1930s* (Boston: Twayne, 1982), p. 2 (quotation).

3. Norman Cousins, "Will Women Lose Their Jobs?" *Current History and Forum* 41 (September 1939), p. 14.

4. Susan Ware, *Beyond Suffrage: Women in the New Deal* (Cambridge: Harvard University Press, 1981), p. 10 (quotation).

5. Susan Ware, "Women and the New Deal," in Harvard Sitkoff, ed., *Fifty Years Later: The New Deal Evaluated* (New York: Alfred A. Knopf, 1985), p. 119 (quotation).

6. See Martha H. Swain, "'The Forgotten Woman': Ellen S. Woodward and Women's Relief in the New Deal," *Prologue: Journal of the National Archives* 15 (Winter 1983), pp. 201–13.

7. Ware, *Holding Their Own*, p. 40 (first quotation); Roger Biles, *Memphis in the Great Depression* (Knoxville: University of Tennessee Press, 1986), p. 76 (second and third quotations).

8. Winifred D. Wandersee, *Women's Work and Family Values, 1920–1940* (Cambridge: Harvard University Press, 1981), p. 122.

9. Susan D. Becker, *The Origins of the Equal Rights Amendment: American Feminism between the Wars* (Westport, Conn.: Greenwood, 1981), pp. 142 (first quotation), 202 (second quotation), 217 (third quotation).

10. Ibid., p. 150 (quotation).

11. Swain, "'The Forgotten Woman,'" p. 213; Ware, "Women and the New Deal," p. 130.

CHAPTER 11: THE NEW DEAL AND URBAN AMERICA

1. John Teaford, *The Twentieth Century American City: Problem, Promise, and Reality* (Baltimore: Johns Hopkins University Press, 1986), p. 78 (quotation).

2. Roger Biles, "The Urban South in the Great Depression," *Journal of Southern History* 56 (February 1990), p. 81 (Jones quotation); Paul Anthony Stellhorn, "Depression and Decline: Newark, N.J., 1929–1941" (Ph.D. diss., Rutgers University, 1982), p. 114 (Reddan quotation); Howard Chudacoff, *The Evolution of American Urban Society* (Englewood Cliffs, N.J.: Prentice Hall, 1975), p. 233 (Buttenheim quotation).

3. Blake McKelvey, *The Emergence of Metropolitan America, 1915–1966* (New Brunswick, N.J.: Rutgers University Press, 1968), p. 81 (first quotation); Roger Biles, *Big City Boss in Depression and War: Mayor Edward J. Kelly of Chicago* (DeKalb: Northern Illinois University Press, 1984), p. 23 (second quotation).

4. Sidney Fine, *Frank Murphy: The Detroit Years* (Ann Arbor: University of Michigan Press, 1975), pp. 299–300 (first quotation); Howard Chudacoff and Judith E. Smith, *The Evolution of American Urban Society*, 3d ed. (Englewood Cliffs, N.J.: Prentice Hall, 1988), p. 240 (second quotation).

5. Mark I. Gelfand, *A Nation of Cities: The Federal Government and Urban America, 1933–1965* (New York: Oxford University Press, 1975), p. 24 (Tugwell quotations), p. 55 (Roosevelt quotations).

6. Ibid., p. 381 (Ford quotation); Jackson, *Crabgrass Frontier*, p. 195 (Tugwell quotation).

7. Paul K. Conkin, *Tomorrow a New World: The New Deal Community Program* (Ithaca: Cornell University Press, 1959), p. 329 (quotation).

8. David R. Goldfield, "The Urban South: A Regional Framework," *American Historical Review* 86 (December 1981), p. 1030.

9. Robert P. Ingalls, *Herbert H. Lehman and New York's Little New Deal* (New York: New York University Press, 1975), p. 182 (quotation).

10. Mary Susan Cole, "Catherine Bauer and the Public Housing Movement" (Ph.D. diss., George Washington University, 1975), p. 352n.

11. Badger, *The New Deal: The Depression Years, 1933–1940,* p. 241 (editor quotation).

12. Edward O'Connor, *The Last Hurrah* (Boston: Little, Brown, 1956); Lyle W. Dorsett, *Franklin D. Roosevelt and the City Bosses* (Port Washington, N.Y.: Kennikat, 1977), p. 113.

13. Bruce M. Stave, *The New Deal and the Last Hurrah: Pittsburgh Machine Politics* (Pittsburgh: University of Pittsburgh Press, 1970), p. 182.

14. Biles, *Memphis in the Great Depression,* p. 81 (quotation).

15. Charles H. Trout, *Boston, the Great Depression, and the New Deal* (New York: Oxford University Press, 1977), pp. x (Wade quotation), 315 (Trout quotation).

16. Gelfand, *A Nation of Cities,* p. 68.

17. Jackson, *Crabgrass Frontier,* p. 190 (quotation).

CONCLUSION

1. Otis L. Graham, Jr., and Meghan Robinson Wander, eds., *Franklin D. Roosevelt, His Life and Times: An Encyclopedic View* (Boston: G. K. Hall, 1985), p. 285 (first quotation); Harvard Sitkoff, "Introduction," in Sitkoff, *Fifty Years Later,* p. 5 (second quotation).

2. Richard S. Kirkendall, "The New Deal as Watershed: The Recent Literature," *Journal of American History* 54 (March 1968), p. 847 (quotation).

3. Graham and Wander, *Franklin D. Roosevelt, His Life and Times,* p. 228 (quotation).

4. Leuchtenburg, "The Achievement of the New Deal," p. 220 (first quotation); Patterson, *America's Struggle against Poverty, 1900–1980,* p. 56 (second quotation).

5. Louchheim, *The Making of the New Deal: The Insiders Speak,* p. 15 (quotation).

6. John Braeman, "The New Deal: The Collapse of the Liberal Consensus," *Canadian Review of American Studies* 20 (Summer 1989), p. 77.

7. David Burner, *The Politics of Provincialism: The Democratic Party in Transition, 1918–1932* (New York: Alfred A. Knopf, 1968).

8. Mark Leff, *The Limits of Symbolic Reform,* p. 287 (quotation).

9. James T. Patterson, *The New Deal and the States: Federalism in*

Transition (Princeton: Princeton University Press, 1969), p. 202.

10. Barry D. Karl, *The Uneasy State: The United States from 1915 to 1945* (Chicago: University of Chicago Press, 1983), p. 124.

Bibliographical Essay

On the stock market boom and bust in the 1920s, see Robert Sobel, *The Great Bull Market* (1968); and John Kenneth Galbraith, *The Great Crash* (1954). The causes of the Great Depression are discussed in Peter Temin's *Did Monetary Forces Cause the Great Depression?* (1976); and Milton Friedman and Anna Schwartz, *The Great Contraction* (1965). Broadus Mitchell, *Depression Decade* (1947); and Michael A. Bernstein, *The Great Depression: Delayed Recovery and Economic Change in America* (1987), provide an overview of the economic collapse. Numerous oral histories describe life in the 1930s, including Studs Terkel, *Hard Times* (1970); Ann Banks, *First-Person America* (1980); Robert S. McElvaine, ed., *Down and Out in the Great Depression: Letters from the Forgotten Man* (1983); and Tom Terrill and Jerrold Hirsch, *Such As Us* (1978). Reports of depression conditions are detailed in Richard Lowitt and Maurine Beasley, eds., *One Third of a Nation: Lorena Hickok Reports on the Great Depression* (1981); and John F. Bauman and Thomas H. Coode, *In the Eye of the Great Depression: New Deal Reporters and the Agony of the American People* (1988). Irving Bernstein, *The Lean Years: A History of the American Worker, 1920–1933* (1960), remains the definitive account of that topic. On violent protest see Tony Bubka, "The Harlan County Coal Strike of 1931," *Labor History* 11 (Winter 1970), pp. 41–57; and John L. Shover, "The Farmers' Holiday Association Strike, August 1932," *Agricultural History* 39 (October 1965), pp. 196–203. For a case study of one city's response to the depression see Bonnie Fox Schwartz, "Unemployment Relief in Philadelphia, 1930–1932: A Study of the Depression's Impact on Voluntarism," *Pennsylvania*

Magazine of History and Biography 92 (January 1969), pp. 86–108. For background on public works and government see Udo Sautter, "Government and Unemployment: The Use of Public Works Before the New Deal," *Journal of American History* 73 (June 1986), pp. 59–86.

There is a vast and growing Herbert Hoover literature, much of it now revisionist. The best biographies are Joan Hoff Wilson, *Herbert Hoover, Forgotten Progressive* (1975); Albert U. Romasco, *The Poverty of Abundance: Hoover, the Nation, the Depression* (1965); and David Burner, *Herbert Hoover: A Public Life* (1979). The Hoover presidency is examined in Martin L. Fausold, *The Presidency of Herbert C. Hoover* (1985); Martin L. Fausold and George T. Mazuzan, eds., *The Hoover Presidency: A Reappraisal* (1974); and Jordan A. Schwarz, *The Interregnum of Despair: Hoover, Congress, and the Depression* (1970). More specialized studies include Ellis W. Hawley, "Herbert Hoover, the Commerce Secretariat, and the Vision of an 'Associative State,'" *Journal of American History* 61 (June 1974), pp. 116–40; Susan Estabrook Kennedy, *The Banking Crisis of 1933* (1973); James Stuart Olson, *Herbert Hoover and the Reconstruction Finance Corporation, 1931–1933* (1977); Donald J. Lisio, *The President and Protest: Hoover, Conspiracy, and the Bonus Riot* (1974); Donald J. Lisio, *Hoover, Blacks, and Lily-Whites: A Study of Southern Strategies* (1985); Roger Daniels, *The Bonus March: An Episode of the Great Depression* (1971); William Mullins, "Self-Help in Seattle, 1931–1932," *Pacific Northwest Quarterly* 72 (January 1981), pp. 11–19; William Mullins, "'I'll Wreck the Town If It Will Give Employment': Portland in the Hoover Years of the Depression," *Pacific Northwest Quarterly* 79 (July 1988), pp. 109–18; William Mullins, *The Hoover Depression and the Urban West Coast: Los Angeles, San Francisco, Seattle, and Portland, 1929–1933* (1991); and Elliot A. Rosen, *Hoover, Roosevelt, and the Brains Trust: From Depression to New Deal* (1977). Portions of Arthur M. Schlesinger, Jr., *The Cycles of American History* (1986), are relevant.

Numerous biographies provide insight into the character of Franklin D. Roosevelt. The first four volumes of Frank Freidel's *Franklin D. Roosevelt—The Apprenticeship* (1952); *The Ordeal* (1954); *The Triumph* (1956); and *Launching the New Deal* (1973)—comprehensively cover the years through 1933. His *Franklin D. Roosevelt: A Rendezvous with Destiny* (1990), is a comprehensive one-volume biography. James MacGregor Burns, *Roosevelt: The Lion and the Fox* (1956), remains the best one-volume biography.

Kenneth S. Davis, *FDR: The New Deal Years 1933–1937: A History,* is part of a multivolume work in progress. Also see Ted Morgan, *FDR: A Biography* (1985); Bernard Bellush, *Franklin D. Roosevelt as Governor of New York* (1952); Alfred Rollins, Jr., *Roosevelt and Howe* (1962); Michael R. Beschloss, *Kennedy and Roosevelt: The Uneasy Alliance* (1980); Graham J. White, *FDR and the Press* (1979); Richard W. Steele, *Propaganda in an Open Society: The Roosevelt Administration and the Media, 1933–1941* (1985); and Robert E. Sherwood, *Roosevelt and Hopkins* (1948).

Many New Dealers wrote memoirs of their experiences. Rexford G. Tugwell wrote several, including *The Democratic Roosevelt* (1957), *The Brains Trust* (1968), and *In Search of Roosevelt* (1972). Also see Eleanor Roosevelt *This Is My Story* (1937), and *This I Remember* (1949); Samuel I. Rosenman, *Working for Roosevelt* (1952); Raymond Moley, *The First New Deal* (1967); Harry L. Hopkins, *Spending to Save: The Complete Story of Relief* (1936); Frances Perkins, *The Roosevelt I Knew* (1946); David Lilienthal, *TVA: Democracy on the March* (1944); Harold L. Ickes, *The Autobiography of a Curmudgeon* (1943), and the three volumes of *The Secret Diaries of Harold L. Ickes* (1954).

Biographies of other key figures from the New Deal era include George McJimsey, *Harry Hopkins: Ally of the Poor and Defender of Democracy* (1987); John Kennedy Ohl, *Hugh S. Johnson and the New Deal* (1985); J. Joseph Huthmacher, *Senator Robert F. Wagner and the Rise of Urban Liberalism* (1968); Richard Lowitt, *George W. Norris: The Triumph of a Progressive, 1933–1944* (1978); John M. Blum, *From the Morgenthau Diaries*, 3 vols. (1959–65); Jordan Schwarz, *Liberal: Adolf A. Berle and the Vision of an American Era* (1987); John A. Salmond, *A Southern Rebel: The Life and Times of Aubrey Willis Williams, 1890–1965* (1983); Martha H. Swain, *Pat Harrison: The New Deal Years* (1978); Sidney Fine, *Frank Murphy: The New Deal Years* (1979); George Martin, *Madam Secretary: Frances Perkins* (1976); Chester M. Morgan, *Redneck Liberal: Theodore G. Bilbo and the New Deal* (1985); Polly Ann Davis, *Alben Barkley: Senate Majority Leader and Vice President* (1979); John E. Miller, *Governor Philip F. LaFollette, the Wisconsin Progressives, and the New Deal* (1983); Bernard Sternsher, *Rexford Tugwell and the New Deal* (1964); Michael V. Namorato, *Rexford G. Tugwell: A Biography* (1988); George H. Mayer, *The Political Career of Floyd B. Olson* (1951); Donald R. McCoy, *Landon of Kansas* (1967); T. Harry Williams, *Huey Long* (1969); Edward C. Blackorby, *Prairie*

Rebel: The Public Life of William Lemke (1963); Roy Talbert, Jr., *FDR's Utopian: Arthur Morgan of the TVA* (1987); Samuel B. Hand, *Counsel and Advise: A Political Biography of Samuel I. Rosenman* (1979); and Graham White and John Maze, *Harold Ickes of the New Deal: His Private Life and Public Career* (1985).

Among the general studies of the New Deal, the most detailed is Arthur M. Schlesinger, Jr., *The Age of Roosevelt*. It includes *The Crisis of the Old Order, 1919–1933* (1957), *The Coming of the New Deal* (1959), and *The Politics of Upheaval* (1960), which concludes in 1936. William E. Leuchtenburg's *Franklin D. Roosevelt and the New Deal* (1963) remains the best one-volume analysis. Carl Degler's "The Third American Revolution," in *Out of Our Past: The Forces That Shaped Modern America* (1959), has been influential. A conservative critique of the New Deal is Edgar Eugene Robinson, *The Roosevelt Leadership* (1955). New Left interpretations are found in Paul Conkin, *The New Deal* (1967); Barton J. Bernstein's essay in his edited book, *Towards a New Past* (1968); Howard Zinn, ed., *New Deal Thought* (1966); and Ronald Radosh's "The Myth of the New Deal," in Ronald Radosh and Murray Rothbard, eds., *A New History of Leviathan: Essays on the Rise of the American Corporate State* (1972). Also see Basil Rauch, *The History of the New Deal* (1944); John Braeman, Robert H. Bremner, and David Brody, eds., *The New Deal: The National Level* (1975); Barry D. Karl, *The Uneasy State: The United States from 1915 to 1945* (1983); Robert S. McElvaine, *The Great Depression: America, 1929–1941* (1984); Stephen W. Baskerville and Ralph Willett, eds., *Nothing Else to Fear: New Perspectives on America in the Thirties* (1985); Anthony J. Badger, *The New Deal: The Depression Years, 1933–1940* (1989); Steve Fraser and Gary Gerstle, eds., *The Rise and Fall of the New Deal Order, 1930–1980* (1989); Robert Eden, ed., *The New Deal and Its Legacy: Critique and Reappraisal* (1989); Wilbur J. Cohen, ed., *The New Deal Fifty Years After: A Historical Assessment* (1984); Harvard Sitkoff, ed., *Fifty Years Later: The New Deal Evaluated* (1985); Alonzo L. Hamby, ed., *The New Deal: Analysis and Interpretation* (1981); Katie Louchheim, ed., *The Making of the New Deal: The Insiders Speak* (1983); James E. Sargent, *Roosevelt and the Hundred Days: Struggle for the Early New Deal* (1981); Richard S. Kirkendall, "The New Deal as Watershed: The Recent Literature," *Journal of American History* 54 (March 1968), pp. 839–52; Jerold S. Auerbach, "New Deal, Old Deal, or Raw Deal: Some Thoughts on New Left Historiography," *Journal of Southern*

History 35 (February 1969), pp. 18–30; and Samuel B. Hand, "Al Smith, Franklin D. Roosevelt, and the New Deal: Some Comments on Perspective," *Historian* 27 (May 1965), pp. 366–81.

On New Deal politics see Kristi Andersen, *The Creation of a Democratic Majority, 1928–1936* (1979); John M. Allswang, *The New Deal and American Politics: A Study in Political Change* (1978); Samuel Lubell, *The Future of American Politics*, 3d rev. ed. (1965); Allan J. Lichtman, "Critical Election Theory and the Reality of American Presidential Politics, 1916–1940," *American Historical Review* 81 (April 1976), pp. 317–51; James T. Patterson, *Congressional Conservatism and the New Deal* (1967); George Q. Flynn, *American Catholics and the Roosevelt Presidency, 1932–1936* (1968); and David L. Porter, *Congress and the Waning of the New Deal* (1980). The reaction of Progressives to the New Deal is discussed in Otis L. Graham, Jr., *An Encore for Reform: The Old Progressives and the New Deal* (1967); Ronald L. Feinman, *Twilight of Progressivism: The Western Republican Senators and the New Deal* (1981); and Ronald A. Mulder, *The Insurgent Progressives in the U.S. Senate and the New Deal, 1933–1939* (1979).

Political opposition to the New Deal is discussed in Donald R. McCoy, *Angry Voices: Left-of-Center Politics in the New Deal Era* (1958); David H. Bennett, *Demagogues in the Depression: American Radicals and the Union Party, 1932–1936* (1969); Alan Brinkley, *Voices of Protest: Huey Long, Father Coughlin, and the Great Depression* (1982); Abraham Holtzman, *The Townsend Movement: A Study in Old Age Pressure Politics* (1963); George Wolfskill, *The Revolt of the Conservatives: A History of the American Liberty League, 1934–1940* (1962); Charles J. Tull, *Father Coughlin and the New Deal* (1965); Frank Warren, *Liberals and Communism: The "Red Decade" Revisited* (1966) and *An Alternative Vision: The Socialist Party in the 1930s* (1974); Harvey Klehr, *The Heyday of American Communism: The Depression Decade* (1984); Glen Jeansonne, *Gerald L. K. Smith: Minister of Hate* (1988); William Anderson, *The Wild Man from Sugar Creek: The Political Career of Eugene Talmadge* (1975); Richard Polenberg, "The National Committee to Uphold Constitutional Government, 1937–1941," *Journal of American History* 52 (December 1965), pp. 582–98; John Robert Moore, "Senator Josiah W. Bailey and the 'Conservative Manifesto' of 1937," *Journal of Southern History* 31 (February 1965), pp. 21–39; and James T. Patterson, "The Failure of Party Realignment in the South, 1937–1939," *Journal of Politics* 27 (August 1965), pp. 602–17.

Much has been written about agriculture in the 1930s. The most comprehensive treatment is Theodore Saloutos, *The American Farmer and the New Deal* (1982). Also see Theodore Saloutos, "New Deal Agricultural Policy: An Evaluation," *Journal of American History* 61 (September 1974), pp. 394–416; Richard S. Kirkendall, *Social Scientists and Farm Politics in the Age of Roosevelt* (1966); Christiana Campbell, *The Farm Bureau and the New Deal: A Study in the Making of National Farm Policy, 1933–1940* (1962); and the relevant chapters in Gilbert C. Fite, *American Farmers: The New Minority* (1981). On the cotton crisis of 1931 see Robert E. Snyder, *Cotton Crisis* (1984). On farm violence see John L. Shover, *Cornbelt Rebellion: The Farmer's Holiday Association* (1965). Biographies of key New Deal figures include Gilbert C. Fite, *George N. Peek and the Fight for Farm Parity* (1954); Edward L. and Frederick A. Schapsmeier, *Henry A. Wallace: The Agrarian Years, 1919–1940* (1968); William D. Rowley, *M. L. Wilson and the Campaign for the Domestic Allotment* (1970); Roy V. Scott and J. G. Shoalmire, *The Public Career of Cully A. Cobb: A Study in Agricultural Leadership* (1973); and Wilma Dykeman and James Stokely, *The Seeds of Southern Change: The Life of Will Alexander* (1962). Van L. Perkins, *Crisis in Agriculture: The Agricultural Adjustment Administration and the New Deal, 1933* (1969), tells the story of the critical first year. On the New Deal and southern agriculture, see Gilbert C. Fite, *Cotton Fields No More: Southern Agriculture, 1865–1980* (1984); Pete Daniel, *Breaking the Land: The Transformation of Cotton, Tobacco, and Rice Cultures Since 1880* (1985); Jack Temple Kirby, *Rural Worlds Lost: The American South, 1920–1960* (1987); and portions of Gavin Wright, *Old South, New South: Revolutions in the Southern Economy Since the Civil War* (1986). More specific studies of the southern rural poor are Paul E. Mertz, *New Deal Policy and Southern Rural Poverty* (1978); David E. Conrad, *The Forgotten Farmers: The Story of the Sharecroppers in the New Deal* (1965); and Donald H. Grubbs, *Cry from the Cotton: The STFU and the New Deal* (1971). Also on the South, see Anthony J. Badger, *Prosperity Road: The New Deal, Tobacco, and North Carolina* (1980). Sidney Baldwin, *Poverty and Politics: The Rise and Decline of the Farm Security Administration*, is a useful study of one agency. F. Jack Hurley, *Portrait of a Decade: Roy Stryker and the Development of Documentary Photography in the Thirties* (1972), discusses the FSA photographers. Resettlement programs are detailed in Donald Holley, *Uncle Sam's Farmers: The New Deal Communities in the Lower Mississippi Valley* (1975);

Joseph L. Arnold, *The New Deal in the Suburbs: A History of the Greenbelt Town Programs 1935–1954* (1971); and Paul K. Conkin, *Tomorrow a New World: The New Deal Community Program* (1959). The New Deal in the West is examined in Richard Lowitt, *The New Deal and the West* (1984); Leonard J. Arrington, "Western Agriculture and the New Deal," *Agricultural History* 44 (October 1970), pp. 337–53; Donald C. Swain, "The Bureau of Reclamation and the New Deal, 1933–1940," *Pacific Northwest Quarterly* 61 (October 1970), pp. 137–46; Donald Worster, *Dust Bowl: The Southern Plains in the 1930s* (1979); and Walter Stein, *California and the Dust Bowl Migration* (1973). On rural electrification, see D. Clayton Brown, *Electricity for Rural America: The Fight for the REA* (1980); and H. S. Person, "The Rural Electrification Administration in Perspective," *Agricultural History* 24 (April 1950), pp. 70–89.

The most thorough discussion of the NRA is Bernard Bellush, *The Failure of the NRA* (1975). For background see Robert F. Himmelberg, *The Origins of the National Recovery Administration: Business, Government, and the Trade Association Issue, 1921–1933* (1976). The contemporary analysis by the Brookings Institute is recorded in Leverett S. Lyon et al., *The National Recovery Administration: An Analysis and Appraisal* (1935). In *Recovery and Redistribution under the NIRA* (1980), Michael M. Weinstein questions traditional views of the NRA's impact on the economy. So does Donald R. Brand in *Corporatism and the Rule of Law: A Study of the National Recovery Administration* (1988). Several studies highlight NRA policies affecting particular industries. On textiles, see Louis Galombos, *Competition and Cooperation: The Emergence of a National Trade Association* (1966); and James A. Hodges, *New Deal Labor Policy and the Southern Cotton Textile Industry, 1933–1941* (1986). On petroleum, see Linda J. Lear, "Harold L. Ickes and the Oil Crisis of the First Hundred Days," *Mid-America* 63 (January 1981), pp. 3–17. On coal, see James P. Johnson, "Drafting the NRA Code of Fair Competition for the Bituminous Coal Industry," *Journal of American History* 53 (December 1966), pp. 521–41; and John W. Hevener, *Which Side Are You On? The Harlan County Coal Miners* (1978). On automobiles, see Sidney Fine, *The Automobile under the Blue Eagle: Labor, Management, and the Automobile Manufacturing Code* (1963). The NRA's labor relations are discussed in Irving Bernstein, *The New Deal Collective Bargaining Policy* (1950). Ellis W. Hawley, *The New Deal and the Problem of*

Monopoly (1966), is an incisive look at New Deal economic policy. The recovery role played by the RFC is examined in James S. Olson, *Saving Capitalism: The Reconstruction Finance Corporation and the New Deal, 1933–1940* (1988); and Arthur M. Schlesinger, Jr., "Getting FDR's Ear," *New York Review of Books* 36 (February 16, 1989), pp. 20–23. Also see Theodore Rosenof, *Dogma, the Depression, and the New Deal: The Debate of Political Leaders over Economic Recovery* (1975).

Several comprehensive treatments of New Deal social welfare policy exist, including William R. Brock, *Welfare, Democracy, and the New Deal* (1988); William W. Bremer, "Along the 'American Way': The New Deal's Work Relief Program for the Unemployed," *Journal of American History* 62 (December 1975), pp. 636–52; Charles H. Trout, "Welfare in the New Deal Era," *Current History* 65 (July 1973), pp. 11–14, 39; Judith Ann Trolander, *Settlement Houses and the Great Depression* (1975); and Frances Fox Piven and Richard A. Cloward, "The New Deal and Relief," in Donald T. Critchlow and Ellis W. Hawley, eds., *Poverty and Public Policy in Modern America* (1989), pp. 147–50. The subject is also treated in the following: Anthony J. Badger, "The New Deal and the Localities," in Rhodri Jeffreys-Jones and Bruce Collins, eds., *The Growth of Federal Power in American History* (1983), pp. 102–15; James T. Patterson, *The New Deal and the States: Federalism in Transition* (1969); and James T. Patterson, *America's Struggle against Poverty, 1900–1980* (1981).

The impact of New Deal relief can be seen in numerous state studies, most published recently. Begin with John Braeman, Robert H. Bremner, and David Brody, eds., *The New Deal: The State and Local Levels* (1975). Useful state studies include George T. Blakey, *Hard Times and New Deal in Kentucky, 1929–1939* (1986); Bruce D. Blumell, *The Development of Public Assistance in the State of Washington during the Great Depression* (1984); Thomas H. Coode and John F. Bauman, *People, Poverty, and Politics: Pennsylvanians during the Great Depression* (1981); Richard C. Keller, *Pennsylvania's Little New Deal* (1982); Richard M. Judd, *The New Deal in Vermont: Its Impact and Aftermath* (1979); Ronald L. Heinemann, *Depression and New Deal in Virginia: The Enduring Dominion* (1983); Frances W. Schruben, *Kansas in Turmoil, 1930–1936* (1969); Michael S. Holmes, *The New Deal in Georgia: An Administrative History* (1975); Robert P. Ingalls, *Herbert H. Lehman and New York's Little New Deal* (1975); Michael P. Malone, *C. Ben Ross and the New Deal in*

Idaho (1970); John Dean Minton, *The New Deal in Tennessee, 1932–1938* (1979); Robert E. Burke, *Olson's New Deal for California* (1953); James F. Wickens, *Colorado in the Great Depression* (1979); and Larry Whatley, "The Works Progress Administration in Mississippi," *Journal of Mississippi History* 30 (February 1968), pp. 35–50. Also see the relevant chapters in George B. Tindall, *The Emergence of the New South, 1913–1945* (1967).

Several specialized studies on New Deal relief agencies merit attention. See John A. Salmond, *The Civilian Conservation Corps, 1933–1942: A New Deal Case Study* (1967); Donald S. Howard, *The WPA and Federal Relief Policy* (1943); and Bonnie Fox Schwartz, *The Civil Works Administration, 1933–1934: The Business of Emergency Employment in the New Deal* (1984). On surplus relief, see Janet Poppendieck, *Breadlines Knee-Deep in Wheat: Food Assistance in the Great Depression* (1986). Two sources on social security are Roy Lubove, *The Struggle for Social Security, 1900–1935* (1986); and W. Andrew Achenbaum, *Social Security: Visions and Revisions* (1986). On WPA's Project One, see Alan Lawson, "The Cultural Legacy of the New Deal," in Harvard Sitkoff, ed., *Fifty Years Later: The New Deal Evaluated* (1985); Jane DeHart Matthews, *The Federal Theatre, 1935–1939: Plays, Relief, and Politics* (1967); Jane DeHart Matthews, "Arts and the People: The New Deal Quest for Cultural Democracy," *Journal of American History* 62 (September 1975), pp. 316–39; Monty Noam Penkower, *The Federal Writers' Project: A Study in Government Patronage of the Arts* (1977); Richard McKenzie, *The New Deal for Artists* (1973); William F. McDonald, *Federal Relief Administration and the Arts* (1969); and Joanne Bentley, *Hallie Flanagan: A Life in the American Theatre* (1988).

On labor the preeminent work is still Irving Bernstein, *Turbulent Years: A History of the American Worker, 1933–1941* (1971). Also see his *A Caring Society: The New Deal, the Worker, and the Great Depression* (1985). Consult Christopher L. Tomlins, *The State and the Unions: Labor Relations, Law, and the Organized Labor Movement in America, 1880–1960* (1985), and "AFL Unions in the 1930s: Their Performance in Historical Perspective," *Journal of American History* 65 (March 1979), pp. 1021–42; Stanley Vittoz, *New Deal Labor Policy and the American Industrial Economy* (1987); David Brody, *Workers in Industrial America: Essays on the Twentieth Century Struggle* (1980), and "Labor and the Great Depression: The Interpretive Prospects," *Labor History* 13 (Spring 1972), pp. 231–44;

Peter Friedlander, *The Emergence of a UAW Local, 1936–1939: A Study in Class and Culture* (1975); Daniel Nelson, "The CIO at Bay: Labor Militancy and Politics in Akron, 1936–1938," *Journal of American History* 71 (December 1984), pp. 565–86; John A. Salmond, *Miss Lucy of the CIO: The Life and Times of Lucy Randolph Mason, 1882–1959* (1988); James A. Gross, *The Making of the National Labor Relations Board, 1933–1937* (1974); Bruce Nelson, *Workers on the Waterfront: Seamen, Longshoremen, and Unionism in the 1930s* (1988); George G. Suggs, Jr., *Union Busting in the Tri-State: The Oklahoma, Kansas, and Missouri Metal Workers' Strike of 1935* (1986); and Bernard Sternsher, "Great Depression Labor Historiography in the 1970s: Middle-Range Questions, Ethnocultures, and Levels of Generalization," *Reviews in American History* 11 (June 1983), pp. 300–319. For a discussion of the New Deal in the broader context of American labor history, see Robert H. Zieger, *American Workers, American Unions, 1920–1985* (1986).

The New Deal's impact on minorities has been examined in several studies. The most comprehensive treatments of blacks are Harvard Sitkoff, *A New Deal for Blacks: The Emergence of Civil Rights as a National Issue, the Depression Decade* (1978); John B. Kirby, *Black Americans in the Roosevelt Era: Liberalism and Race* (1980); and Raymond Wolters, *Negroes and the Great Depression: The Problem of Economic Recovery* (1970). Also see Ralph J. Bunche, *The Political Status of the Negro in the Age of FDR* (1973); Bernard Sternsher, ed., *The Negro in Depression and War: Prelude to Revolution, 1930–1945* (1969); Nancy J. Weiss, *Farewell to the Party of Lincoln: Black Politics in the Age of FDR* (1983); Mark Naison, *Communists in Harlem during the Depression* (1983); Robert Zangrando, *The NAACP Crusade against Lynching* (1980); Richard Weiss, "Ethnicity and Reform: Minorities and the Ambience of the Depression Years," *Journal of American History* 66 (December 1979), pp. 566–85; B. Joyce Ross, "Mary McLeod Bethune and the NYA," *Journal of Negro History* 60 (January 1975), pp. 1–28; Mark W. Kruman, "Quotas for Blacks: The PWA and the Black Construction Worker," *Labor History* 16 (Winter 1975), pp. 37–51; John A. Salmond, "The CCC and the Negro," *Journal of American History* 52 (June 1965), pp. 75–88; Nancy L. Grant, *TVA and Black Americans: Planning for the Status Quo* (1990); and Dona Cooper Hamilton, "The National Urban League and New Deal Programs," *Social Service Review* 58 (June 1984), pp. 227–43. Studies of Native Americans include Don L. Parman, *The Navajos and the New Deal* (1975); Kenneth R. Philip, *John Collier's Crusade for Indian Reform* (1977); Graham D. Taylor, *The New Deal and American Indian Tribalism: The Administration of the Indian Reorganization Act, 1934–1945* (1980); and Lawrence C. Kelly, *The Assault on Assimilation: John Collier and the Origins of Indian Policy Reform* (1983). Also see Leonard Dinnerstein, "Jews and the New Deal," *American Jewish History* 72 (June 1983), pp. 461–76.

The literature on women and the New Deal is recent and growing. Begin with Susan Ware, *Holding Their Own: American Women in the 1930s* (1982), *Beyond Suffrage: Women in the New Deal* (1981), and *Partner and I: Molly Dewson, Feminism, and New Deal Politics* (1987); Lois Scharf, *To Work and to Wed: Female Employment, Feminism, and the Great Depression* (1980); Ruth Milkman, "Women's Work and Economic Crisis: Some Lessons of the Great Depression," *Review of Radical Political Economics* 8 (Spring 1976), pp. 72–97; Winifred D. Wandersee, *Women's Work and Family Values, 1920–1940* (1981); Julia Kirk Blackwelder, *Women of the Depression: Caste and Culture in San Antonio, 1929–1939* (1984); Phyllis Palmer, *Domesticity and Dirt: Housewives and Domestic Servants in the United States, 1920–1945* (1989); Susan D. Becker, *The Origins of the Equal Rights Amendment: American Feminism between the Wars* (1981); Martha H. Swain, "'The Forgotten Woman': Ellen S. Woodward and Women's Relief in the New Deal," *Prologue: Journal of the National Archives* 15 (Winter 1983), pp. 201–13, and "A New Deal for Mississippi Women, 1933–1943," *Journal of Mississippi History* (August 1984), pp. 191–212. Biographies of Eleanor Roosevelt include Tamara Hareven, *Eleanor Roosevelt: An American Conscience* (1968); Joseph P. Lash, *Eleanor and Franklin* (1971); Blanche Wiesen Cook, *Changes over Time: The Many Lives of Eleanor Roosevelt* (1985); and Joan Hoff Wilson and Marjorie Lightman, eds., *Without Precedent: The Life and Career of Eleanor Roosevelt* (1984). Martha Swain is preparing a biography of Ellen Sullivan Woodward.

The impact of the New Deal on cities is discussed in Mark I. Gelfand, *A Nation of Cities: The Federal Government and Urban America, 1933–1965* (1975); John H. Mollenkopf, *The Contested City* (1983); Bernard Sternsher, ed., *Hitting Home: The Great Depression in Town and Country* (1970); and Douglas L. Smith, *The New Deal in the Urban South* (1988). Studies of individual cities are Jo Ann E. Argersinger, *Toward a New Deal in Baltimore: People and Government in the Great Depression* (1988); Charles H. Trout,

Boston, the Great Depression, and the New Deal (1977); Barbara Blumberg, *The New Deal and the Unemployed: The View from New York City* (1979); and Roger Biles, *Memphis in the Great Depression* (1986). On the New Deal and machine politics see Lyle W. Dorsett, *Franklin D. Roosevelt and the City Bosses* (1977) and *The Pendergast Machine* (1968); Bruce M. Stave, *The New Deal and the Last Hurrah: Pittsburgh Machine Politics* (1970); and Roger Biles, *Big City Boss in Depression and War: Mayor Edward J. Kelly of Chicago* (1984). On public housing see Timothy L. McDonnell, *The Wagner Housing Act: A Case of the Legislative Process* (1957); John F. Bauman, "Safe and Sanitary without the Costly Frills: The Evolution of Public Housing in Philadelphia, 1929–1941," *Pennsylvania Magazine of History and Biography* 101 (January 1977), pp. 114–28; and Roger Biles, "Nathan Straus and the Failure of U.S. Public Housing, 1937–1942," *Historian* 53 (Autumn 1990), pp. 33–46. For the impact of the FHA and HOLC on urban America see Kenneth T. Jackson, *Crabgrass Frontier: The Suburbanization of the United States* (1985).

Other topics of interest are found in Mark Leff, *The Limits of Symbolic Reform: The New Deal and Taxation, 1933–1939* (1984); Ralph F. deBedts, *The New Deal's S.E.C.: The Formative Years* (1964); Michael Parrish, *Securities Regulation and the New Deal* (1970); Thomas K. McCraw, *TVA and the Power Fight: 1933–1939* (1971); Michael J. McDonald and John Muldowny, *TVA and the Dispossessed: The Resettlement of Population in the Norris Dam Area* (1982); Philip J. Funigiello, *Toward a National Power Policy: The New Deal and the Electric Utility Industry* (1973); William R. Childs, *Trucking and the Public Interest: The Emergence of Federal Regulation, 1914–1940* (1985); Barry Dean Karl, *Executive Reorganization and Reform in the New Deal* (1963); Richard Polenberg, *Reorganizing Roosevelt's Government* (1966); Joan M. Crouse, *The Homeless Transient in the Great Depression: New York State, 1929–1941* (1986); Dean L. May, *From New Deal to New Economics: The American Liberal Response to the Recession of 1937* (1981); A. L. Riesch Owen, *Conservation under FDR* (1983); Marion Clawson, *New Deal Planning: The National Resources Planning Board* (1981); Frank Freidel, *FDR and the South* (1965); Richard H. Pells, *Radical Visions and American Dreams: Culture and Social Thought in the Depression Years* (1973); Michael E. Parrish, "The Hughes Court, the Great Depression, and the Historians," *Historian* 40 (February 1978), pp. 286–308; and Peter H. Irons, *The New Deal Lawyers* (1982).

Index